AF706429

In *Epistemology in Spinoza, Marx-Freud-Lacan*, Kiarina Kordela gives us what has been sorely lacking in recent work on biopower: a reflection on how the commodification of self-actualization anchors the current moment of late capitalism. Through a series of joyful readings of Spinoza, Marx, Freud, and Lacan, Kordela opens a perspective not just on biopower, but on our own singular essence irreducible to capitalism's incessant repetition of the same old same old. This is a work to be reckoned with, to be thought about, and above all to be enjoyed.

Timothy Campbell, *Professor of Italian, Department of Romance Studies, Cornell University*

At a moment when philosophy appears blocked in pointless antinomies, between either constructivism, or new materialism and speculative realism, Kiarina Kordela breaks with these antinomies and reveals those seemingly radical opponents as tacit accomplices – or "couples" in Bachelardian sense. Kordela's couragious advance aims for what philosophy can do best: it takes a position, it draws clear lines of demarcation, and it gives a superb overview of the current situation on philosophy's battleground.

Robert Pfaller, *University of Art and Industrial Design, Linz*

Epistemontology in Spinoza-Marx-Freud-Lacan

A. Kiarina Kordela steps beyond extant commentaries on Marx's theory of commodity fetishism – from A. Sohn-Rethel to L. Althusser, É. Balibar, Slavoj Žižek, and others – to show that in capitalism value is the manifestation of the homology between thought and being, while their other aspect – power – is foreclosed and becomes the object of biopower.

Using monistic Marxian/Lacanian structuralism as an alternative to dominant models from Plato and Kant to phenomenological accounts, deconstruction, and other contemporary approaches, Kordela expertly argues that Marx's theory of commodity fetishism is a reformulation of the Spinozian thesis that thought (mind) and things (bodies or extension) are manifestations of one and the same being or substance. Kordela's link between Spinoza and Marx shows that being consists of two aspects, value and power, the former leading to structuralist thought, the latter becoming the object of contemporary biopower. *Epistemontology in Spinoza-Marx-Freud-Lacan* intervenes between two dominant lines of thought in the reception of Marx today: on the one hand, an approach that relates Marxian thought to psychoanalysis from a Hegelian/dialectical perspective and, on the other hand, an approach that links Marxism to Spinozian monism, at the total exclusion of psychoanalysis.

This book will interest scholars and researchers who study Marxism, (post)structuralism, psychoanalysis, critical theory, ontology, epistemology and theories of representation, theoreticians of cultural studies and comparative literature, aesthetic theory, including the relation of art to economy and politics, and biopolitics.

A. Kiarina Kordela is Professor of German and Director of the Critical Theory Program at Macalester College, and Honorary Adjunct Professor at the Writing and Society Research Center, University of Western Sydney, Australia. She publishes on topics such as literature, philosophy, psychoanalysis, critical, political, and film theory, intellectual history, and biopolitics.

Routledge Innovations in Political Theory

For more information about this series, please visit: https://www.routledge.com/Routledge-Innovations-in-Political-Theory/book-series/IPT

Rethinking Utopia
Place, Power, Affect
David M. Bell

Hugo Grotius and the Modern Theology of Freedom
Jeremy Seth Geddert

Critical Urban Theory, Common Property, and "the Political"
Desire and Drive in the City
Dan Webb

Democracy Beyond the Nation State
Practicing Equality
Joe Parker

Reclaiming Representation
Contemporary Advances in the Theory of Political Representation
Edited by Mónica Brito Vieira

Dignity and Human Rights
Language Philosophy and Social Realizations
Stephan P. Leher

A Conceptual Investigation of Justice
Kyle Johannsen

Compromise and Disagreement in Contemporary Political Theory
Edited by Christian F. Rostbøll and Theresa Scavenius

Democratic Political Tragedy in the Postcolony
The Tragedy of Postcoloniality in Michael Manley's Jamaica and Nelson Mandela's South Africa
Greg A. Graham

Epistemontology in Spinoza-Marx-Freud-Lacan
The (Bio)Power of Structure
A. Kiarina Kordela

Epistemontology in Spinoza-Marx-Freud-Lacan

The (Bio)Power of Structure

A. Kiarina Kordela

Routledge
Taylor & Francis Group
LONDON AND NEW YORK

First published 2018
by Routledge

2 Park Square, Milton Park, Abingdon, Oxfordshire OX14 4RN
52 Vanderbilt Avenue, New York, NY 10017

Routledge is an imprint of the Taylor & Francis Group, an informa business

First issued in paperback 2019

Library of Congress Cataloging in Publication Data
A catalog record for this book has been requested

ISBN: 978-1-138-06835-3 (hbk)
ISBN: 978-0-367-37208-8 (pbk)

Typeset in Times New Roman
by Taylor & Francis Books

Contents

List of tables ix
Acknowledgments x
Note on citing Spinoza's Ethics *and the Treatises* xi
Epigraph xii

Introduction 1

Chapter summaries 7

1 Words and things in the era of value, power, and biopower 13

Dominant secular epistemology, and epistemontology 13
Commodity fetishism and structuralism 22
Being qua *value, and the methodology of commodity fetishism 24*
Other attempts to challenge the dominant secular epistemology 27
Being qua *power-of-self-actualization 41*
Classical ideology and commodity fetishism or biopolitical ideology 43
Being qua *power-of-self-actualization and* qua *value, or fallen being 46*

2 Materialist epistemontology: Marx and Sohn-Rethel with Spinoza and psychoanalysis 53

Two lines of secular epistemology 53
Real abstraction, and intellectual and manual labor 54
The capitalist (mutual) abstractification of productive labor and value 59
Parmenides's coins do not accrue 62

God, or substance, or labor-power 64
The law of historical materialism 67
Sohn-Rethel's methodology: commodity fetishism 68

3 Psychoanalysis and structuralism 73

Object and time 75
Drive, lack, desire 86
Postscript on fantasy 90

4 Dialectics, or valences of structuralism 95

Dialectics 96
Structuralism 105
Kafka's valences 111
Coda 114

5 Value: The aesthetic itinerary from content to structure 126

6 Marx and psychoanalysis 151

Conceptual, methodological, epistemontological affinities 152
Commodity fetishism and materialist epistemology: from bourgeois ideology to the constitutive imaginary, and from interiority-exteriority to extimacy 155
From surplus-value to surplus-enjoyment 160

7 The other side of value: Substance, labor and enjoyment, or biopolitics according to Spinoza, Marx and Lacan 166

Jouissance *of the real* 169
Temporality of the jouissance *of the real* 172
Aspects of labor and their temporalities 179
Labor and the historical modes of its "loss" and "counting" 181
Imitation enjoyment as a religious practice 187
Spinoza's democracy and secular salvation 190

Index 201

Tables

4.1 Dialectics in Adorno and Lukács 103
4.2 Structure of Postmodern Dialectics 109

Acknowledgments

I would like to thank Alya Ansari (Macalester '19) and Nick Chun (Macalester '19) for helping with the editing process and composing the index during our 2017 summer research collaboration. A big thank you to Parker Field, Macalester alumnus and freelance editor, researcher and writer based in New York, who generously volunteered his professional expertise in editing. I would also like to thank Natalja Mortensen, the senior editor of the Political Science sector of Routledge, for her interest in my work. My gratitude to Macalester College and my friends and colleagues there, and to the international intellectual community with all the conferences, symposia, and talks that have offered the opportunity to discuss several of the ideas presented here. I would like to thank in particular Andrew Benjamin, Marie-Hélène Brousse, Tony Brown, Cesare Casarino, Joan Copjec, Tim Dean, Filippo De Lucchese, Jeff Diamanti, Jonathan Michael Dickstein, Heiko Feldner, Nathan Gorelick, Sean Grattan, Christian Haines, Maire Jaanus, Jan Jagodzinski, Sigi Jöttkandt, Onur Kartal, Lydia R. Kerr, Sheila Kunkle, Franco Milanesi, J.D. Mininger, Mariana Roa Oliva, Brian D. O'Neil, Jason M. Peck, Andrew Pendakis, Luis Recoder, Juan Robaina, Bastian Ronge, Matthias Rothe, Arun Saldanha, Hoon Song, Yannis Stavrakakis, Imre Szeman, Gautam Basu Thakur, Andrea Ughetto, Dimitris Vardoulakis, Véronique Voruz, Elizabeth Weed, and Caroline A. Williams – for generously showing their appreciation of my work by inviting me to contribute to their edited collections and journal issues, or by translating and/or commenting on my work in other languages, and generally promoting its dissemination. Last but not least, my gratitude goes to the greatest and most permanent source of inspiration, my students, for their unmitigated thirst for knowledge and for challenging convenient thinking.

Note on citing Spinoza's *Ethics* and the Treatises

In citing Spinoza's *Ethics* I am using Edwin Curley's translation in his *The Collected Works of Spinoza*, and the following code:

A	axiom
C	corollary
D	demonstration
Def.	definition
DOE	definitions of the emotions
E	explication
L	lemma
P	proposition
S	scholium

TTP stands for Spinoza's *Theologico-Political Treatise*, and *TP* for his *Political Treatise*.

The question as to what value really is, like the question as to what being is, is unanswerable. And precisely because they have the same formal relation to objects, they are as alien to each other as are thought and extension for Spinoza. Since both express the same absolute substance, each in its own way and perfect in itself, the one can never encroach upon the other. They never impinge upon each other because they question the concepts of objects from completely different points of view. But this disjunctive parallelism of reality and value does not divide the world into a sterile duality, which the mind with its need for unity could never accept – even though its destiny and the method of its quest may be to move incessantly from diversity to unity and from unity to diversity. What is common to value and reality stands above them: namely … that which can be signified and expressed in our concepts of reality and value, and which can enter into either one or the other series … Reality and value are, as it were, two different languages by which the logically related contents of the world, valid in their ideal unity, are made comprehensible to the unitary soul … These two compilations made by the soul, through perceiving and through valuing, may perhaps once more be brought together in a metaphysical unity, for which there is no linguistic term unless it be in religious symbols. There is perhaps a cosmic ground where the heterogeneity and divergencies that we experience between reality and value no longer exist, where both series are revealed as one; this unity either being unaffected by the two categories, and standing beyond them in majestic indifference, or signifying a harmonious interweaving of both, which is shattered and distorted into fragments and contrasts only by our way of regarding it, as if we had an imperfect visual faculty.

(Georg Simmel, *The Philosophy of Money*, 62)

Introduction

The present work pursues a double movement. The first movement begins with unfolding epistemontology as a theory of unified ontology and epistemology (particularly regarding the question of truth and representation) that derives from Marx's theory of commodity fetishism in connection to Spinozian monism. In this regard, this work takes a decisive step beyond extant commentaries on the theory of commodity fetishism, from Georg Simmel and Alfred Sohn-Rethel to Étienne Balibar, Slavoj Žižek, and others. This epistemontology is a secular account of the relation between representation and reality, or words and things, and their relation to being, in the era of capitalist modernity roughly since the seventeenth century. The initial thesis that propels this work is that Marx's theory of commodity fetishism is a reformulation of the principle of monism, with which Spinoza overcame the dualism between representation and external reality. According to Spinoza's monistic principle, thought (mind) and things (bodies or extension) are manifestations of one and the same being or substance, as a result of which "the order and connections of ideas is the same as the order and connections of things" (*Ethics* IIP7). In spite of the incommensurable difference between ideas and things, their relations share the same structures, and both, ideas and things, express the same substance or being. As we shall see, Marx's commodity fetishism postulates the same "parallelism" (see e.g., Curley 1988: 62) or "complementarity" (see e.g., Yovel 1989: 159) or homology between the order of ideas and the order of things.

In this respect, Spinoza and Marx stand together against, on the one hand, the dominant modern Western dissociation of representation and being and, eventually, between representation and reality, as it has been developed from Kant to deconstruction. On the other hand, Spinoza and Marx stand together against the attempts to challenge the above dominant conception and access either being or reality by bypassing representation. The (post-)Kantian line severs representation from being and ultimately reality to the point that representation becomes self-referential (De Man, Derrida). Opposing this line, attempts to access being or reality without the mediation of representation include: Martin Heidegger's "disclosure of being"; Alain Badiou's call for a return to Platonism, as a philosophy that "does not take as its point of departure words, but things" (Badiou 2003: 50); Gilles Deleuze's conception of expression which postulates that the "opposition of expressions and signs is one of the fundamental principles of Spinozism," and that "the object … expresses itself" without any involvement with the sign (Deleuze 1990: 182, 22); and Quentin Meillassoux's "speculative materialism" that wants "to consider the realms of subjectivity and objectivity independently of one another," and assumes that "absolute reality is an *entity without thought*" (Meillassoux 2008: 5, 36). These latter approaches separate thought from reality and from being, and claim that, in some way or other, things reveal themselves without the mediation of representation or thought, which they equate with consciousness, whether empirical or transcendental.

Against these two approaches, I shall argue that Spinozian monism and Marx's theory of commodity fetishism entail that the two realms are homologous, that is, thought and reality or things share the same structures, for they are manifestations of the same being. However, first we should point out that, in Gilles Deleuze's words, in Spinoza "thought … surpasses the consciousness that we have of it" and amounts to the "discovery of the unconscious" (Deleuze 1988: 18–9). Similarly, as we shall later see in more detail, when Marx's theory of commodity fetishism states that in capitalism "the characteristic which objects of utility have of being values is as much men's social product as is their language" (Marx 1990: 167) – that is, their thought – he means (a) that there is a parallelism between economic and linguistic values, and (b) that these linguistic values or "men's … language" are not their consciousness but the unconscious. Marx's connection of exchange-value and language already points to the connection between his theory of political economy and Saussure's structuralist linguistics. When, finally, Lacan says that "*the unconscious is structured like language*" (Lacan 1981: 20), he does not mean that it is structured in the way language is thought or spoken by consciousness; rather it means that the unconscious is structured as a system of linguistic values each of which is defined in differential relations with the other linguistic values – just as economic exchange-values in capitalism are defined in differential relations with the other exchange-values. The network of economic and linguistic values is the unconscious structure that reflects the concatenation or constitutive relations of all things that exist in reality.

This is why, *in one respect*, substance or Nature or God – which for Spinoza are one and the same – is a structure, or rather structurality itself: the potential of any concrete structure to constitute itself, or in Deleuze's words, "God [is] the source of all the constitutive relations of things" (Deleuze 1990: 297).[1] This explains, for instance, the possibility of modern natural sciences, that is, the translation of natural phenomena into laws *qua* purely formal structures. As we shall see, it also explains the parallel development of knowledge within fields of the Humanities toward formal structuralism. "Structuralism" here does not mean specifically the eponymous twentieth-century theoretical movement, even as some of its aspects remain central in approaching structuralism as meant here. Structuralism here means the specific episteme required for the study of value within secular capitalist modernity – which is also to say, for the study of things insofar as, in capitalism, they are also values.

The corollary of the thesis that the structures of thought and of reality are homologous and both express one and the same being, is that when thought is by necessity distorted, the distortion is objective (rather than a subjective illusion), that is, the reality of being is itself distorted. To spell out this point more clearly, we need first to approach being not as structurality but in its other aspect – which motivates the second movement of the present work.

As we know since Spinoza, being or substance can be conceived by secular thought – that is, a thought that does not presuppose a creator of being – only as self-caused. This means that being is the power or potential of being to actualize itself (for if being were not the power of bringing itself into existence, then there should be something else prior to it that created it). If the sole secular conception of being is the power of self-actualization, then, in secular modernity, both extension and thought should be direct manifestations of the potential of self-actualization. To translate this in Marx's terms, both objects of utility and exchange-values should be direct manifestations of human labor-power. For humans partake most directly in being (the potential of self-actualization) through their labor-power, since "labour-power … is not materialized in a product … thus exists not really, but only in potentiality" (Marx 1993: 267). Labor-power is the potentiality of labor to actualize itself – but *in itself*, labor-power can actualize itself only as a product, not as an exchange-value.

The actualization of labor-power as both a product and exchange-value presupposes the commodification of labor-power. In capitalism, the potentiality of labor's self-actualization is for the first time commodified (Virno 2004: 82–4), as a result of which surplus-value is, again, for the first time in history, accumulated. In turn, this new economic organization is necessarily accompanied by commodity fetishism: "commodity fetishism … is … inseparable from the production of commodities" (Marx 1990: 165). This fetishism consists, on a most immediate level, in the fact that, on the one hand, we assume, subjectively or consciously, that we exchange concrete objects of utility and that we actualize our labor-power through concrete labor practices in concrete products; on the other hand, objectively or from the perspective of the unconscious, we are vehicles for the circulation of abstract exchange-values, just as our labor is congealed as abstract labor (labor-time) in the commodities we produce, thereby becoming alienated and autonomous (from the laborer). The result of the commodification of things and labor is that commodities no longer matter as products of concrete modes of actualization of labor-power or as concrete objects of utility; rather they matter only insofar as they are the manifestations of value, as "both the money and the commodity function only as different modes of existence of value itself, the money as its general mode of existence, the commodity as its particular or, so to speak, disguised mode" (Marx 1990: 255). In other words, the result of commodification is that the being or substance of which both concrete things and abstract exchange-values are "different modes of existence" appears to be not the power of self-actualization but exclusively value – that is, as an element of structure.

To recapitulate so far, according to its secular conception, being is the undifferentiated union of the power of self-actualization and of structurality. However, as we can conceive of substance only through its attributes – i.e., after a minimum of differentiation – we could say that from the perspective of the attribute of thought substance is structurality, that is, the potential of structures to be constituted and actualized. From the perspective of the attribute of extension, substance is the potential of bodies to be actualized, and both the body's power of self-actualization and structure (thought) express the same being. This would entail that use-values (bodies) and exchange-values (thoughts) should be the expression of being as both power-of-self-actualization and of structurality (value). However, this is not the case because capitalism – the economic system of secular modernity – is inseparable from commodity fetishism, according to which both thought and bodies appear as concrete modes *exclusively* of value. Due to the capitalist economy, thought and bodies express being exclusively as value and are prevented from expressing being *qua* power-of-self-actualization – at the very moment when this conception of being is the very foundation of the secular *épistémé* as such.

However, if commodity fetishism forces both thought and reality to express being in a distorted way, as exclusively value, then the appearance of being as value is not a subjective illusion but an effect of the objective capitalist transformation of reality. As Alfred Sohn-Rethel has argued, the abstraction of the commodity as exchange-value is not a fiction of our mind but rather real (*Realabstraktion*), objectively occurring within the social reality of capitalism. Henceforth, both thought and reality express being as value, while the fact that the commodification of being also means the commodification of the power of self-actualization escapes consciousness to become, as we shall see, a biopolitical factor in the sustenance of contemporary biopower. On the one hand, insofar as thought and reality in capitalist modernity express being as value, value becomes the ubiquitous object of knowledge, from economics, aesthetics, ethics, and accounts of subjectivity and society, to ontology. As a result, a tendency toward formalization and structuralism – the model of thought capable of grasping the logic of value – marks and defines the philosophical and theoretical paradigm of secular capitalist modernity. "Secular" indicates that the structuralist episteme in question must be non-creationist – that is, it must be predicated on the monist premise that being is the power of self-actualization. Identifying this monist structuralist episteme, examining its relation to its traditional competitor (dualism and dialectics), and unfolding the conceptual relations among certain central fields of knowledge that examine value – Marx's political economy, aesthetics and ethics, and psychoanalysis – are the focus of the larger part of this work.

The last chapter focuses on the commodification of being *qua* power-of-self-actualization. In this chapter, Marx's labor-power is linked to Jacques Lacan's conception of enjoyment, insofar as for Lacan being is libido or the *jouissance* (enjoyment) of the real, which is the power of life to actualize itself ("*se faire*"). The commodification of both labor-power and of enjoyment amounts to the commodification of being *qua* power-of-self-actualization. However, to approach the effects of this commodification beyond their contribution to the accumulation of surplus-value, we have to treat labor-power and enjoyment as excesses supposed to fall outside the realm of value. Lacan's link between labor and enjoyment in his XVII seminar and Spinoza's conception of the third kind of knowledge, singular essence, and secular salvation will help us grasp the biopolitical appropriation of the power-of-self-actualization and the impediment of Spinoza's secular salvation through capitalism's double secular religion of debt and distraction.

The agenda of the present project can become more clear also through a juxtaposition with a very relevant book, Samo Tomšič's *The Capitalist Unconscious* (2015), which came out after I had completed this manuscript but prior to its publication process, which gives me the opportunity to make the following remarks. The principal affinity between my work in general, at least since *$urplus: Lacan, Spinoza* (2007), and Tomšič's recent book lies in their partly similar agendas, namely, to show that "psychoanalysis, structuralism, and the critique of political economy participate in the same movement of thought" (Tomšič 2015: back cover). This means that, as Žižek put it, "[t]o be a Marxist today, one HAS to go through Lacan!" (Tomšič 2015: back cover). I do not have the slightest objection to either Tomšič or Žižek. However, I maintain further that in order to be a Marxist today, beyond structuralism and Lacan, one must go through Spinoza. This means, above all, to understand, as the present work argues, that the other side of structure – its loss or lack, or *jouissance* – far from being negativity, is the power of being to actualize itself. Note also that, as we shall see, this conception of *jouissance* or the loss to structure is not a "corrective" to Lacanian theory but constitutive of it. This conception, in turn, means, on the one hand, that one must understand that not only "Lacan's Marx" but also Spinoza "is a structuralist *avant la lettre*" (Tomšič 2015: 77) – which involves broadening the historical field of applicability of "structuralism" to secular capitalist modernity since its inception. On the other hand, perhaps more importantly, it means that one must understand labor-power not simply in terms of structure but also in terms of the power of self-actualization – which is the true excess to structure. As mentioned above, Spinoza's God is indeed structure, but only in one respect, which is the respect of the imaginary.

My reference to the imaginary does not, of course, mean that this respect is not part of reality; it simply means that we need also to approach the real from the perspective of the symbolic. Then we see that at the same time that God is structure – or in Lacan's words that Tomšič also quotes, "structure is real" (Lacan 2006: 30; Tomšič 2015: 77) – God or the real is the power of self-actualization. God or the real is structure without, however, being reducible to structure or to its loss understood as pure negativity. This is why, as Tomšič writes, "alienation *is* structure" (Tomšič 2015: 66). To this Tomšič adds: "The equivalence between alienation and structure … leaves no doubt that the flip side of the production of surplus is the reproduction of lack – the true 'matter' by which the subject is constituted" (Tomšič 2015: 66). Tomšič is on the right track, except having left Spinoza entirely out of his examination, he does not take the further step to infer that the lack or "matter" by which the subject is constituted is *jouissance* not as pure negativity but as substance *qua* power of self-actualization. Thus, Tomšič's account of the capitalist unconscious remains within the logic of structure, even when it examines lack and loss. One may want to see the difference between the two works as exemplifying the difference between the Hegelian and the Spinozian ways of establishing the connection among the critique of political economy, structuralism, and psychoanalysis. And, as the present work argues about Spinoza and Hegel, the two works compared here may also be not opposites but compatible.

These last comments relate to the crucial difference pointed out by Pierre Macherey between negative and positive determination, which we shall revisit in more detail in the third chapter. In Macherey's words, "to determine something negatively is to represent it abstractly according to its limits" (Macherey 2011: 141). When we do this to a thing, we "relate it … to that which it is not," including to "its possible disappearance" – which is why that which determines the thing can appear as pure negation. By contrast, "to determine something positively … is to perceive it … according to the immanent necessity that engenders it within substance, according to the law of causality that is the same one through which substance produces itself" – that is, according to the power of self-actualization. Now, these two determinations, far from excluding each other, are both operative in any thing: the negative from the perspective of time (Hegel's Concept), the positive from the perspective of eternity (Spinoza's Concept). The difference is not that between error and truth, but between perspectives. As we shall see in the fourth chapter, to treat the difference between Spinoza and Hegel as one concerning the question regarding which of the two is true and which false is to approach them from the perspective of the imaginary. From the perspective of the symbolic, the only possible error is for either perspective to ignore the existence of the other perspective.

Chapter summaries

Chapter 1, "Words and things in the era of value, power, and biopower," shows how Marx's theory of commodity fetishism undermines the dominant epistemological paradigm of secular capitalist modernity that, at least since Kant to deconstruction, severs things from their representations. By postulating a simultaneous and parallel constitution of objectivity and subjectivity, Marx's theory entails a structural homology between things and thought, as the two manifestations of being. The examination of the structural homology between things and thought is the task of epistemontology. Although, with Spinoza, secular thought postulates that being is both the power of self-actualization and structurality or value, commodity fetishism makes being appear only as value (Marx). This appearance, however, is real; that is, it is not a subjective illusion but part of objectivity, not unlike the abstraction of commodities as values, which is a real abstraction ("*Realabstraktion*"; Sohn-Rethel). Hence, epistemontology must examine being both as value and as the power of self-actualization. The former examination explains the tendency of secular thought toward formalization and structuralism; the latter reveals the link between labor-power and enjoyment (*jouissance*) – two modulations of the power of self-actualization – and calls for a psychoanalytic revision of the theory of biopower and biopolitics.

The chapter also differentiates the position of this Spinozian-Marxian psychoanalytic epistemontology from Deleuze's conception of "expression," as well as from other attempts to oppose the dominant epistemological tradition (the dualism between words and things) by claiming cognitive access to things or to being, such as those by Martin Heidegger, Alain Badiou, and Quentin Meillassoux. This chapter engages recurrently with Étienne Balibar's (and, more or less directly, Louis Althusser's) reading of Marx, including his differentiation between ideology and commodity fetishism, which leads to an examination of the relation between ideology and biopolitics.

Chapter 2, "Materialist epistemontology: Marx and Sohn-Rethel with Spinoza and psychoanalysis," first explains that Sohn-Rethel's theory undermines the (post-)Kantian dissociation of representation and things, by showing that the Kantian *a priori* categories of thought (representation) are *a posteriori* effects of the relations of things (a point also emphasized by Žižek). The relations of things determine the *a priori* categories of thought to the point that, in Sohn-Rethel's words, "[e]rst mit dieser Warensprache im Bewußtsein werden die Warenbesitzer zu rationalen Wesen [it is only through the language of commodities in consciousness that their owners become rational beings]" (Sohn-Rethel 1989: 24, translation mine). The "Realabstraktion" (real abstraction) that occurs in things when commodified is to be taken in a "literal sense," that is, the commodification of things amounts to their transformation into the language that provides the *a priori* categories of human thought. As a result, far from being inaccessible to representation, the relations between things are precisely what is revealed in the transcendental categories of representation. And both the relations between things and our representations are manifestations of being, so that we are led not only to a "materialist epistemology" (Sohn-Rethel's goal) but to a materialist epistemontology.

Further, I argue that Sohn-Rethel's distinction between intellectual and manual labor concerns primarily the distinction between consciousness and the unconscious *within* the market. For "in commodity exchange the action and the consciousness of people go separate ways. Only the action [of the exchange] is abstract[ed]" from the useful thing (Sohn-Rethel 1978: 30). The split, then, between consciousness and the unconscious occurs within the realm of exchange itself, as the split between the (unconscious) action of hands and the (conscious) intentions of the mind. The commodity's essence as abstract value is inaccessible to the consciousness of the very persons whose acts bring it about. Beyond the division of labor within production, commodity fetishism involves a division between manual and intellectual labor within the realm of exchange, which corresponds to the split between the unconscious and consciousness. The chapter also presents a series of corrections that Marx's own theory indicates that need to be made in Sohn-Rethel's account, particularly regarding the source of abstraction, the role of coined money, and the difference between capitalist and precapitalist modes of production and exchange.

Chapter 3, "Psychoanalysis and structuralism," shows the necessary interconnection between capitalist economy and (monist structuralist) psychoanalytic thought. It does so by reading together (a) Spinozian monism – as the first philosophical system that conceived of being (substance) in structural terms; (b) Marx's theory of commodity fetishism – as the groundwork for a secular epistemontological theory; (c) Freudian-Lacanian psychoanalysis – as instrumental in the formulation of properly structuralist thought; and (d) Deleuze's account of structuralism – both as a systematic presentation of structuralist thought and as an attempt to preempt possible criticisms from a Hegelian/dialectical perspective. While Laplanche and Pontalis serve as background for teasing out the structuralist epistemology of psychoanalysis, I set Deleuze in dialogue with Alexandre Kojève in order to reveal Deleuze's theoretical trajectory as an attempt to preempt possible objections (of Hegelian origin) to all three: Spinoza, structuralism, and psychoanalysis.

Chapter 4, "Dialectics, or valences of structuralism," turns to dialectics as the line of thought traditionally perceived as the alternative, if not opponent, to monism. By setting in dialogue Fredric Jameson, Georg

Lukcács, and Deleuze, and through an analysis of Kafka's short story "Prometheus," I show both the differences between the two modes of thought and their intrinsic interconnection. Dialectics is an inevitable parallel effect-formation of structuralism that is required in order to give an account of value from the perspective of the imaginary. Thus, I supplement Pierre Macherey's thesis that Hegel had to misread Spinoza in a specific way and for specific reasons (Macherey 2011), but adding that, nevertheless, Hegel's "misreading" is not simply an error that needs to be dismissed but rather is the supplement to Spinozian monism that emerges with objective necessity.

Chapter 5, "Value: the aesthetic itinerary from content to structure," shows the impact of value's permeation of the economy and epistemontology in secular capitalist modernity on aesthetic, as well as ethical, value. I identify four phases in this development: first, the movement of "ideal content," an incubator of modern value, lasting until Kant's intervention; second, the new paradigm of "abstractism" or "formalization," which emerges out of the Enlightenment; third, "structuralism," in which Romanticism advances the paradigm of formalization; and, fourth, "performative self-referentiality," a modern consequence of the third, formulated by, notably, Heidegger and Benjamin. The chapter traces this development through Baumgarten, Winckelmann, Lessing, Goethe, Kant, Hegel, Fichte, Novalis, Schlegel, Schelling, Hölderlin, Schiller, Schopenhauer, Nietzsche, Heidegger, Benjamin, and Adorno. Moreover, the chapter extends further the discussions on the relation between aesthetics and political economy offered in Howard Gaygill's *Art of Judgment* and John Guillory's chapter on Adam Smith in *Cultural Capital* by linking the conceptual transitions from Hume through Adam Smith to Marx with the formalization that increasingly imbued both fields of knowledge. The chapter also engages in the dialogue between Paul de Man and Jochen Schulte-Sasse regarding romantic irony in order to show that structuralism, and any aesthetic theory informed by it, is a new transcendental theory (Deleuze) where, as follows from Lacan's formula of atheism ("God is unconscious"), the function of God is replaced by that of the unconscious.

Chapter 6, "Marx and psychoanalysis," shows that, far from requiring a conciliation, psychoanalysis and Marx's theory are intrinsically intertwined due to their conceptual, methodological, epistemological, and ontological affinities. Beyond the attempts of the Frankfurt School, the most decisive step in revealing this interconnection was taken by Jacques Lacan's reading of Freudian psychoanalysis. Lacan's structuralism-inflected perspective foregrounded the objectivity of the unconscious, thereby eventually enabling Marxist theorists – notably Louis Althusser and Étienne Balibar – to revise Marxist theory from a psychoanalytic lens. The chapter traces the homologous developments in Marx's and Freud's thought toward the obliteration of traditional binaries, such as nature-culture and biology-psychology.

Focusing then particularly on Marx's theories of value and commodity fetishism in *Capital: Volume 1*, the chapter pursues the obliteration, within both theories, of further dualisms, such as subject and object or interiority and exteriority, that led to the shift in the conceptualization of the imaginary and ideology from an illusion and a means of bourgeois oppression to a function constitutive of subjectivity. After briefly recapitulating the relation between ideology and biopolitics, as well as the introduction of the split between consciousness and the unconscious within the field of the market (examined in the first and second chapters, respectively), the chapter focuses on the relations between surplus-volume, surplus-enjoyment, and labor, as they are revealed particularly through Lacan's XVII seminar and his introduction of the four discourses, notably the discourses of the Master and of the University. This link between enjoyment and labor anticipates the discussion of being *qua* power-of-self-actualization and of biopower in the next and last chapter.

Chapter 7, "The other side of value: substance, labor and enjoyment, or biopolitics according to Spinoza, Marx and Lacan," turns away from value to the "other side" of being, that is, being *qua* power-of-self-actualization. The issue here becomes the function of being beyond its subjugation to the accumulation of economic value. It is through labor and enjoyment that we can obtain access to this aspect of being that exceeds economic valorization. Labor involves three elements (Marx) – (a) concrete physical and mental activity, (b) abstract labor *qua* labor-time, and (c) labor-power as the power of labor to actualize itself. Therefore, labor-power is for human beings the bridge between their finitude in duration and eternal substance – not unlike Spinoza's singular essence of finite modes. The three elements of labor correspond to three temporalities, respectively: (a) diachrony or finite linear time, (b) synchrony, and (c) eternity (singular essence, like substance or the power of self-actualization, exists under the "species of eternity" – Spinoza). A commodity contributes to the accumulation of value only in its aspect as exchange-value, while its aspect as use-value falls out of the circulation of value, as Marx's reduction of the formula of capital from M – C – M to M – M′ indicates. Similarly, labor contributes to the accumulation of value only in its two latter aspects (b and c), while the concrete physical and mental activity, and its finite diachrony, fall out of the circulation of value.

This examination of the aspects of labor and their temporalities reveals that biopolitics operates through the administration of the subject's relation to these three temporalities, as a means of fostering secular illusions of immortality combined with a surrogate experience of ecstatic eternity. This means that, on the one hand, the exclusion of finite diachrony (and hence of mortality) from the universe of value induces the biopolitical urge to hide death from the horizon of human experience (Foucault); on the other hand, the concomitant commodification of labor-power/*jouissance* amounts to the commodification of eternity. While *jouissance* is by definition impossible (as is the experience of eternity), its commodification (through media, drugs, etc.) makes it seem possible in the form of "semblance of surplus *jouissance*" (Lacan 2007: 93). This semblance of surplus *jouissance*, I argue, consists in distraction (losing the sense of self and of time), as a kind of semblance experience of eternity – the closest modern societies can come to the religious ecstatic experience. Through George Bataille's theory of religion and Benjamin's fragment "Capitalism as Religion," I show the profoundly religious character of particularly late, hyper-mediatized, secular capitalism, which also explains the predominance of religious references in contemporary international political conflicts. I conclude by juxtaposing the capitalist biopolitical mechanisms and Spinoza's conception of the third kind of knowledge – which understands the body and mind in terms of their singular essence – as the means to secular salvation.

Note

1 Unless otherwise indicated, brackets in citations are inserted by me.

References

Badiou, A. (2003) *Infinite Thought: Truth and the Return to Philosophy*, Oliver Feltham and Justin Clemens (trans. and eds), London: Continuum.

Curley, E. (1988) *Behind the Geometrical Method: A Reading of Spinoza's Ethics*, Princeton, NJ: Princeton University Press.

Deleuze, G. (1988) *Spinoza: Practical Philosophy*, Robert Hurley (trans.), San Francisco, CA: City Light Books.

Deleuze, G. (1990) *Expressionism in Philosophy: Spinoza*, Martin Joughin (trans.), New York: Zone Books.

Lacan, J. (1981) *The Four Fundamental Concepts of Psychoanalysis*, Jacques-Alain Miller (ed.), Alan Sheridan (trans.), New York: W.W. Norton.

Lacan, J. (2006) *Le Séminaire: Livre XVI: D'un Autre à l'autre*, Paris: Seuil.

Lacan, J. (2007) *The Seminar of Jacques Lacan: Book XVII: The Other Side of Psychoanalysis*, Russell Grigg (trans.), Jacques-Alain Miller (ed.), New York: W.W. Norton & Co.

Macherey, P. (2011) *Hegel or Spinoza*, Susan M. Ruddick (trans.), Minneapolis: University of Minnesota Press.

Marx, K. (1990) *Capital: A Critique of Political Economy (Volume 1)*, Ben Fowkes and David Fernbach (trans.), New York: Penguin.

Marx, K. (1993) *Grundrisse: Foundations of the Critique of Political Economy (Rough Draft)*, Martin Nicolaus (trans.), London: Penguin Books.

Meillassoux, Q. (2008) *After Finitude: An Essay on the Necessity of Contingency*, Ray Brassier (trans.), London: Continuum.

Simmel, G. (2004) *The Philosophy of Money*, Tom Bottomore and David Frisby (trans.), New York: Routledge.

Sohn-Rethel, A. (1978) *Intellectual and Manual Labor: A Critique of Epistemology*, ed. J. Young and P. Walton, trans. Martin Sohn-Rethel, London: Macmillan.

Sohn-Rethel, A. (1989) *Geistige und körperliche Arbeit: zur Epistemologie der abendländischen Geschichte*, revidierte und ergänzte Neuauflage, Weinheim: VCH Acta Humaniora.

Spinoza, B. (1985) *The Collected Works of Spinoza*, Edwin Curley (ed. and trans.), Princeton, NJ: Princeton University Press.

Tomšič, S. (2015) *The Capitalist Unconscious: Marx and Lacan*, London: Verso.

Virno, P. (2004) *A Grammar of the Multitude: For an Analysis of Contemporary Forms of Life*, Isabella Bertoletti, James Cascaito, and Andrea Casson (trans.), New York: Semiotext(e).

Yovel, Y. (1989) *Spinoza and Other Heretics: The Marrano of Reason*, Princeton, NJ: Princeton University Press.

1 Words and things in the era of value, power, and biopower

Dominant secular epistemology, and epistemontology

An underlying thesis of the present work is that generally Marx's account of value in *Capital, Volume 1*, and more specifically his theory of commodity fetishism are further elaborations, developments, and re-articulations of the Spinozian thesis that thought (mind) and things (bodies or extension) are manifestations of one and the same being or substance. Commodity fetishism is a milestone in the Spinozian-Marxian line of thought that, to repeat from the introduction, stands, on the one hand, against the dominant modern Western conception of the relation between words and things or representation and reality, from Kant to deconstruction; and, on the other hand, against the attempts to challenge this conception by bypassing representation. The (post-)Kantian line severs representation from reality to the point that representation becomes self-referential (De Man, Derrida). Opposing this line, attempts to access things without the mediation of representation include: Martin Heidegger's "disclosure of being"; Alain Badiou's call for a return to Platonism, as a philosophy that "does not take as its point of departure words, but things" (Badiou 2003: 50); and Quentin Meillassoux's "speculative materialism" that wants "to consider the realms of subjectivity and objectivity independently of one another" and assumes that "absolute reality is an *entity without thought*" (Meillassoux 2008: 5, 36). These latter approaches grant access to reality (or things) as something authentic that, in some way or other, succeeds in revealing itself against its corrupted representations.

Turning first to the dominant secular tradition, its position is that words and things follow their separate ways. Indicative of the extent to which this position is dominant is Michel Foucault's account in his *The Order of Things* (*Les mots et les choses*) of the epistemic shift from theocratic feudalism – or, in Foucault's terms, the "Classical system of order" – to secular capitalist modernity. During the "Classical system of order," Foucault writes, one could say: "Language is simply the representation of words; nature is simply the representation of beings; need is simply the representation of needs" (Foucault 1970: 209). That is, representation coincided with what it represented. "The end of Classical thought," that long process marking the seventeenth and eighteenth centuries, was to "coincide with the decline of representation" (Foucault 1970: 209), that is, with the gradual demolition of the "organic" links or "similitudes" that "since the Stoics ... link the marks [words] to the things," so that eventually "things and words were to be separated" (Foucault 1970: 42–3). The reason why the organic link between words and things had gradually to disintegrate was the fact that its divine foundation (God) was itself destined to be increasingly undermined through the process of secularization. Thus, modern thought is defined by an escalating chasm between things and words, according to which "the order of words and the order of things no longer intersect except along an artificially defined line," as "there is talk of things that take *place* in another space than that of words" (Foucault 1970: 230).

This development was to be sealed by German Idealism in the heart of the Enlightenment, with Immanuel Kant's absolute severance of the thing-in-itself from its appearance, that is, from the way the thing appears to the transcendental subject or consciousness through the latter's *a priori* categories of thought. By "the end of the eighteenth century," and after the advent of "Ideology and critical philosophy ... of Destutt de Tracy and Kant," the "very being of that which is represented is ... going to fall outside representation itself" (Foucault 1970: 240). The represented thing or reality became the referent, exiled from language. By the nineteenth century it will have been established that things "turn in upon themselves, posit their own volumes, and define for themselves an *internal* space which, to our representation, is on the *exterior*" (Foucault 1970: 239). From then onward, "it is possible to know phenomena, but not substances; laws, but not essences; regularities, but not the beings that obey them" (Foucault 1970: 245). Eventually, with Ferdinand de Saussure, even the link between word (signifier) and concept (signified) was to become "*arbitrary* and *differential*," not unlike the link between money's symbolic value and its material worth (de Saussure 1959: 118; see also Foucault 1970: 174–80) – a parallel that foregrounds homologies between the structures of thought and economy. It is no longer the inherent qualities of each linguistic or monetary sign (e.g., coin) that matters but their differential relations to other linguistic or monetary signs. Both words and economic values are gradually transformed into members of differential structures, while things, evidently immune to this entire development, increasingly enjoy their massive solidity in some transcendent space.

The legacy of this position finds its culminating point in deconstruction. According to Paul de Man, "the paradigmatic structure of language is rhetorical rather than representational or expressive of a referential, proper meaning" (de Man 1979: 106). To be sure, de Man does not deny the referentiality of language altogether, but deprives it of all "extra-linguistic referent or meaning," reducing the referent to "the intralinguistic resources of figures" – a distinction predicated on the dualism between a presumed extralinguistic essence (thing-in-itself) and language, and hence on the dualism between object and subject (de Man 1979: 105).

I leave the opposing line of thought – the attempts to access the authenticity of things in spite of their misrepresentation – for later, as it will be easier to address it after we have seen how Marx's theory of commodity fetishism and Spinozian monism challenge this dominant tradition and point to a unified epistemontology.

As a bridge to the alternative, Spinozian-Marxian, position regarding the relation between words and things, I turn to Jim Hansen's concise comparison between Paul de Man's and Walter Benjamin's approaches to the relation between language and nature. For Benjamin there is no dualism between nature and language, for, as Hansen writes, "nature is never a first principle in itself for Benjamin because it is always involved in a dialectic with history and, thus, is only open to us through history and language," so that "history and the historicity of understanding are subject to nature, and nature is acknowledged as a category subject to historical thought" (Hansen 2004: 678). For de Man, by contrast, language remains wholly confined within history, with no access to nature, because "the linguistic context or constructedness of an allegory, its situatedness, always collapses that allegory's pretension to be transcendentally or transhistorically true," and this should serve as a lesson for the "critic" that "the trick is to be aware of this aporia, to see allegory … as the ironic 'pseudoknowledge' of its own impossibility" (Hansen 2004: 672). This amounts to saying that the sole possible cognitive object of allegory is itself, or, that language's function is exhausted within its own self-referentiality. Accordingly, "in de Man [allegory] reflects a deconstructive move on the part of either a piece of writing or an individual writer" (Hansen 2004: 672). By contrast, for Benjamin, "allegorical form itself … is produced by certain kinds of historical crises" so that "allegory reflect[s] some historical failure of or crisis in human perception en masse," which, as such, points to something other than history and perception. For de Man, "'[t]he Truth' gets replaced by contextual and discursive truths of various hermeneutic circles," whereas for Benjamin the "allegory's apparently arbitrary linking of an unrepresentable idea to a material emblem indicates that the idea itself was dialectically enfolded into a material history strewn with similarly transient ideas" (Hansen 2004: 675–6). That is, however arbitrary the linking of a piece of reality (the "unrepresentable idea") with some signifier (the "material emblem") may be, the mere possibility of a link between the two series presupposes that they both share a common element. "Common" means that this element belongs neither in the one series (the realm of the immutable "idea") nor in the other (the realm of transient "material history"), and, yet, permeates both. This is the element of the "transient ideas," which imbues both the idea with transience, and history with the idea. In this way, allegory gives an account of the "unrepresentable idea" of the real object insofar as it "represents the irrecoverable loss of the object's originary sense" (Hansen 2004: 675). Thus, "allegory historicizes itself, and immanent critique, then, becomes an allegorical method for discussing and meditating on lost forms," whereby "formalism itself becomes allegorical," that is, "a formalism capable of doubting its own truth-claims without giving up on the object's *Warheit-Gehalt* (truth-content) wholesale" (Hansen 2004: 675–6, 680).

In Hansen's concise conclusion, although both "in de Man and in Benjamin, formalism" and the question of the allegorical form "become the way for modern thought to negotiate the problem of historicity," Benjamin "enfolds the transcendent into the immanent while de Man's approach deconstructs the transcendent via the immanent" (Hansen 2004: 669). I would argue that it is this *enfolding of the transcendent into the immanent* that constitutes proper secular thought. The sheer deconstruction of transcendence only reduces "transient ideas" (and, thereby, representation itself) to pure transience, while leaving the ideatic aspect of transcendence intact. In short, Benjamin's position is that the constructedness and deconstructibility of truths can only mean that similar effects occur in nature itself – if language has "fallen" it is because nature itself has "fallen"; therefore, in being deconstructed, truth reveals "the object's *Warheit-Gehalt* (truth-content)."

Benjamin belongs to the alternative, Spinozian-Marxian, line of thought, according to which words and things (or, to put it in Spinoza's terms, thought and extension) are the two aspects (attributes) in which one and the same substance expresses itself. Being the expression of one and the same substance, words and things are structurally homologous, so that our knowledge about our thought (epistemology) is also knowledge about the things in the external world, and these structures shared by both thought and things point to the structures of the substance or being that they express (ontology). In other words, our epistemology is always also ontology, and vice versa – whence the concept of *epistemontology.* However, even as epistemology is a recapitulation of ontology and vice versa, this does not mean that things reveal themselves transparently to thought – the metaphors of revelation and transparency do not even apply here. Nor does it mean that, as we shall see, things and thought are mirror images of each other. To recall Spinoza's words, "the order and connections of ideas is the same as the order and connections of things" (*Ethics* IIP7), not because they see in each other their mirror image. There is no kind of communication between body and mind. Yet both express the same order because they both express one being: the third element that belongs to neither but is in both.

In this context it seems imperative to address the following famous and multiply commented-upon passage from Althusser's commentary regarding "the transition from Volume One to Volume Three" (Althusser and Balibar 2009: 209) in Marx's *Capital*. This transition, Althusser emphatically remarks, is associated both in Marx and several of his commentators with a:

> confusion between the thought-concrete, which Marx completely isolated from the real-concrete in the *Introduction*, and this same real-concrete ... in reality, the concrete of Volume Three, i.e., the knowledge of ground rent, profit and interest, is, like all knowledge, *not the empirical concrete but the concept*, and therefore still always an abstraction ... still a product of thinking, the *knowledge* of an empirical existence and not that empirical *existence* itself ... We never leave abstraction on the way from Volume One to Volume Three, i.e., we never leave knowledge ... *we never leave the concept* ... never for an instant do we set foot beyond the absolutely impassable frontier which separates ... the concept from ... things – and for a very good reason: *this frontier is impassable in principle because ... there is no homogeneous space (spirit or real) between the abstract of the concept of a thing and the empirical concrete of this thing which could justify the use of the concept of a frontier.*
>
> (Althusser and Balibar 2009: 209–10)

In this, Althusser could not be more correct: it is an echo of Spinoza's adamant insistence on the fact that there is absolutely no communication whatsoever between the two attributes, thought and extension. The homology between thought and things or concrete reality owes not to any trespassing of a presumed frontier between them but, to repeat from the introduction, it owes to the parallelism between them, that is, the fact that "the order and connections of ideas is the same as the order and connections of things" (*Ethics* IIP7). The real confusion, evidenced both in Althusser and several of his commentators, is the assumption that in order for thought to produce adequate knowledge of reality it would have to go outside itself and touch, or itself become, that reality. In this internal contradiction within Althusser's work we encounter one of those points that exemplify one of Althusser's own theses regarding the writings of any thinker, including Althusser himself. Applied to Althusser, his own thesis entails, in Balibar's words, that "what Althusser 'thought' is of course not what he 'wanted to think'" (Balibar 1996: 112). I think this contradiction relates to Althusser's zeal to define any scientific knowledge (including, by the way, structuralism) "not" – as Warren Montag puts it in recapitulating Althusser's critique of Deleuze's essay on structuralism that we shall revisit in detail in the third chapter – "by the real object that it studies ... but by that with which it has broken: ... 'historicism and empiricism'" (Montag 2013: 99). One of the defining characteristics of this tradition with which scientific knowledge must break is the supposition of a pre-given object of reality (including, for instance, an authentic past) that it must reconstruct. However, as I hope it has already begun, and will continue, to become clear, this is not what is meant by reality here. I also do not know the extent to which those moments in Althusser's work that seem to subscribe to the Kantian severance of knowledge from the thing-in-itself may also owe simply to the latter's hegemonic dominance in intellectual history.

Moreover, epistemontology must not be misunderstood as a continuation of the theocratic motif of the "organic" link between words and things. Epistemontology fully recognizes the arbitrary nature of the secular sign, linguistic or economic; in the Foucauldian idiom, epistemontology is part of the era for which the divinely guaranteed continuum between being and thought has been broken. There is no bond whatsoever between being and thought in secular capitalist modernity, yet the two are homologous, and this is so not because of any transcendent ground. Quite the contrary, what enables their homology is the enfolding of transcendence within immanence, that is, within the material and historical conditions of production and the exchange of value (economic and linguistic). We shall approach this matter with regard to Marx's theory of commodity fetishism more directly in the second chapter. For now let us note that the crux of Marx's theory of commodity fetishism consists in revealing the homology between being and thought in the episteme of secular capitalist modernity, and in fact as constitutive of this episteme.

By this token, in Pierre Macherey's words, "[t]he presentation of the classical *épistémé*, defined as an order of representation, given by Foucault in *The Order of Things*" – as we saw it above – "left no place for [either] Spinoza" or Marx, and both thinkers, as Deleuze remarks regarding Spinoza, belong to "a rather hidden and a rather forbidden history of philosophy" (Macherey 1998: 124; Deleuze 1990: 322, as cited in Macherey 1998: 124, with translation modified). However, as we shall see below in this chapter, the Spinozian-Marxian parallelism between extension and thought is not to be understood as an "[e]xpression" that, as Macherey puts it following Deleuze, "is the opposite of a representation" (Macherey 1998: 123). To be sure, the homology of extension and thought indeed means that for "Spinoza knowledge is not 'representation' of the thing to the mind through the mediation of a mental image itself capable of being relayed through a system of signs; rather, knowledge is expression, that is, production and constitution of the thing itself in the mind" (Macherey 1998: 123). However, this does not mean that "expression … does not require the mediation of signs in order to take place" (Macherey 1998: 123). Rather, it means that this dynamic production and constitution of the thing is inseparable from a dynamic production and constitution of the sign. Not that the sign constitutes the thing – as idealism would have it – but thing and sign are produced and constituted in one and the same movement, and they do so in homologous ways, so that the order of things and that of signs are the same. It is for this reason that Spinozian monism and Marx's theory of commodity fetishism entail a unified epistemontology.

We can begin approaching this simultaneous production and constitution of signs and things or thought and extension by reflecting on Étienne Balibar's insightful commentary on Marx's theory of commodity fetishism in his short book *The Philosophy of Marx*. Here is Balibar's citation of a relevant passage from Marx's *Capital, Volume 1*:

> "The fetishism of the commodity," Marx tells us, is the fact that a "definite social relation between men themselves … assumes here, for them, the fantastic form of a relation between things." Or, alternatively, "to the producers … the social relations between their private labours appear … as material [*dinglich*] relations between persons and social relations between things."
>
> (Balibar 2007: 56, citing Marx 1990: 165–6)

(Note that the German "*dinglich*" means literally "thingly," that is, as relations made out of things or nature.) Paradoxically, this fetishistic inversion is possible not because of the thingliness or materiality of the commodities, but because "commodities," while being "useful material objects … also possess another quality, which is immaterial but no less objective: their exchange-value … expressed … as a certain sum of money" (Balibar 2007: 58). In fact, this "intrinsic relation between the commodity and *its* value … confer[s] on [the commodity] an added objectivity," insofar as it is "the 'objective laws' of the circulation of commodities" or the objective and independent movement of the "fluctuation of values which determines the conditions in which individuals have access to commodities"; by contrast, "the personalities of the individuals who carry out" the act of sale and purchase "are quite irrelevant to it" and, as such, "they are entirely interchangeable" (Balibar 2007: 58–9).

Therefore, what makes Marx's "theory of fetishism … one of the great theoretical constructions of modern philosophy" is that it shows "that there is no theory of objectivity without a theory of subjectivity. *By rethinking the constitution of social objectivity, Marx at the same time virtually revolutionized the concept of the 'subject'*" (Balibar 2007: 56, 64–5). The dominant (Kantian) transcendentalism posits the "separation of the natural from the moral world" along with the opposition between subject and object, and postulates "a consciousness [that] 'constitutes a world,' i.e., makes it intelligible by means of its own categories or forms of representation – space, time, causality." As opposed to this model, Marx introduces "the mechanism of fetishism" as "indeed … a constituting of the world: the social world, structured by relations of exchange, which clearly represents the greatest part of the 'nature' in which human individuals live, think, and act today" (Balibar 2007: 65–6).[1] Commodity fetishism means that "the constitution of the world is not … the work of a subject, but a genesis of subjectivity (*a* form of determinate historical subjectivity) as part (and counterpart) of the social world of objectivity" (Balibar 2007: 67).

What is more, this simultaneous genesis of objectivity and subjectivity is determined not so much by the content of these objects or "the personalities" of the subjects, which, to repeat, become "entirely interchangeable," but by their "relations of exchange" and the "fluctuation of values" (Balibar 2007: 58). If objects and subjects are not pre-given entities with inherent qualities but are rather constituted purely through "relations of exchange," then objects and subjects are nothing else than expressions of value. In capitalism, the being expressed through objects (reality) and subjects (thought) is value. Since objects and subjects are expressions of value, they themselves are constituted not on the basis of any inherent individual qualities of each object or subject but through formal relations with all other objects or subjects, as members of purely differential structures. This is the reason why secular thought had to develop toward formalization and to produce knowledge that treats its objects as structures.

*

Here we have arrived at two interrelated crucial inferences regarding the epistemontology of secular capitalist modernity: being is value, and, as a corollary of this, thought tends toward formalization and structuralism. (We know from the introduction here that being is not only value, but for now we are focusing on the effect of commodity fetishism which consists in making being appear precisely as only value.) We shall return to these interrelated inferences shortly, after we continue to pursue briefly Balibar's line of thought that points to the need for an epistemontology.

*

The simultaneous genesis of objectivity and subjectivity indicated in Marx's theory of commodity fetishism has as its corollary, Balibar continues, the fact that:

> the real and the imaginary (what Marx terms the "suprasensible," the "fantastic form" of autonomous commodities which dominate their producers) are immediately combined, or, alternatively, the *givenness* of the objects of experience is immediately combined with the *norm* of behaviour they call forth.
>
> (Balibar 2007: 66)

This move constitutes a radical subversion of the "three viewpoints" of classical thought, "which were, respectively, those of science (intelligibility of phenomena), metaphysics (necessary illusions of pure thought), and morality or 'practical reason' (behavioral imperative)" (Balibar 2007: 66). Hence, seen "from the standpoint of classical idealism, it might seem that" Marx's theory of commodity fetishism "merely combined" or, even worse, "*confused*" these "three viewpoints." However, a comparison between "those which proceeded it in the history of philosophy" and Marx's commodity fetishism "brings out the originality of this theory of the constitution of the world," which lies in the fact that, on the one hand, the world "does not arise out of the activity of any subject," while, on the other hand, commodity fetishism "does constitute subjects or forms of subjectivity and consciousness *in* the very field of objectivity." With commodity fetishism, "subjectivity has shifted" from "its 'transcendent' or 'transcendental' position … into a position of effect or result of the social process" (Balibar 2007: 66). This means that the individual subject in Marx "is one that is practical, multiple, anonymous, and by definition not conscious of itself" (Balibar 2007: 67). Marx's sole reference to an autonomous "dominant subject [*übergreifendes Subjekt*]" is with regard to capital (Marx 1990: 255), that is, at least in a sense, "a *non-subject* … namely, 'society,' i.e., the whole set of activities of production, exchange and consumption the combined effect of which is perceptible to each person outside himself, as a 'natural' property of things" (Balibar 2007: 67). If it is not a universal subject but this non-subject or society that constitutes the world, then, it is also "this non-subject or complex of activities which produces social *representations* of objects at the same time as it produces representable *objects*" (Balibar 2007: 67). It follows that the "commodity, like money, to say nothing of capital and its various forms, is preeminently both a representation and, at the same time, an object; it is an object always already given in the form of a representation" (Balibar 2007: 67). It is an object always already given in the form of thought since it is an object always already given in the form of (exchange) value. In short, Marx's theory of commodity fetishism amounts to the philosophical thesis that the object, whose part and counterpart is the subject, is both thing and signifier.

Therefore, the episteme of secular capitalist modernity requires a coherent epistemontological theory that treats subject, object and word as structurally homologous, or, what amounts to the same, as series of the same structure. Subject, object, and representation are series that replicate the structure of one and the same being, in its aspect as value. However, to repeat, and as we shall see particularly in the third chapter, this does not mean that the series are mirror images of each other; rather they stand in a symbolic or properly structuralist relation. Nor does this mean that structure forms a totality or that all domains of reality and its knowledge are reducible to their unity. I am of course alluding here to Althusser's and Macherey's criticisms of Deleuze's aforementioned account of structuralism on the basis that, again in Montag's summary of this exchange, "Deleuze's essay" – "How do we recognize structuralism?" – "points to [the] direction" of "positing … a unity where it does not exist, a unity moreover guaranteed by the identity of the object of knowledge across domains" – the object being "language" or value (Montag 2013: 97).

Thus, even while striving to focus on the aspect of being as value, we must keep in the back of our minds the fact that value and structure concern only the one aspect of being, the other involving, as we shall see in the last chapter, the singularity of every single thing so that there is disorder and non-unity not only between different series but also within each series.

Commodity fetishism and structuralism

With this reference to structuralism, let us return to our two earlier inferences to address first the second one, namely, that thought in secular capitalist modernity tends toward formalization and structuralism. As Balibar remarks, the capitalist market obeys only the "model of objectivity of economic phenomena in general and their laws," which are as inexorable as "the objectivity of the laws of nature" (Balibar 2007: 58). This owes to the fact that in capitalism "economic objects are *always already quantifiable* ('that is how things are,' it is their nature)," so that "the social imperative [is] to *submit* them (and the human activities which produce them) to an endless quantification and rationalization, transcending any pre-ordained limit, be it 'natural' or 'moral'" (Balibar 2007: 66). From this Balibar infers that there is a "double language 'spoken' by the world of commodities: the language of equivalence and measurement, given formal expression in the monetary sign, and the language of obligation and contract, formally expressed in law" (Balibar 2007: 71). This, in turn, means that the theory of commodity fetishism amounts to "the analysis of symbolic structures," which "finds its ultimate expression in structural Marxism" (Balibar 2007: 71 and 56). However, Balibar links Marx's conception of the law exclusively to the legal and juridical realm and, thus, locates the "structuralist-inspired reading" of Marx's theory in thinkers such as E.B. Pashukanis and Jean-Joseph Goux, who have argued respectively, in Balibar's words, that "just as there is an economic fetishism of *things*, so there is a juridical fetishism of *persons*," or that "the structure common to economic and juridical (and moral) fetishism is *generalized equivalence*" which "subjects individuals to the [double] form of circulation (circulation of values, circulation of obligations)" (Balibar 2007: 71–2). Although Pashukanis's and Goux's theories are possible also because of the theory of commodity fetishism, we must not forget that the concept of law both in Marx and in structuralism transcends its legal or moral sense. This means that symbolic structures are not limited to economic and the juridical systems.

Beyond the laws that can be broken, there are scientific and properly structural laws that are unbreakable. Marx refers to such laws as "eternal laws," for example, when Marx writes that "commodity fetishism … is … inseparable from the production of commodities," it follows that commodity fetishism is one of "the eternal laws of commodity-exchange" (Marx 1990: 165, 301). As long as I exist under the conditions of capitalist commodity-exchange, I can be aware of, examine, analyze, study, or ignore the law of commodity fetishism, but I cannot break it. That commodity fetishism is an eternal law of capitalism means that it is what Ferdinand de Saussure calls a "synchronic law." As de Saussure writes:

> It is a popular practice to speak of laws in linguistics … what are they like? Since language is a social institution, one might assume *a priori* that it is governed by prescriptions analogous to those that control communities. Now every social law has two basic characteristics: it is *imperative* and it is *general* … Do the laws of language fit this definition?
>
> (de Saussure 1959: 91)

As an example, de Saussure compares models that describe the development of Greek in time – such as that the "final *m* changed to *n*: **jugom – zugón* (cf. Latin *jugum*)" – to laws of the Greek language such as that "the accent never falls farther back than the antepenult" (de Saussure 1959: 91–2). Examples of the first type describe "diachronic facts," while those of the second type state "synchronic facts" (de Saussure 1959: 95). Because "diachrony … supposes a dynamic force through which an effect is produced … diachronic events are always accidental and particular" and "force themselves upon language but are in no way general" (de Saussure 1959: 93, 95). By contrast, "the synchronic law is general but not imperative," so that when "one speaks of law in synchrony, it is in the sense of an arrangement, a principle of regularity" (de Saussure 1959: 92–3). The eternal laws of commodity-exchange are of this latter type, describing general principles of regularity, like mathematical laws or what Spinoza calls "eternal truths," as opposed to imperatives, which Spinoza links to revelation as the presentation of the law in the form of moral decrees to be obeyed out of fear. Synchronic laws are "eternal" insofar as they remain "eternally" the same within the historically specific episteme that they govern – in our case, the era of secular capitalist modernity. Far from being imperative, these laws are performed by people even "without being aware of it" (Marx 1990: 166–7). A fundamental task of a (monist) structural Marxism consists in identifying these laws or principles of general regularities in all homologous series of value.

In the third chapter, we shall also see how structuralist thought conceives the relation between structure and diachrony. As a reminder to the reader, by "structuralism" I do not mean the specific movement labeled as such and which became the object of poststructuralist critique. Rather, as it will become more clear in the course of the present work, I mean a form of thought specific to the episteme whose object of knowledge is value (in all its varied manifestations) and whose development is coextensive with secular capitalist modernity since the seventeenth century. In terms of its historical aspect, this thesis might appear similar to "Althusser's identification … of Montesquieu as the founding moment of structuralism's prehistory" in his 1962–1963 seminar on "The Origins of Structuralism" (Montag 2013: 26). A major difference, however, lies in the fact that, as follows from the above references to Althusser, he (along with Macherey) eventually (i.e., by the late 1960s) thought that, if structuralism is something of which to take heed at all, then it should be a fragmentary system of thought, in the sense that each field of knowledge would have a different object, rather than value as a universal object. Conversely, to posit value as the universal object meant for Althusser to produce an imaginary unity – and this is an error to be avoided. By contrast, as will become increasingly evident, I argue that this permeation of everything with value is not a subjective fallacy but part of the objective imaginary constituted by and in commodity fetishism. Further, I argue that there is something that exceeds this objective fantasy – the excess to structure – which, as we shall see in the last chapter, relates to Spinoza's third kind of knowledge.

The corollary other difference between Althusser's and my theses consists in that for Althusser, Spinoza and structuralism seem to be alternatives that do not overlap. As Montag comments, after his turn away from structuralism to a "theory of the encounter" and "a philosophy of the conjuncture, according to which 'history is a process without a subject or goals,'" Althusser was "inspired by Epicurus and Lucretius … as well as Machiavelli, Spinoza, and Nietzsche, for whom structure might be thought to be a reduction of real complexity and heterogeneity to an imaginary order" (Montag 2013: 16). I maintain, as we shall have the occasion to see, that structuralism is part of Spinoza's system and, in fact, does not pertain to the imaginary order (first kind of knowledge) but to that of reason (second kind of knowledge) – which, by the way, is also Deleuze's position.[2] However, it is true that there is a further real complexity and heterogeneity – what Spinoza calls singular essence – that eludes reason or structuralism, and is accessible only to intuition (third kind of knowledge). Nevertheless, for Spinoza, in opposition to the imaginary which is the source of error, both reason and intuition access truth – for, to repeat, the "illusion" that everything is value is an objective truth of capitalism. Incidentally, the present thesis agrees entirely with Althusser that history is a process without a subject or goals.

The next section returns to our first inference above – namely, that due to commodity fetishism, in capitalism being appears exclusively as value – and concludes in its last paragraph with some further remarks on the structuralist nature of secular thought.

Being *qua* value, and the methodology of commodity fetishism

The first lesson we learn from Spinoza is that being can be conceived by secular thought – that is, a thought that does not presuppose a creator of being – only as that which is the cause of itself: "substance cannot be produced by anything else … [and] therefore it … [is] the cause of itself" (*Ethics* IP7D). Being or substance is the power of being to actualize itself; it is the power of self-actualization. Therefore, both extension and thought – since they both express being – should be direct manifestations of the power of self-actualization. However this is not the case, precisely because of commodity fetishism, which, as Marx tells us, turns thought and reality into manifestations of value. The era of secular capitalist modernity is one that, on the one hand – due to its secular character – necessitates the conception of being as the power of self-actualization, while, on the other hand – due to its capitalist economy and its commodity fetishism – prevents thought from conceiving of being as the power of self-actualization. Another way of formulating the effect of commodity fetishism is to say that in capitalism the power-of-self-actualization is excluded from consciousness.[3] However, if commodity fetishism forces thought to conceive of being in a distorted way, as exclusively value, this is because reality itself is distorted within a capitalist economy. As we have seen in the introduction, in capitalism, being expresses itself in distorted ways in *both* thought and reality. To repeat, "both the money and the commodity function only as different modes of existence of value itself, the money as its general mode of existence, the commodity as its particular or, so to speak, disguised mode" (Marx 1990: 255). As a result of commodification, both concrete things and abstract exchange-values are "different modes of existence" of being *qua* exclusively value (and not also *qua* power-of-self-actualization).

*

At this point one may object: why should we take Marx's theory of commodity fetishism at face value? Should we not instead take a more sober approach and simply try to demystify the fetish? Should we not simply try to enlighten ourselves by pointing out that being is also the power of self-actualization and that its appearance as exclusively value is only an illusion produced by commodity fetishism?

The key in Marx's methodology regarding commodity fetishism is that he treated this *appearing* not just as an error to be rectified but as constitutive of reality and being. Balibar, to whom we are once again returning, spells out the logic of Marx's methodology. Initially there appear to be two alternative approaches to commodity fetishism and its inversion of relations between subjects and objects, which we could call the enchanted and the disenchanted approaches:

> One may … construe this relation either as the effect of a "supernatural" power of money, which creates and animates the movement of commodities, embodying its own imperishable value in the perishable bodies of commodities, or, on the other hand, as a "natural"

> effect of the relation between commodities, which establishes an expression of their values and the proportions in which they can be exchanged by way of social institutions.
>
> (Balibar 2007: 59)

As Balibar adds right after this remark, "[i]n reality, these two conceptions are symmetrical and interdependent" (Balibar 2007: 59). "On the one hand, by a movement akin to demystification or demythification, he is concerned to *dissolve* that phenomenon" of fetishism and "to show that it is an appearance based, in the last instance, on a 'misunderstanding'" (Balibar 2007: 60). On the other hand, however, he pursued this "misunderstanding" or "appearance" as far as only two thinkers before him had done, Spinoza and Hegel. That is, Marx understood:

> that active "appearing" (both *Schein* and *Erscheinung*, i.e., both illusion and phenomenon) constitutes a mediation or necessary function without which, in given historical conditions, the life of society would be quite simply impossible. To suppress the appearance would be to abolish social relations.
>
> (Balibar 2007: 61)

To suppress the appearing – both illusion and objectively given phenomenon – would be to abolish reality itself. This is why, in Spinoza's terms, "truth is the standard both of itself and of the false" (*Ethics* IIP43S). Knowing the truth presupposes knowing both itself (objective phenomena) and the false illusions that are engendered by these objective phenomena. Or, to put it in the parlance of Lacanian psychoanalysis, Marx understood that we cannot constitute, or have cognitive access to, a symbolic order (an objective system of "social relations") without the mediation of the imaginary. (Parenthetically, in the fourth chapter we shall see that, nevertheless, there are differences in the ways Spinoza and Hegel relate truth to appearing.) This is why, as Balibar continues:

> To the first stage of the critique, which consists in dissolving the *appearance of objectivity*, there must be added, then, another which is, in actuality, the precondition for it, and demonstrates the constitution of *the appearance in objectivity.*
>
> (Balibar 2007: 61)

It is because the appearance (illusion) is constituted *in* objectivity that "fetishism is not a subjective phenomenon or a false perception of reality, as an optical illusion or a superstitious belief would be. It constitutes, rather, the way in which reality (a certain form of social structure) cannot but appear" (Balibar 2007: 60). In other words, we can demystify commodity fetishism only by also taking it seriously, as an objective fact.

The fact that in secular capitalist modernity value appears to be the being of which everything within reality is a manifestation is not a subjective illusion or *just* a false perception of reality and being. Rather, it is the sole way in which reality and being can appear in the specific social structure of secular capitalist modernity, due to objective necessity. Put differently, when thought is by necessity distorted (illusory), the distortion is objective, that is, the reality of being is itself distorted. It is *as such an objective necessity that epistemontology*, and hence, this work, *treats seriously being* qua *value*. The supplementary parallel movement of this is, of course, to foreground the aspect of being *qua* power-of-self-actualization, to which we shall return at the end of this chapter.

The fact that in secular capitalist modernity being appears exclusively as value means that its episteme can have the most immediate cognitive access to being by approaching its manifestations as systems of values – that is, as structures consisting of purely formal, relational, and differential elements. Hence, value becomes the ubiquitous object of knowledge, from economics, ethics, and aesthetics, to linguistics, psychoanalysis, and ontology. Consequently, the tendency to formalization and eventually structuralism defines the entire philosophical and theoretical paradigm of secular capitalist modernity both in its monist and dualist (dialectical) variants. While demonstrating these points, the present work will reconceptualize "structuralism" as the (tacit or not) force in thought throughout secular modernity. Structuralism is produced by capitalism but it also provides the very rules of thought that condition revolutionary thought and practice. The quasi-universal principle of formalization invites us to examine the relation between the two modern lines of thought, as represented by, on the one hand, the line Spinoza-Marx-structuralism-psychoanalysis, and, on the other hand, dialectics, from Hegel to Lukács, Adorno, Jameson, and Žižek, including the Hegelian reading of psychoanalysis. This original reinstating of structuralism bears affinities to Žižek's reading of Lacan and Lacanian structuralist thought, but it is primarily based on Spinozian monism, while also specifying the exact importance of Hegel.

Other attempts to challenge the dominant secular epistemology

Let us now turn to the line opposing the dominant (post-)Kantian epistemological position. Eminent in this tradition is Heidegger, for whom the question remains throughout how authentic being, as well as authentic truth and tradition, can disclose itself within the ontic realm of historical time, in spite of the fallenness of Dasein. The latter is due to none other than the imaginary and ideological distortions involved in representation. As I am juxtaposing extensively Heidegger's position to Marx's theory of commodity fetishism (and to Benjamin) elsewhere, here I will only try to summarize briefly from that piece a central aspect of their difference. At first sight, Heidegger appears to concur with the position of the theory of commodity fetishism (and of psychoanalysis) that the objectively produced imaginary "distortions" of representation reflect objective "distortions" of reality – that is, they reflect that there is no "authentic" being, except insofar as so-called "authentic" being is itself "distorted." In *Being and Time* Heidegger recurrently stresses that "falling [*Verfallen*]" – the "basic kind of Being which belongs to everydayness" – "has mostly the character of Being-lost in the publicness of the 'they,'" whereby "Dasein has … fallen away [*abgefallen*] from itself as an authentic potentiality for Being its Self"; nevertheless, "falling is a definite existential characteristic of Dasein itself" and "reveals an *essential* ontological structure of Dasein itself" (Heidegger 2008: 219–20, 224; Heidegger 1974ff, 2: 233–4, 238).

Statements such as the above seem to indicate that, for Heidegger, the imaginary is integral to the ontological structure of Dasein. He also categorically declares that Dasein is always "fallen" and, hence, always prey to the untruths and illusions of the "they," and cautions us not to "take the fallenness of Dasein as a 'fall' from a purer and higher 'primal status,'" for "not only do we lack any experience of this [primal status] ontically, but ontologically we lack any possibilities or clues for Interpreting it" (Heidegger 2008: 220; Heidegger 1974ff: 2: 233–4). In short, there is no pre- or non-fallen state of Dasein. Yet, instead of this distinction Heidegger speaks of the difference between Dasein's "inauthenticity" and "authenticity." Heidegger defines this difference as one between, on the one hand, "a quite distinctive kind of Being-in-the-world – the kind which is completely fascinated by the 'world' and by the Dasein-with of Others in the 'they,'" and, on the other hand, "*authentic* existence," the latter initially being modestly defined as "not something which floats above falling everydayness" but as "only a modified way in which such everydayness is seized upon" (Heidegger 2008: 220 and 224; Heidegger 1974ff: 2: 233, 238). Now, Dasein's means to its authenticity is "resoluteness" (*Entschlossenheit*), a term which "signifies letting oneself be summoned out of one's own lostness in the 'they,'" and which Heidegger further defines as "*the resolution* [*Entschluß*]" that "*is precisely the disclosive projection and determination of what is factically possible at the time* [*ist gerade erst das erschließende Entwerfen und Bestimmen der jeweiligen faktischen Möglichkeiten*]" (Heidegger 2008: 345; Heidegger 1974ff: 2: 395). Even here Heidegger again cautions that even "resoluteness, as *authentic Being-one's-Self*, does not detach Dasein from its world" and its fallenness, and that, "disclosed in its 'there,' [Dasein] maintains itself both in truth and untruth with equal primordiality" (Heidegger 2008: 344–5; Heidegger 1974ff, 2: 395–6). In fact, "this 'really' holds in particular for resoluteness as authentic truth [*Das gilt 'eigentlich' gerade von der Entschlossenheit als der eigentlichen Wahrheit*]" (Heidegger 2008, 345; Heidegger 1974ff: 2: 396).

Yet, this equo-primordiality of truth and untruth is fully undermined in the next step that states – and herein occurs Heidegger's leap – that in the case of "resoluteness as authentic truth … resoluteness appropriates untruth authentically [*eignet sich die Unwahrheit eigentlich zu*]" (Heidegger: 2008, 345; Heidegger 1974ff: 2: 396). In other words, although the essential ontological characteristic of Dasein is to be primordially submerged in both truth and untruth, the moment that Dasein lets itself be summoned out of its lostness in the "they," truth appropriates untruth authentically. This is why for Heidegger, as Howard Caygill puts it, "the moment of origin is potentially a moment of clarity and resolute decision" within history, a moment "of historical decision, enabling Dasein to choose as a subject its own destiny" (Caygill 2005: 308–9). For Heidegger, "the site of tradition is surrendered to the subject of tradition, be it the hero, the poet, the leader or the people" (Heidegger 2008: 305). A juxtaposition to Benjamin makes the point more clear. While Heidegger "very rapidly translated the handing over of tradition into the agonal, or dialectical, logic of subjectivity" and "grants the possibility of gathering tradition on the ground of the subject," Benjamin "insisted upon the destruction of tradition" and "avoided any temptation to transform the site of tradition into the place of the subject" (Caygill 2005: 301, 305–6). For, as Benjamin writes, "that which is original is never revealed in the naked and manifest existence of the factual," for "on the one hand it needs to be recognized as a process of restoration and re-establishment, but, on the other hand, and precisely because of this, as something imperfect and incomplete" (Benjamin 1977: 45). If the factual treats the original as something that needs restoration and re-establishment, it is because the original or authentic itself is imperfect and incomplete. Reality and thought distort being because being itself is from the outset distorted. There is no prototype free of distortion; the distortion of being does not have an opposite or other. Heidegger's attempt fails because it obstinately upholds the ideal of a perfect original, in comparison to which any factual is inauthentic and inferior (ironically, a rather Platonic model).

While Heidegger opposed the philosophical tradition of *parousia* (presence) ever since Plato, Alain Badiou exhibits, as Peter Hallward put it in his commentary on Badiou, an "unusual fidelity to Plato … once you have renounced its transcendent aspect" (Badiou 2001: 119), and takes Platonism as a philosophy that "does not take as its point of departure words, but things" (Badiou 2003: 50). Does this mean that in Badiou "things" become a new locus of authentic origin? At least in a generous reading, and as in Heidegger above, it initially appears that the origin itself may be immanent in its effects, as, for instance, in the following passage:

> Certainly, it is true that sense [in Plato] is distributed according to the One and that beings are of the order of the simulacra … But it in no way follows from this, as Deleuze assumes is the case with Plato, that the simulacra or beings are necessarily depreciated or considered as nonbeings. On the contrary, it is necessary to affirm the rights of

> simulacra as so many equivocal cases of univocity that joyously attest to the univocal power of Being.
>
> (Badiou 2000: 26)

As in Plato, the distinction between Being and beings or simulacra is neither one between Thing and words, nor between Word/Idea and things. Rather, it is one between authentic Being/Idea and simulacra (things or ideas) within empirical reality. Badiou seems to argue here against Deleuze that the simulacra in Plato are not to be depreciated as inferior "non-beings" (imaginary), but rather that the right should necessarily be acknowledged of the many equivocal cases of the simulacra to attest to the univocal power of Being. From the perspective of the monist theory of commodity fetishism, one would formulate the point in stronger terms, as it is not simply a matter of the simulacra's "rights" but a necessary presupposition for the univocity of being that it be attested by the simulacra – as it (being) itself is an effect of this attestation. That is, Being does not exist but as a (non-actualizable) effect of its simulacra.

What is here manifest as a slight, perhaps only rhetorical rather than essentially conceptual, discrepancy between Badiou and the present epistemontological position becomes magnified in Badiou's turn to mathematical formalization and logical proof, as the means through which things express themselves. In "What is a Proof in Spinoza's *Ethics*?" Badiou argues that "a proof explains the proposition in terms of what has gone before," that is, what is already known. As Joseph Hughes has shown in his commentary on Badiou's essay, to attend to a proof is "to notice that it is not merely a recuperative gesture which becomes clear only after everything is already known." Rather, for Spinoza, attending to a proof requires "an inescapable apprenticeship through which thought learns *to create.*" Spinoza's concept of proof exceeds the "merely logical proof" and its linearity in time because it includes an inventive dimension, that is, for Spinoza, true ideas "can only be *discovered*, in so far as they are *invented*, and once invented will ground, at a later stage of history, the discovery of still more," including about what has gone before. This means, Hughes continues, that for Spinoza, (a) method "has a history which is the history of invention," (b) "science must be invented," (c) both reading and demonstrating are "discovery," and – what is presupposed for the above three – (d) that "there is a temporality to the process of demonstration," because of which "there always persists, in any given utterance, a horizon of potentiality, specifically the potentiality for radical, perhaps savage, future specification." In short, Hughes historicizes proof and method in the most Spinozian, Benjaminian, and psychoanalytic sense; that is, he shows that the temporality of demonstration is not linear – proceeding from one known to the next – but rather involves retroactivity – bringing a future known back to a past unknown so as to render it known, that is, so as to bring it into existence.[4]

Now I would like to turn to Deleuze, a thinker whose work is generally a source of inspiration for the present work, but from which the present theory needs to be differentiated particularly regarding his concept of expression, the role of imagination in knowledge, and the third kind of knowledge in Spinoza.[5] Note that by imagination Spinoza means, beyond what we usually call imagination, all sensory perception and bodily affections and emotions – all of which he calls passive affects (even as under specific circumstances we can have active affects). In his *Expressionism in Philosophy: Spinoza*, Deleuze aligns truth with "expression," and rejects "impression" and the "sign" (representation) as a purely imaginary distortion of truth that occurs mostly through anthropomorphic projections. For Deleuze, philosophy and truth lie unambiguously on the side of expression, while revelation and faith lie equally unambiguously on the side of the sign. In Deleuze's words, a "revelatory" or "imperative sign is not an expression but a confused impression which leads us to believe that the true expressions of God, the laws of nature, are so many commandments" (Deleuze 1990: 181). Here we see a concurrence between Deleuze and Badiou's claim that only mathematical formalism – the laws of nature *qua* geometrical laws – expresses truth, that is, "an eternal truth," not unlike the truth "that God … has from eternity decreed that three angles of a triangle are equal to two right angles" (*TTP* 63). If in God's decree regarding the eternal law of the triangle we see a commandment – something that we obey only out of fear of punishment – then we perceive it as revelation, the latter consisting in an imaginary mirror-like projection: "[r]evelation is not an expression, but a cultivation of the inexpressible, a confused and relative knowledge through which we lend God determinations analogous to our own (Understanding, Will)" (Deleuze 1990: 181–2).

What Deleuze presents here is indeed an accurate description of a point repeated by Spinoza throughout the *Theologico-Political Treatise* and elsewhere. However, it is inaccurate to infer that the "opposition of expressions and signs is one of the fundamental principles of Spinozism" (Deleuze 1990: 182). In fact, such an inference is fundamentally wrong, for one of Spinoza's fundamental principles is actually that "*truth* is the standard both of itself and of the false" (*Ethics* IP43S) – or, to put it in the present terms, truth is the standard of both expression and the sign. Truth cannot just be expressed; it must be both expressed (as a mathematical law or logical structure) and revealed (narrated as [an imaginary] article of faith). And both, expression (mathematical law) and sign (revelation/fable), are the two sides of representation – both equally required for truth to be told.

The following passage from Deleuze can be read in support of this thesis:

> *Expression itself no longer emanates, no longer resembles anything.* And such a result can be obtained only within a perspective of

> univocity … Things in general are modes of divine being, that is, they implicate the same attributes that constitute the nature of this being … The things that are produced are not imitations any more than their ideas are models. There is nothing exemplary even in the idea of God, since this is itself, in its formal being, also produced.
> (Deleuze 1990: 180–1)

From a monist (anti-emanetist and pro-univocity) perspective, what follows from this passage is that signs (modes) implicate the same attributes that constitute the nature of the divine being. Therefore, if modes involve a confused knowledge through which they endeavor to rescue God's superiority, this is due to the fact that the divine attributes *are themselves fallen* from their (transcendentalist) divine status and are craving to be restored in their superiority. To put it once again in Benjamin's idiom, the "fallenness" of signs expresses that being (or the absolute) itself is fallen, that is, recalling Hansen's words, that it, too, is "enfolded into a material history strewn with … transient ideas" (Hansen 2004: 675). This can be the only coherent meaning of Deleuze's statement that there is nothing exemplary even in the idea of God, since this is itself also produced. If so, then it follows that one of the fundamental principles of Spinozism is that expressions and signs stand *not in opposition but in an immanent relation* with each other, as the true and the false ways in which substance makes itself known.

Indeed, there are some passages in the same work by Deleuze that undermine his own thesis that, to repeat, the "opposition of expressions and signs is one of the fundamental principles of Spinozism," and that can be taken as supporting the position presented here. For instance, in the chapter "Toward the Third Kind of Knowledge," Deleuze presents the three kinds of knowledge (imagination, reason, and intuition) as a sequence in which each kind depends on and cannot exist without the preceding ones. Having established that imagination operates through images, and reason through common notions, Deleuze writes that "[i]f we consider their origin, common notions find in imagination the very conditions of their formation"; and, moreover, considered "in their practical function," common notions "apply only to things that can be imagined" (Deleuze 1990: 294). So, reason (expression) and imagination (sign) are here unambiguously presented as imbricated.

Deleuze makes also a smooth transition from the first two kinds of knowledge (imagination and reason) to the third (intuition), in a way that we also find in Yirmiyahu Yovel. Both thinkers identify the shift from reason to intuition in the shift from "common notions" in the sense of common to all modes, to "common notions" in the sense of notions common between a singular mode and God (Deleuze 1990: 300; and Yovel 1989: 156). This commonality has, however, diametrically different consequences for each thinker. For Yovel, Spinoza's third kind of knowledge provides access to secular redemption, conceived as the "realization of eternity within time" through a kind of ecstatic experience like those attained by mystics – but obtained instead through knowledge (Yovel 1989: 170). This is the knowledge of the community between one's singular essence and substance. Like substance, my essence is eternal, whereas my body and mind are finite (mortal). Given that "particular essences are eternal while minds are perishable," salvation "consists in uniting … the perishable mind and the eternal essence" through intuition, that is, through Spinoza's "rational translation of the ideal of *unio mystica*" (Yovel 1989: 170, 168). This is also to say that secular salvation can be obtained only while alive: "Thus Spinoza keeps to his strict immanent philosophy even when offering a theory of salvation" (Yovel 1989: 170). This kind of secular redemption is crucial to the working of biopolitics, as we shall see in the last chapter. By contrast, Deleuze eventually regresses to a transcendentalist model of salvation, despite his assertion that "we should not imagine that the soul endures beyond the body: it endures while the body itself endures, and it is eternal insofar as it expresses the body's essence" (Deleuze 1990: 314). Nevertheless, Deleuze proceeds to allude to afterlife: "While we existed … we could hope for only partial beatitude. But death seems to put us in a situation where we can only be affected by affections of the third kind, which are themselves explained by our essence" (Deleuze 1990: 315–6). Further, our conduct while alive is the measure of our rewards in afterlife:

> In fact, our capacity to be affected will not, according to Spinoza, be exercised (after death) by active affections of the third kind, if we did not succeed during existence itself in experiencing a maximum proportion of active affections of the second kind and (already) of the third. Spinoza … entirely preserves the positive content of the notion of salvation. Existence itself is still conceived as a kind of test.
>
> (Deleuze 1990: 317)

For Deleuze, Spinoza's feat consists in guaranteeing that this test is "[n]ot … a moral one but a physical or chemical test, like that whereby workmen check the quality of some material, of a metal or a vase" (Deleuze 1990: 317). Deleuze's conclusion is all the more unconvincing given that the very last proposition of the entire *Ethics* emphatically admonishes us against a notion of redemption conceived in terms of any kind of test and rewards: "*Blessedness is not the reward of virtue, but virtue itself*" (*Ethics* VP42).

One might think that the reason why Deleuze, unlike Yovel, ultimately fails to sustain Spinoza's immanentism might owe to the following difference between their readings of the three kinds of knowledge. For Yovel, reason accounts for diachronic (mechanical) laws, and only intuition for synchronic (structural) laws, whereas for Deleuze, diachrony pertains to the imaginary, synchronic laws to reason, and intuition relates to being in terms of neither diachrony nor synchrony (quasi-eternity) but eternity proper, the (a-)temporality of power/potentiality. However, on the contrary, Deleuze has an advantage in having figured out that diachrony is imaginary. Spinoza states so explicitly: "time … is a product of the imagination" (*Ethics* IIP44S). For this reason Deleuze is also correct in seeing in reason a knowledge that understands its object not in time (mechanical laws) but under a certain species of eternity (synchronic laws): reason's "[c]ommon notions express God as the source of all the constitutive relations of all things" (Deleuze 1990: 297), and "it is in the nature of reason to perceive things under a certain species of eternity (sub quadam specie aeternitatis)" (*Ethics* IIP44C2, translation modified). This is why Deleuze feels compelled to differentiate between "two kinds of eternity, one characterized by the presence of common notions [reason], the other by the *existence* of singular essences [intuition]" (Deleuze 1990: 398, n. 11).[6] In short, Deleuze's reading of the three kinds of knowledge is overall more accurate than Yovel's.

Then – in spite of his professed devotion to anti-emanetism and to the univocity between the One substance and the multiplicity of its modes – there remains one explanation for Deleuze's persistence in afterlife: his conception of substance as ultimately transcendent to its modes. It is this transcendentalist proclivity that is divulged as much through Deleuze's emphatic rejection of "impression" or the "sign" (i.e., of imagination) as through his final invocation of afterlife. For even as he acknowledges the imagination as a necessary step toward the next kind of knowledge, the only thing that imagination – i.e., all knowledge based on perception and affects – can produce, according to Deleuze, is confused knowledge. In this case, given that only death "relieves" us from imagination – "*The mind can exercise neither imagination nor memory save while the body endures*" (*Ethics* VP21) – we can see the true light only after death.

What Deleuze seems to forget is that the loss of imagination and memory after death means that "we" are no longer "we," for "I" am "I" only as long as I have memory, something which I lose when the body no longer endures. Having forgotten this, Deleuze infers that "[i]n losing existence we lose nothing: we lose only our extensive parts" (Deleuze 1990: 317), and ignores that we also lose our identity. For Deleuze, while we are alive we are subject to representation which amounts to an illusion, and expressionism can grant us access to the knowledge of being only in afterlife. In this way, Deleuze's reading commits one of the most common errors of humans: "they are indeed conscious of the eternity of the mind, but they confuse it with duration and assign it to imagination or to memory, which they believe to continue after death" (*Ethics* VP34S). Any devaluation of representation reverts to the same transcendentalist dualism that upholds the immunity of what is represented above and beyond the corruption of that which does the representation, or – in more Spinozian terms – the dualism that upholds the sanctity of the attributes against the corruption of the modes.

Finally, I turn to Quentin Meillassoux, as a representative of a more recent tendency among the attempts to bypass representation, speculative materialism or realism. Speculative materialism proposes itself as the alternative to all post-critical or post-Kantian philosophy, which is based on "*correlation*," that is "the idea according to which we only ever have access to the correlation between thinking and being, and never to either term considered apart from the other" (Meillassoux 2008: 5). In other words, Meillassoux continues, "correlationism consists in disqualifying the claim that it is possible to consider the realms of subjectivity and objectivity independently of one another" (Meillassoux 2008: 5). Based on this definition Marx's theory of commodity fetishism and the present epistemontology are clearly correlationist. The thesis that things and thought are homologous manifestations of being stands in opposition to "every materialism that would be speculative," that is, that would hold that "absolute reality is an *entity without thought*" (Meillassoux 2008: 36). However, for Meillassoux, Kant and the whole Kantian paradigm are also correlationists, in spite of their severance between absolute reality (thing in itself) and thought. Let us pursue Meillassoux's reasoning.

The case through which Meillassoux attempts to ascertain absolute reality as prior to and independent of thought is "ancestrality," that is, "any reality anterior to the emergence of the human species – or even anterior to every recognized form of life on earth" (Meillassoux 2008: 26). In the face of the fact that "today's science formulates a certain number of ancestral statements bearing upon the age of the universe, the formation of stars, or the accretion of the earth," Meillassoux asks: "*How is correlationism liable to interpret these statements?*" (Meillassoux 2008: 10).

He responds that correlationism cannot take such ancestral statements at face value, unless it degrades itself to the level of a "metaphysics" willing to "hypostatize the correlation" and to uphold that "the eternal-correlate can point to the existence of an 'ancestral witness,' an attentive God, who turns every event into a phenomenon" by functioning as the consciousness that witnesses it (Meillassoux 2008: 10–1). Now, Kant himself would reproach Meillassoux for committing here a "transcendental subreption," that is, for mistaking a regulative rule of reason for a constitutive rule of reason, or, to put it more simply, for assuming that he is talking about an event as absolute reality when he is talking about it only as a phenomenon.[7] For even if one presupposed an "ancestral witness" – whether God or a transcendental subject – the most one could take at face value is the experience of (the phenomenon given to) that witness, not the existence of an absolute reality in itself, outside this experience. Nevertheless, Meillassoux is right to assert that "where science is concerned, philosophers have become modest – and even prudent," assuring scientists that philosophy's "theories in no way interfere with the work of the scientist" (Meillassoux

2008: 13). In granting this assurance, what the philosopher truly "means is that although it is normal and even natural for the scientist to adopt a spontaneously realist attitude, which she shares with the 'ordinary person,' the philosopher possesses a specific type of knowledge which imposes a correction upon science's ancestral statements," namely, if the "ancestral statement" is "Event Y occurred x number of years before the emergence of humans," the philosopher "will simply add" at the end of the statement: " – *for humans* (or even, for *the human scientist*)" (Meillassoux 2008: 13).

I share Meillassoux's desire to legitimize epistemologically the knowability of things – as long as one does not revert to a pre-critical dogmatism, which is also to say, as long as one recognizes that both the human scientist and her thing ("absolute reality") share the same objective distortions, necessarily imposed by the mode of the fallenness of being under the specific historical circumstances in which the scientist and the thing encounter each other. It is not a matter of subjectivism or relativism, of the personality, ideology, idiosyncrasies, or other individuating characteristics of the human scientist – which indeed may or may not contribute to errors that should not be taken at face value. It is a matter of fact that the scientist's "thing" could not emerge without the science that she is practicing, and hence, without the historical conditions that enable the emergence of this science. That statements about "absolute reality" should be taken at face value does not mean that "absolute reality" itself does not change; on the contrary, it does, and by objective socio-historical necessity. Which is why "absolute reality" does not mean either a reality without history or without thought.

This objection notwithstanding, I partly sympathize with Meillassoux's frustration in the face of the false modesty that characterizes the attitude of (dominant) contemporary philosophy toward science, for, in truth, this modesty is a gesture of impotent arrogance. As Meillassoux puts it, the philosopher's above codicil, "– *for humans* (or even, for *the human scientist*)," is:

> the codicil of modernity: the codicil through which the modern philosopher refrains (or at least thinks she does) from intervening in the content of science, while preserving a regime of meaning external to and more originary than that of science.
>
> (Meillassoux 2008: 13–4)

I say I "partly" sympathize because there is a limit to this sympathy. The present materialist epistemontology shares Meillassoux's aspiration "to achieve what modern philosophy has been telling us for the past two centuries is impossibility itself: *to get out of ourselves*, to grasp the in-itself" (Meillassoux 2008: 27). However, this same epistemontology does not aspire "to know what is *whether we are or not*" (Meillassoux 2008: 27, emphasis added). This would amount to a reversion to an idealism that lacks any consciousness of the material, historical conditions of the constitution of thought, let alone of the historical constitution of things. My invocation of material and historical conditions, as we shall presently see, does not refer to human consciousness.

Meillassoux's account is predicated on the pre-psychoanalytic premise that thought equals consciousness – (a premise that prior to psychoanalysis was undermined by Spinoza and, as we shall see in the fifth chapter, also by Friedrich Wilhelm Joseph von Schelling). This is particularly evident in Meillassoux's consistent equation of the transcendental subject with consciousness. Drawing on "Kantian idealism," Meillassoux describes "the transcendental subject" as follows:

> There can only be a transcendental subject on condition that such a subject *takes place*.
>
> What do we mean by "taking place"? We mean that the transcendental, insofar as it refuses all metaphysical dogmatism, remains indissociable from the notion of a *point of view*.
>
> (Meillassoux 2008: 24)

Removing this "point of view," Meillassoux continues, "would violate the essential finitude of the transcendental subject" and could not "ascribe sensible receptivity and its spatio-temporal form"; without a "point of view," the transcendental subject "would no longer be bound to knowledge by perceptual adumbration, and since the world for it would no longer be a horizon but rather an exhaustively known object," it "could no longer be conceived as a transcendental subject of the Husserlian type" (Meillassoux 2008: 24). Meillassoux then asks:

> But how do notions such as finitude, receptivity, horizon, regulatory idea of knowledge, arise? They arise because, as we said above, the transcendental subject is posited as a point of view on the world, and hence as taking *place* at the heart of the world. The subject is transcendental only insofar as it is positioned in the world, of which it can only ever discover a finite aspect, and which it can never recollect in its totality.
>
> (Meillassoux 2008: 24–5)

A materialist epistemontology also positions the transcendental subject in the world, yet it diverges from the rest of Meillassoux's conditions. These may indeed conform to the Kantian and Husserlian conceptions of the transcendental subject, insofar as they describe a transcendental subject of a correlative empirical subject that is conceived as exhaustible (both empirically and transcendentally) to consciousness. By definition, this subject can only have a certain point of view from which it discovers only a finite aspect of the world, and for which the world can never be an exhaustively known object. Only a thought which is coextensive with the entirety of the world, and which takes place everywhere in the world and from any possible point of view in the world, could know the totality of the world. No consciousness, empirical or transcendental, can know this thought, which, therefore, is unconscious. This is why, from the perspective of consciousness, the unconscious is "nonsensical" (Lacan 1981: 250). That "*the unconscious is outside*" means precisely that it does not coincide with the point of view of consciousness, whether defined as an empirical or transcendental category (Lacan 1981: 123). That "the Other, the capital Other, is already there in every opening … of the unconscious," and that "*the unconscious is structured like language*" does not mean that it is structured in the way language is thought or spoken by consciousness (Lacan 1981: 130, 20). It means that it is structured like linguistic structure: "What is there … when it is a question of the unconscious of the subject … [is] intended to bring out irreducible, nonsensical – composed of non-meanings – signifying elements" (Lacan 1981: 250). The corollary of this linguistic structure of purely differential signifying and nonsensical values is the network of the constitutive relations of things – including what the scientist identifies as natural laws. The unconscious is outside because things think, and this does not mean that things have consciousness.

It is because things think, *whether we are or not*, that the scientist can make true statements about "absolute reality" whether ancestral or not. However, also, from within what episteme the observer thinks makes an important difference in the statements that she will be able to produce regarding "absolute reality." It is because things think that we can make true statements about "absolute reality," but it is only because our era's network of the constitutive relations of reality is a system of differential values that there can be an observer called "scientist" in the specific sense of a science that also enables ancestral statements.

Speculative materialism with its belief in an absolute reality conceived as the other of thought may expose itself to the same perilous predicament about which Meillassoux warns the correlationists of the Kantian idealist or Husserlian type. Due to "extreme idealism," this type of correlationist "is incapable of admitting that what science tells us about these occurrences of matter independent of humanity effectively occurred as described by science." As a result:

> our correlationist then finds herself dangerously close to contemporary creationism: those quaint believers who assert today, in accordance with a "literal" reading of the Bible, that the earth is no more that 6,000 years old, and … that God also created at the same time as the earth 6,000 years ago those radioactive compounds … in order to test the physicist's faith.
>
> (Meillassoux 2008: 18)

Let us assume that speculative materialism could convince us, on the basis of its logic, that we should take at face value the scientific evidence that the world was not created 6,000 years ago. How could it then, again on the basis of the same logic, respond to the question: If matter does not think, where does thought come from? Would this not amount to opening the back door for a new reentry of God? The reference to the complexity of the "brain organ" rather than the mind is an impotent attempt to bypass the impediment posed by this question. For the question concerns precisely this: *How is it possible that a material organ produces something immaterial?* If the philosopher does not want to revert to presecular metaphysics and refuses to hypostatize the immaterial, then she has to assert that the material itself is already relational and differential – something which, since Einstein and quantum physics, is reconfirmed also by science. To recall Simmel's epigraph to the present work, if matter and the immaterial have the same formal relations to being it is because they constitute a "disjunctive parallelism," that is, they are both radically different and formally similar. If only thought were relational and differential and matter were not, how could they ever share the same form, and, hence, to repeat an old philosophical question, how could the subject think the object?

As mentioned above, in the face of this question Schelling came to the conclusion that the object (nature) itself thinks. However, because Meillassoux equates thought and consciousness he assumes that "Schelling's nature" belongs to the line of thought that "hypostatizes some mental, sentient, or vital term" (Meillassoux 2008: 37). It is also for the same reason that when Meillassoux pursues the (for him inadmissible) hypothesis of a transcendental subject with no point of view he does not recognize that, in effect, he offers an accurate description of the unconscious:

> Let us suppose a subject without any point of view on the world – such a subject would have access to the world as a totality, without anything escaping from its instantaneous inspection of objective reality … [T]he world for it would … be … the transparent object of an immediately achieved and effective knowledge … [It] would therefore be capable of totalizing the real infinity of whatever is contained in each of these forms.
>
> (Meillassoux 2008: 24)

This omniscience is one of the reasons why Lacan stated that in secular thought, "*God is unconscious*" (Lacan 1981: 59). Of course, for Meillassoux's statement to be indeed an accurate description of the unconscious we must specify that by "subject" is meant not the "ego" (consciousness) but "the subject of the unconscious" (Lacan 1981: 37). Similarly, unconscious thought indeed "*remains indissociable from its incarnation in a body*" (Meillassoux 2008: 25), under the condition that we understand that this body is no particular body but the continuum of all materiality, as it follows from the substance's attribute of extension. If we agree on this, then we can concur with Meillassoux that:

> Granted, the transcendental is the condition for knowledge of bodies, but it is necessary to add that the body is also the condition for the taking place of the transcendental. That the transcendental subject has *this* or that body is an empirical matter, but that it *has* a body is a non-empirical condition of its taking place.
>
> (Meillassoux 2008: 25)

If by "a body" Meillassoux means the continuum of bodies or materiality deriving from the attribute of extension – which is the other, inseparable, side of the continuum of mind or intellect, deriving from the attribute of thought – he is correct in arguing that there can be no thought without extension. The inverse is equally true: there can be no extension without thought. However, as we have seen, this inverse position is exactly what Meillassoux wants to discard, maintaining instead that "[e]very materialism that would be speculative … must assert … that thought is not necessary (something can be independently of thought)" (Meillassoux 2008: 36). In his attempt to rescue the connection between word and thing, Meillassoux seems to guide us back to the old Cartesian dualism, only turned upside-down: it is not the thought (soul) that can exist without a body, it is the body that can exist without thought.

If, as Meillassoux argues, the "science" that studies ancestral matter "reveals a time that … does not need conscious time," this is so because the thought of matter is unconscious thought (Meillassoux 2008: 22). For, as Meillassoux rightly puts it, "though ancestrality is a temporal notion, its definition does not invoke distance in time" but rather a time "which is not ancient in any vague sense, nor some sort of lacuna in that which is temporally given, but which must rather be identified with that which is *prior to givenness in its entirety*" (Meillassoux 2008: 22–3). Structuralism teaches us that that which is "*prior to givenness in its entirety,*" that is, prior to anything actual, is the virtual – an ontologically different category, rather than something temporally distant from the actual. To conceive of a temporality specific to the virtual (and to the unconscious) is indeed "*to conceive of a time in which the given as such passes from non-being into being,*" a time in which Being passes from the virtual to the actual (Deleuze 2004: 21). This is why, as Deleuze writes regarding the "position of structuralism[,] … time is always a time of actualization" (Deleuze 2004: 180). This relation between the virtual and the actual relates to the aforementioned problematic of the relation between structure and (conscious) diachrony, to which we shall return in the third chapter.

Marx's collapse of the traditional opposition between subject and object entails both that thought is part of reality or objectivity and that it cannot be reduced to consciousness. This is why, as we shall see in the next section, in addition to structuralism, commodity fetishism entails the logic and methodology of psychoanalysis. Like Spinoza, Marx understood that a secular conception of the relation between thought and things must necessarily presuppose thought as inherent in matter. Otherwise one faces the unsurpassable problem of having to account for the emergence of thought in the midst of materiality.

In the third chapter we shall pursue in more detail the itinerary of Freud's thought toward both structuralism and the collapse of traditional oppositions, as postulated also by commodity fetishism.

Let us conclude this section on psychoanalysis by noting that, beyond structuralism, the capitalist mode of production and exchange of commodities has as its corollary the psychoanalytic logic and cognitive approach. As we have seen, Marx's theory of commodity fetishism and its entailed epistemontology collapse traditional oppositions such as object and subject or exteriority and interiority – and this collapse is the founding and defining premise of psychoanalysis. Moreover, psychoanalysis is the first field of knowledge that defined its object as the unconscious – a function introduced within social reality by dint of precisely commodity fetishism, that is, the fact that in the market, while we consciously assume that we exchange objects of utility, objectively we are vehicles of the circulation of exchange-values "without being aware of it" (Marx 1990: 167). In the sixth chapter we shall examine in more detail several fundamental conceptual, methodological, epistemological, and ontological affinities between Marx's theory and psychoanalysis. By focusing on Lacan's concept of *jouissance*, in the last chapter we shall see that psychoanalysis is also the field that can account for the commodification of being *qua* power-of-self-actualization in terms that go beyond the subjugation of being to value.

Being *qua* power-of-self-actualization

As a way of turning to being *qua* power-of-self-actualization let us begin by noting that fetishism consists in the redoubling of value. Value is both that which is manifested – being – and one of the two modes of its manifestation – exchange-value or thought (the other mode being use-value). One of the tasks of epistemontology is to discern the difference between these two aspects of value – as being and as exchange-value or thought. The most conspicuous difference consists in the fact that while exchange-value is an adequate empirical manifestation of value, value *qua* being obfuscates the fact that being is also the power of self-actualization.

This obfuscated other side of being is the topic of the last chapter,[8] but I would like to explain already here why the examination of being *qua* power-of-self-actualization is connected to biopower. The reason has to do with the fact that, as we have seen, labor-power directly partakes in being *qua* power-of-self-actualization, insofar as it is labor's power to actualize itself. As we also have seen, in capitalism this power is commodified, thereby being objectively subjugated to value and serving the latter's accumulation. Further, as we shall see in the last chapter, we also partake of being *qua* power-of-self-actualization through our enjoyment (Lacan's *jouissance*). Now, it is only one part of the epistemontology of commodity fetishism to take the illusory or mystifying appearance at face value and, thus, to pursue being *qua* value. The other, demystifying part is to raise the question about the function of being *qua* power-of-self-actualization – and, hence, of labor-power and enjoyment – beyond its subjugation to the accumulation of value.

This interrogation leads to an examination of the three distinct aspects of labor (Marx): (a) concrete physical and mental activity, (b) abstract labor *qua* labor-time, and (c) labor-power as the power of labor to actualize itself. These correspond to three distinct temporalities: (a) diachrony or finite linear time, (b) synchrony, and (c) eternity (substance or the power of self-actualization exists under the species of eternity – Spinoza). Any commodity other than labor-power consists of only two aspects, use-value (in diachrony) and exchange-value (in synchrony), and it contributes to the accumulation of value only in its aspect as exchange-value; its aspect as use-value falls out of the circulation of value, as Marx's reduction of the formula of capital from M – C – M to M – M′ indicates. Labor, which consists of three elements, contributes to the accumulation of value only in its two latter aspects (b and c), while the concrete physical and mental activity, with its finite diachrony, fall out of the circulation of value.

This examination of the aspects of labor and their temporalities reveals that biopower is truly "a new form of pastoral power" that is "coextensive and continuous with life" and "is salvation oriented" (Foucault 1999: 422). To be sure, it is "no longer a question of leading people to their salvation in the next world but rather ensuring it in this world" (Foucault 1999: 422). For this power operates through the administration of the subject's relation to these three temporalities, as a means of fostering a secular illusion of immortality combined with a surrogate experience of ecstatic eternity, as described by Spinoza in the context of his third kind of knowledge. The elimination of finite diachrony (and hence of mortality) from the universe of value contributes to the biopolitical task of hiding death from the horizon of human experience. As Foucault put it, "death has become … something to be hidden away. It has become the most private and shameful thing of all (and ultimately, it is now not so much sex as death that is the object of a taboo)" (Foucault 2003: 247). Simultaneously, the concomitant commodification of labor-power/enjoyment amounts to the commodification of eternity. While *jouissance* is by definition impossible (as is the experience of eternity), its commodification (through media, drugs, etc.) makes it seem possible in the form of "imitation surplus *jouissance* [semblant de plus-de-jouir]" (Lacan 2007: 81; Lacan 1991: 93).

This semblance of enjoyment consists in distraction (losing the sense of self and of time), as a kind of semblance experience of eternity – the closest modern societies can come to the religious ecstatic experience. As we shall see in the last chapter, secular capitalism is of a profoundly religious character, with this very fact being increasingly repressed. The progress of this repression is directly proportional to the permeation of the discourse of international politics and contemporary forms of warfare with religious references.

In other words, biopower operates by fulfilling religious functions in apparently secular ways, and serves the same main function as ideology, namely: while ideology or biopolitics may not directly serve the accumulation of value, they are the underside required for sustaining the system of the accumulation of value. Biopolitics, therefore, does not signal the end of ideology but rather is its late capitalist version,[9] the one that corresponds to the dominance of the market, as opposed to the state. However, as we shall presently see, this historical difference entails that even as biopolitics is ideology, it has to be differentiated from the classical notion of ideology.

Classical ideology and commodity fetishism or biopolitical ideology

Once again, Balibar's commentary can help us discern the difference between classical ideology and biopolitics, as the contemporary form of ideology. Balibar does not speak of biopolitics; rather he juxtaposes ideology to commodity fetishism itself, on the basis of the difference between "idea" or "idol" and "fetish." In both cases, ideology and fetishism (whose corollary is biopolitics), there occurs a "*splitting up* of the real community of individuals," which:

> is followed by a *projection* or transposition of the social relation onto an external "thing," a third term. Only, in the one case [ideology], the thing is an "idol," an abstract representation which seems to exist all on its own in the ethereal realm of ideas (Freedom, Justice, Humanity, Law), whereas in the other [fetishism/biopolitics] it is a "fetish," a material thing which seems to belong to the earth, to nature, while exerting an irresistible power over individuals (the commodity and, above all, money).
>
> (Balibar 2007: 76)

Ideology is marked by a dualism between immanence and transcendence, the earthly world and the "ethereal realm of ideas," which is why "the theory of ideology is fundamentally a *theory of the State* (by which we mean the mode of domination inherent in the State)" (Balibar 2007: 77–8). Accordingly, its corollary view regarding "the conditions and objectives of the revolutionary struggle" is that "of overthrowing a bourgeois domination which has entered into contradiction with the development of civil society" (Balibar 2007: 77–8). Here domination is perceived as emanating from a realm above or transcendent to civil society. By contrast, in the world of the fetish, it is the earthly material thing that assumes a supernatural and, hence, "irresistible power over individuals." Fetishism folds transcendence fully within the plane of immanence, which is why "fetishism is fundamentally a *theory of the market* (the mode of subjection or constitution of the 'world' of subjects and objects inherent in the organization of society as market and its domination by market forces)" (Balibar 2007: 78).

With the shift from ideology (State) to fetishism (market), we pass from the question of domination to the problematic of "subjection." "Subjection" is not simply subjugation but, foremost, subjectivation or "constitution" of subjects, as well as objects. This is what Balibar means when he writes that Marx's "*The German Ideology* is a theory of the constitution of *power*, whereas what is described in *Capital*, by way of its definition of fetishism, is a mechanism of subjection" (Balibar 2007: 76–7).

However, classical ideology also constitutes subjects (this was Althusser's point), but it does so through an ideal imposed from above, which is why it can be resisted by means of direct confrontation; by contrast, fetishism and biopolitics constitute subjects not from above – from the transcendent space of Ideals – but horizontally, from the realm of earthly objects and affects (including enjoyment). Biopower's primary target of manipulation is our affect, not our ideas, even as discursive signs (visual and verbal) are employed in order to manipulate our affects.[10]

Moreover, fetishism as the attribution of a supernatural power to a mundane thing points to the necessity for biopolitics to address bios and the body not as the actual physical things that they (also) are, but as metaphysical, in fact, quasi-religious entities, with supernatural powers. This means that we have to revise radically our conception of the "secular." That the market and fetishism fold transcendence within the plane of immanence, far from entailing the dissolution or deconstruction of transcendence or metaphysics, means that *anything within the plane of immanence can assume transcendent/metaphysical qualities.* This is precisely:

> what Marx has in mind when he describes the perception of the world of commodities as a perception of "sensuous things which are at the same time suprasensible," in which aspects of the natural and the supernatural coexist uncannily, and when he declares the commodity a "mystical" object, full of "theological niceties" (directly suggesting the comparison of economic language with religious discourse).
>
> (Balibar 2007: 59–60)

The lesson from Marx's theory of commodity fetishism, as Balibar succinctly concludes, is that "[c]ontrary to what Max Weber would later assert, the modern world is not 'disenchanted,' but *enchanted*, precisely insofar as it is the world of objects of value and objectified values" (Balibar 2007: 60). The objectivity of value is the very source of enchantment proper to secular thought. Only a theory that takes at face value the enchantment or fetishization of physical things and bodies is capable of understanding the workings of power – which is the task of a psychoanalytic theory of biopower. Therefore, in contrast to the critique of classical ideology that focused on the ways a particular position was raised to the level of the Ideal, the psychoanalytic critique of biopower and biopolitics focuses on the mechanisms through which everyday life and mundane bodies (bios) are bestowed with metaphysical or quasi-religious functions – "quasi," since they are fashioned by materialist conditions – and the ways in which these functions subjectivize and subject individuals.

Such a psychoanalytic theory of biopower goes beyond Balibar's conclusion, namely that the "phenomena of alienation with which we have dealt here," in examining ideology and fetishism, respectively:

> have developed in opposing ways: on the one side, they are of the order of belief and have to do with the "idealism" of individuals (with the transcendent values to which they subscribe: God, the Nation, the People, or even the Revolution); on the other, they are of the order of perception and have to do with the realism or "utilitarianism" of individuals (with the manifest realities of daily life: utility, the price of things, the rules of "normal" behaviour).
>
> (Balibar 2007: 77)

In his description of the era of commodity fetishism as one governed primarily by a sober realistic utilitarianism and normalizing rules Balibar actually concurs with Foucault's conception of biopower not only because of the latter's focus on the norm but, above all, because we are ultimately left with the description of a disenchanted world. Of course, as we have seen, Foucault himself acknowledges that biopower is a power that "is salvation oriented," even as there is a "change in its objective" so that salvation must now occur in this world. However, by ensuring salvation in this world, Foucault understands that a "series of 'worldly' aims took the place of the religious aims of the traditional pastorate," such as "health, well-being (that is, sufficient wealth, standard of living), security, protection against accidents," etc. (Foucault 1999: 422–3). From a disenchanted perspective one may see these aims as purely "worldly," motivated by pragmatic and utilitarian principles; from an enchanted perspective, however, one cannot miss that these aims are animated by a longing for immortality, not in heavens, to be sure, but in this world – and this is their sole "worldly" feature. Commodity fetishism teaches us that pastoral and religious aims are not replaced by "worldly" ones but are folded within the worldly and are disguised in secular garments. Discerning the secular worldliness of the religious and the religious character of the worldly constitutes the core of the critique of biopolitics.

Classical ideology and biopower have indeed developed in different, yet not in opposing ways. Both sustain ideals – of the quasi-religious type – but, instead of putting them on the pedestal and holding to them the candle, biopower strews them throughout the plane of immanence and circulates them in the market. Also, as we shall see in the last chapter, the phenomena constituting fetishism are not of the order of perception, even as they derive from it. Rather they are of the order of the unconscious. The "hottest" (best-selling and most demanded) among them, as we can already suspect from Foucault's observation, is immortality. Now, immortality can, and has been, conceived in both theophilosophy and the popular imaginary as involving either infinite time or eternity – a distinction to which we shall return in the last chapter – which is why the main terrain of biopolitical administration, as I argue in the last chapter, is neither that of ideas nor of physical things, including bodies, but their temporalities.

Being *qua* power-of-self-actualization and *qua* value, or fallen being

Finally, a remark on the fallenness of Being (in the Benjaminian sense), that is, the fact that Being itself is imperfect and incomplete. This thesis does not introduce skepticism or relativism in ontology and in the conception of Being. *Being is* transhistorically and under any circumstances univocal; it is *One and the same substance* – the power of self-actualization – *that*, however, *is always fallen*. This is why Being or the power of self-actualization can appear at times as gods, at other times as God, and at yet other times as Capital/Value. Badiou is right in stating that "the thorny question" of all philosophy is that "of the names of Being" (Badiou 2000: 27). When he asks, "Is the nomination of the univocal itself univocal?," he responds: "a single name is never sufficient … two are required," for "Being needs to be said in a single sense both from the viewpoint of the unity of its power and from the viewpoint of the multiplicity of the divergent simulacra that this power actualizes in itself" (Badiou 2000: 27). Badiou maintains that Being requires two names for its nomination, one from the perspective of substance itself or its attributes, the other from the perspective of its simulacra or modes. This distinction is liable to the inference that multiplicity enters only the level of the modes, that the One (substance) did not already involve multiplicity. In this way one would locate the fallenness of Being on the level of the modes, thereby introducing a hierarchy between the univocal authentic substance/attributes and the multiple inferior modes. On the contrary, fallenness inheres in Being or substance itself, insofar as it expresses itself to us in the form of its attributes.[11] This is why, to repeat Benjamin's words, Being is imperfect – or more accurately, perfection is imperfect.

For the monist materialist epistemontology proposed here, the fallenness occurs not on the level of the modes (actual things and thoughts) but already on the level of the attributes and, further, the "mediation of some infinite modifications," or, as Beth Lord puts it, the "mediate infinite modes" (Lord 2010: 39). Spinoza distinguishes them both from the level of "those things which are produced immediately by God" (Schuller 2002: 917), and from the modes, since these are "infinite modes." When Schuller asked Spinoza in their correspondence for examples clarifying the distinction, Spinoza responded:

> The examples you ask for of the first kind [things which are produced immediately by God] are: in the case of thought, absolutely infinite intellect; in the case of extension, motion and rest. An example of the second kind [produced by the mediation of some infinite modifications] is the face of the whole universe, which, although varying in infinite ways, yet remains always the same.
>
> (Schuller 2002: 919)

In Lord's commentary, "God exists as thinking being, and God exists as extended being. So thinking being and extended being *as such* exist necessarily and eternally" (Lord 2010: 39) – this is the level of the attributes of substance. Now:

> Because each of the attributes has infinite essence, what follows from the nature of the attributes must also be infinite. This means that each of the attributes expresses an *immediate infinite mode*: there is an infinite way in which thinking is expressed and an infinite way in which extension is expressed. What follows from the nature of "thinking being" as such is the infinite intellect ... What follows from the nature of "extended being" as such is infinite motion and rest. Infinite intellect and infinite motion and rest are caused *immediately* by the *absolute nature* of God's attributes.
>
> (Lord 2010: 39)

Next, "from each of these *immediate* infinite modes follows a *mediate* infinite mode" (Lord 2010: 39), as a mediation between the infinite and the finite (mode). This mediate infinite mode is "the face of the whole universe," insofar as, to repeat, it "remains always the same" while "varying in infinite ways" – that is, it is both univocal and multiple. The face of the whole universe or "the whole nature is one individual, whose parts ... vary in infinite ways, without any change of the whole individual" (*Ethics* IIL7S). The whole of nature is "*an infinite physical individual*" or "*continuum*" and "*an infinite thinking individual*" or "*continuum*" (Lord 2010: 40). Finally:

> the finite modes are the "surface features" of these infinite continua. Finite modes of extension – physical things – are the temporary, changeable expressions of the infinite continuum of physicality. Finite modes of thinking – minds and ideas – are the temporary, changeable expressions of the infinite continuum of thinking.
>
> (Lord 2010: 40)

These finite modes are not fallen in relation to the substance because (a) the attributes already introduce the Two within the One and, further, (b) the substance's mediate infinite modes already involve multiplicity, since they vary while remaining the same. Being, the power-of-self-actualization, remains always the same, while it varies in infinite ways – ways that include the appearance of Being as God as much as the appearance of Being as value. The eternal and univocal power of self-actualization can fail in infinite ways – with theocratic feudalism and secular capitalist modernity being only two of them – while always remaining the same.

Notes

1 Note that Hegel remains within this transcendentalist tradition. As Balibar writes, it is true that Hegel rejected "the separation of the natural from the moral world" and "demonstrated that the experience of consciousness was properly located in historical experience" (Balibar 2007: 65). Yet, "in the end, that spirit of reason which has been lost or alienated in the forms of nature or culture merely, in its various experiences, *returns to itself*, to the contemplation of its own structure, its own 'logic'" (Balibar 2007: 65).

2 Knox Peden also identifies a link between the (Kantian) Idea of reason and structure in his commentary on the Deleuze of *Difference and Repetition* (1968), a work published around the same time as his essay on structuralism, stating that there "the Idea itself is 'defined as a structure'" (Peden 2014: 238, citing Deleuze 1994: 183). Moreover, Peden notes that Deleuze equates structure with substance: "this structure is a multiplicity in itself" and, in Deleuze's own words, "multiplicity … is the true substantive, substance itself" (Peden 2014: 238; Deleuze 1994: 182). This equation of structure and substance prior to the turn away from structuralism, Peden continues, "is a common element in both Deleuze's Spinozism and Althusser's. In fact, Althusser is cited affirmatively throughout *Difference and Repetition* for recognizing 'structure' to be, like 'substance,' a name for a process and not an entity" (Peden 2014: 238; Deleuze 1994: 186). My thesis differs insofar as it considers structure to be *only one* aspect of substance. However, for Deleuze, too, at least by 1968, substance is not reducible to structure, as his *Expressionism in Philosophy: Spinoza* (1968) clearly indicates.

3 Of course, since thought exceeds consciousness, being *qua* power-of-self-actualization continues to be operative, but on a level beyond consciousness. This means that the being *qua* power-of-self-actualization operates on the level of both the "*unconscious of thought*" and the "*unknown of the body*" (Deleuze 1988: 19). Which is why, as we shall see in the last chapter, it operates on the level of biopolitics.

4 All passages cited in this paragraph, as well as in this endnote, are from Joseph Hughes (2017; cited from the manuscript, 10, 18, and 17; citing from Badiou 2011). Note also that on the political level, Badiou intends to perform a

"movement from a mathematics of proof to a logical politics," that is, "a transfer of the authority of reason from the sphere of mathematical rationality to that of practical and political rationality." Hughes criticizes the mathematizing "fantasy that the proof can be formalized" in the form of letters or other symbols, and can be "clarified by virtue of deductive relations between them" (cited from the unpublished manuscript). Instead, Hughes proposes that a Spinozian "practical and political rationality" should embrace the inventive dimension involved in its demonstrations. For my account of the function of invention, interpretation, the imaginary, phantasy, and decision – including political decision – in Spinoza, see Kordela and Bermas-Dawes 2017. For my further commentary on Badiou, see Kordela 2007.

5 For more details regarding my account of the role of imagination in Spinoza's work see the afore-cited co-authored article (Kordela and Bermas-Dawes 2017).

6 As I argue elsewhere, Deleuze's "two kinds of eternity" actually refer to the difference between synchrony – the temporality of the relations of structural elements – and eternity – the temporality of potentiality (see Kordela 2013a, particularly the chapter "From Eternity (Attribute) to Immortality (Mode)," 139–44).

7 I am referring here to the following passage from Kant, in which he differentiates a regulative principle or rule of reason from a constitutive principle of reason. The "principle of reason is only a *rule*, prescribing a regress in the series of conditions for given appearances, in which regress it is never allowed to stop with an absolutely unconditioned." Such a rule is not "a *constitutive principle* of reason for extending the concept of the world of sense beyond all possible experience; rather it is a principle of the greatest possible continuation and extension of experience, in accordance with which no empirical boundary would hold as an absolute boundary; thus it is a principle of reason which, as a *rule*, postulates what should be effected by us in the regress, but *does not anticipate* what is given in itself *in the object* prior to any regress. Hence I call it a *regulative* principle" of reason. Kant emphatically draws this distinction so as to prevent "what would otherwise unavoidably happen (through a transcendental subreption) – the ascription of objective reality to an idea that merely serves as a rule" (Kant 1998: 520–1; A509/B537; emphasis in the original).

8 This chapter continues my attempts in advancing a theory of biopower and biopolitics on the basis of Spinoza, Marx, and Freudian-Lacanian psychoanalysis, to which for reasons of brevity, I have been referring to as a psychoanalytic theory of biopower or biopolitics. These attempts include Kordela 2013a and various articles in collections and journals, such as Kordela 2013c, 2016. On biopolitics with an emphasis on Spinoza, see Kordela 2017, and with a focus on Roberto Esposito see Kordela 2013d. Note also that, as I argue in an article, power has always been a power that intervenes on the level of the body and bios; nevertheless, there are distinct historical manifestations of biopower, with capitalist biopower being the one that has drawn the attention of thinkers since Foucault (see Kordela 2013b). In the present work I ignore the fact that sovereignty and all forms of power have always been also forms of biopower, and I use the term referring exclusively to the capitalist form of biopower.

9 Though I disagree with Hilary Neroni's reading of biopolitics, I concur with her thesis that "biopower or biopolitics … functions as the prevailing ideology of our time" (Neroni 2015: 37).

10 Some further comments on what I call bioracism – the biopolitical constitution of racism, with racism being defined as "the break between what must live and what must die" (Foucault 2003: 254) – might shed some more light on this point. In the *predominantly ideological era* (which included the Cold War) affect was subordinated to ideology in their concerted effort to produce a bioracial break on the basis of *ideological criteria*. By contrast, in *the predominantly*

affective era ideology is subordinated to affect, as they again cooperate to produce a racial break, but this time on the basis of *affective criteria*. This is to say, in the latter case, the ultimate unshakable proof of the monstrosity of an act lies explicitly not in the positive (i.e., discursively given) rational/ideological attributes of its perpetrator (e.g., "religious fundamentalist," "enemy of freedom," "enemy of democracy," etc.). It used to be the case that the name (e.g., "communist," etc., or, on the other side of the divide, "capitalist," "bourgeois," etc.) determined who is human and who subhuman. Rather, in our days the ultimate proof of the monstrosity of an act lies in the mere fact that the (representations of the) act succeeds in inducing the affect of horror. Thus, horror – that is, the inability or refusal to remain within a discursive state – comes to be employed as the sensor detecting subhumanity.

Further, Foucault speaks of a "racism of the evolutionist kind, biological racism," as opposed to ethnic or national racism (Foucault 2003: 261). Yet, the term "biological racism" can apply to a racism that draws the line between what must live and what must die by discursively constructing groups of essentialist biological hereditary characteristics, as was, for instance, the case of Nazism. This can no longer be the case in an era in which the West has de-essentialized identities and deems them to be discursive products. In spite of his reference to "biological racism," Foucault himself is aware that the biopolitical racist divide requires no recourse to biology, and that any other ideological construct can succeed in presenting a group of people as an inferior subhuman race that threatens the social body. As he writes, in "States (of the Soviet Union type)," bourgeois convictions sufficed to legitimize the power's "right to kill or … to eliminate, or … to disqualify" (Foucault 2003: 261–2), just as, on the other side of the Iron Curtain, did communist convictions. The operation at hand is indeed bio-racism – a racism in the name of improving bios, life – but its criteria are ideological rather than biological.

Yet, the era of global capital increasingly moves beyond such ideological, and hence purely discursive, criteria that worked up until the end of the Cold War. Today's division falls between what can be at all discursively apprehended, and what cannot (or must not) and is instead supposed to elicit a purely *affect*ive reaction, such as horror. Today's bioracist boundary is drawn between everything that is discursively constructed and comprehended and that which lies outside discourse, a space that today is claimed only by pure states of being, such as affects.

What is thereby forgotten is, of course, one of the major theses of structuralism, namely, to recall Lévi-Strauss, that nature and culture are intertwined in an immanent relation, because of which *human affect is both natural and cultural* – natural as an experiential state, cultural regarding the concrete conditions of its induction. If the predominantly *ideological* era invested energy on *essentializing ideologies*, the predominantly *affective* era invests its energy on *essentializing affect* (see also Kordela 2016).

11 To put it in terms that will not be introduced prior to the last chapter, Being is fallen because it involves two levels of the (Lacanian) real, what Bruce Fink designates as R1 (Real 1) and R2 (Real 2). If Being were exhausted within R1 it would not involve any multiplicity, but because it always actualizes itself in two different ways (attributes), it bears the seed of multiplicity within itself.

References

Althusser, L. and E. Balibar (2009) *Reading Capital*, Ben Brewster (trans.), New York: Verso.

Badiou, A. (2000) *Deleuze: The Clamor of Being*, Louise Burchill (trans.), Minneapolis: University of Minnesota Press.

Badiou, A. (2001) *Ethics: An Essay on the Understanding of Evil*, Peter Hallward (trans.), London: Verso.

Badiou, A. (2003) *Infinite Thought: Truth and the Return to Philosophy*, Oliver Feltham and Justin Clemens (trans.), New York: Continuum.

Badiou, A. (2011) "What is a Proof in Spinoza's *Ethics*?," in Dimitris Vardoulakis (ed.) *Spinoza Now*, Minneapolis: University of Minnesota Press.

Balibar, E. (1996) "Structural Causality: Overdetermination and Antagonism," in *Postmodern Materialisms and the Future of Marxist Theory*, Antonio Callari and David F. Ruccio (eds), Middletown, CT: Wesleyan University Press, pp. 109–120.

Balibar, E. (2007) *The Philosophy of Marx*, Chris Turner and Gregory Elliott (trans.), New York: Verso.

Benjamin, W. (1977) *The Origin of the German Tragic Drama*, John Osborne (trans.), London: Verso.

Caygill, H. (2005) "Benjamin, Heidegger and the Destruction of Tradition," in Peter Osborne (ed.) *Walter Benjamin: Critical Evaluations in Cultural Theory (Volume 1)*, London: Routledge.

Deleuze, G. (1988) *Spinoza: Practical Philosophy*, Robert Hurley (trans.), San Francisco, CA: City Lights Books.

Deleuze, G. (1990) *Expressionism in Philosophy: Spinoza*, Martin Joughin (trans.), Cambridge: Zone Books.

Deleuze, G. (1994) *Difference and Repetition*, Paul Patton (trans.), New York: Columbia University Press.

Deleuze, G. (2004) "How Do We Recognize Structuralism?," in Melissa McMahon and Charles J. Stivale (trans.), David Lapoujade (ed.) *Desert Islands and Other Texts 1953–1974*, Los Angeles, CA: Semiotext(e).

de Man, P. (1979) *Allegories of Reading: Figural Language in Rousseau, Nietzsche, Rilke, and Proust*, New Haven, CT: Yale University Press.

de Saussure, F. (1959) *Course in General Linguistics*, Roy Harris (trans.), New York: The Philosophical Library.

Foucault, M. (1970) *The Order of Things: An Archaeology of the Human Sciences*, New York: Vintage.

Foucault, M. (1999) "The Subject and Power," in Brian Wallis (ed.) *Art After Modernism: Rethinking Representation*, New York: The New Museum of Contemporary Art.

Foucault, M. (2003) *Society Must be Defended: Lectures at the Collège de France*, David Macey (trans.), Mauro Bertani and Alessandro Fontana (eds), New York: Picador.

Hansen, J. (2004) "Formalism and its Malcontents: Benjamin and De Man on the Function of Allegory," *New Literary History*, 35(4): 663–683.

Heidegger, M. (1974) *Gesamtausgabe*, Frankfurt am Main: Vittorio Klosterman.

Heidegger, M. (2008) *Being and Time*, John Macquarrie and Edward Robinson (trans.), New York: Harper.

Hughes, J. (2017) "The Cold Quietness of the Stars: Proof, Rhetoric, and the Authority of Reason in the *Ethics*," in A.K. Kordela, and D. Vardoulakis (eds) *Spinoza's Authority (Volume I): Resistance and Power in the Ethics*, New York: Bloomsbury.

Kant, I. (1998) *Critique of Pure Reason*, Paul Guyer and Allen Wood (trans., eds), Cambridge: Cambridge University Press.

Kordela, A.K. (2007) *$urplus: Spinoza, Lacan*, New York: SUNY Press.

Kordela, A.K. (2013a) *Being, Time, Bios: Capitalism and Ontology*, Charles Shepherdson (ed.), New York: SUNY Press.

Kordela, A.K. (2013b) "Biopolitics, From Tribes to Commodity Fetishism," *Differences*, 24(1) (Spring): 1–29.

Kordela, A.K. (2013c) "(Marxian-Psychoanalytic) Biopolitics & Bioracism," in Sigi Jöttkandt and Joan Copjec (eds) *Penumbr(a)*, Melbourne: Re.Press.

Kordela, A.K. (2013d) "Biopolitics: From Supplement to Immanence – In Dialogue with Roberto Esposito's Trilogy: Communitas, Immunitas, Bios," *Cultural Critique*, 85: 163–188.

Kordela, A.K. (2016) "Monsters of Biopower: Terror(ism) and Horror in the Era of Affect," *Philosophy Today*, 60(1): 193–205.

Kordela, A.K. (2017) "Spinoza's Biopolitics," in *Spinoza's Authority, Volume I: Resistance and Power in the Ethics*, A.K. Kordela and D. Vardoulakis (eds), New York: Bloomsbury.

Kordela, A.K. and Bermas-Dawes, J. (2017) "Spinoza's Immanent Sovereignty: Fantasy and the Decision of Interpretation," in A.K. Kordela and D. Vardoulakis (eds) *Spinoza's Authority (Volume 2): Resistance and Power in the Treatises*, New York: Bloomsbury.

Lacan, J. (1981) *Book XI: The Four Fundamental Concepts of Psychoanalysis*, Alan Sheridan (trans.), Jacques-Alain Miller (ed.), New York: W.W. Norton & Co.

Lacan, J. (1991) *Le Séminaire. Livre XVII: L'envers de la psychanalyse*, Paris: Seuil.

Lacan, J. (2007) *The Seminar of Jacques Lacan: Book XVII: The Other Side of Psychoanalysis*, Russell Grigg (trans.), Jacques-Alain Miller (ed.), New York: W.W. Norton & Co.

Lord, B. (2010) *Spinoza's Ethics*, Edinburgh: Edinburgh University Press.

Macherey, P. (1998) "Deleuze in Spinoza," in *In a Materialist Way: Selected Essays by Pierre Macherey*, Ted Stolze (trans.), Warren Montag (ed.), London: Verso.

Marx, K. (1990) *Capital: A Critique of Political Economy (Volume 1)*, Ben Fowkes and David Fernbach (trans.), New York: Penguin.

Meillassoux, Q. (2008) *After Finitude: An Essay on the Necessity of Contingency*, Ray Brassier (trans.), London: Continuum.

Montag, W. (2013) *Althusser and His Contemporaries: Philosophy's Perpetual War*, Durham, NC: Duke.

Neroni, H. (2015) *The Subject of Torture: Psychoanalysis and Biopolitics in Television and Film*, New York: Columbia University Press.

Peden, K. (2014) *Spinoza Contra Phenomenology: French Rationalism from Cavaillés to Deleuze*, Stanford, CA: Stanford University Press.

Schuller, G.H. (2002) "Letter 63," in *Spinoza's Complete Works*, Indianapolis, IN: Hackett.

Spinoza, B. (1951) *A Theologico-Political Treatise and A Political Treatise*, R.H. M. Elwes (trans.), New York: Dover.

Spinoza, B. (1985) *The Collected Works of Spinoza*, Edwin Curley (trans.), Princeton, NJ: Princeton University Press.

Yovel, Y. (1989) *Spinoza and Other Heretics: The Marrano of Reason*, Princeton, NJ: Princeton University Press.

2 Materialist epistemontology

Marx and Sohn-Rethel with Spinoza and psychoanalysis[1]

Two lines of secular epistemology

Alfred Sohn-Rethel aspired to produce a materialist epistemology that would intertwine Immanuel Kant's critique of pure reason with Karl Marx's critique of political economy. To put it in terms that foreground the paradoxical character of Sohn-Rethel's enterprise – when viewed from the dominant epistemological perspective of modernity – this epistemology would derive the Kantian *a priori* categories of apperception from Marx's analysis of the historical, hence *a posteriori*, reality of capitalism. However, seen from the monist perspective we are becoming familiar with here, there is no paradox, since, as we have seen, thought and things are the expression of being, precisely in all their historical determination. Recalling Benjamin, being or the absolute is itself enfolded into the material history of transient objects and ideas. The mutual enfolding of the *a priori* and the *a posteriori* that Sohn-Rethel discerned in Marx's theory ultimately entails the immersion of being into material history, and concomitantly, the intertwining of ontology and epistemology as epistemontology.

For Sohn-Rethel the path toward such an epistemontology passes through Marx, and not through G.W.F. Hegel – in whom Sohn-Rethel saw the epitome of idealism. That is, Sohn-Rethel did not see this path through dialectical dualism. The latter claims to unify thought and being but only by first opposing them and then trying to synthesize them, a process in which what remains at the end is "the duplication of self-consciousness" (Hegel 1977: 110; §176) – that is, pure (and self-mirrored) thought, with no being.

For Marx, being consists of two aspects: on the one hand, extension or materiality (use-value), subject to decay in linear time and continuous space, and, on the other hand, immateriality or abstraction from materiality (abstract value), whose spatiotemporal categories are those of synchronic differential relations among places devoid of material content (as later formulated by structuralism).[2] However, because secular humans imagine that things pertain only to the material aspect (use-value), Marx's ontology entails that thought – traditionally juxtaposed to things, and understood as consciousness – becomes split between consciousness and the unconscious. As Marx puts it, in capitalism, "men do not bring the products of their labour into relation with each other as values," having recognized "these objects merely as the material integuments of homogeneous human labour" (Marx 1990: 166). Rather, in exchanging these objects we treat them as concrete objects of utility, produced by different kinds of labor, even though in truth they become exchangeable values precisely because they are the material receptacles of homogeneous labor. So, even though we actually exchange abstract values, we "do this without being aware of it" – we do it unconsciously (Marx 1990: 166–7). If we are unable to know what we actually do, then our consciousness must be limited to considering things in their materiality, and not as abstract values. Therefore, our consciousness operates according to the categories of extension (use-value), so that only our unconscious is capable of registering the fact that we are exchanging abstract values. This can be *known* only from the perspective of the exchanged values themselves: the commodities abstracted from their materiality. In Marx's words: "If commodities could speak, they would say this: our use-value may interest men, but it does not belong to us as objects. What does belong to us as objects … is our value … We relate to each other merely as exchange-values" (Marx 1990: 176–7). The language of values, things abstracted from materiality, is the language of our unconscious, and its spatiotemporality is also abstracted in the form of synchronic differentiality. Hence, monist ontology entails both a *monist theory of temporality* (being exists both in diachrony and synchrony) and a *monist epistemology* (thought is split between diachronic consciousness and the synchronic unconscious).

Sohn-Rethel's work endeavors to formulate systematically an ensuing materialist epistemontology and its corresponding theory of temporality.

Real abstraction, and intellectual and manual labor

Taking as his starting point Marx's ontology, Sohn-Rethel approaches being as consisting of two equally real aspects: the material world of use-value and the abstract/formal world of exchange-value. As opposed to the material objects of utility, the "form of commodity is abstract and abstractness governs its whole orbit"; it is "exchange-value," which, "in contrast to the use-value of commodities … is subject only to quantitative differentiation" (Sohn-Rethel: 19).[3] Citing Marx: "Not an atom of matter enters into the objectivity of commodities as values; in this it is the direct opposite of the coarsely sensuous objectivity of commodities as physical bodies" (Sohn-Rethel: 27; Marx 1990: 138). "[E]ven labour," whether intellectual or manual, "when determining the magnitude and substance of value, becomes 'abstract human labour,' human labour purely as such" (Sohn-Rethel: 19). Money, the "form in which commodity-value takes on its concrete appearance … be it as coinage or bank-notes" (which as such is a material thing), loses all its materiality by dint of the fact that it functions as exchange-value – the exchange-value *par* excellence – and "is an abstract thing" (Sohn-Rethel: 19). Finally, "as owner of such riches, man himself becomes an abstract man, a private property-owner" (Sohn-Rethel: 19). In short, "a society in which commodity exchange forms the *nexus rerum* is a purely abstract set of relations," not unlike a structural system (Sohn-Rethel: 19). By contrast, any activity in which the commodity resumes its materiality belongs exclusively in the world of material extension, which is why "'Gebrauch' versteht sich hier als produktiver wie als konsumtiver und als synonym mit dem gesamten Bereich des Stoffwechsels des Menschen mit der Natur im Sinne von Marx ['use' designates here the productive and consumptive realms, that is, the entirety of the metabolic interaction of humans with nature, in Marx's sense]." This is in opposition to "'abstrakt,'" that is, "abzüglich aller Merkmale möglichen Gebrauchs der Waren [excluding all traits of any such possible use of commodities]" (Sohn-Rethel 1989: 18).

This means that the "abstract" and the "material" are determined not by the chemical consistency of a given thing but contextually: within utility (production/consumption) everything is material; within exchange, everything is abstracted from materiality and its spatiotemporal determinations, existing only as pure value. A pound of iron or 10MB of information are equally material within the realm of utility, and equally immaterial in the circulation of exchange. Both Marx and Sohn-Rethel establish, therefore, a distinction between an "ersten oder primären Natur [first or primary Nature]" (the world of utility) and a "zweiten … Natur [second … Nature]" (abstract value). The latter "kommt zustande durch die Notwendigkeit einer Vergesellschaftung in Ablösung von allen Betätigungsweisen des materiellen Stoffwechsels zwischen Mensch und Natur [arises out of the necessity of a socialization detached from all activities relating to the human's material metabolic interactions with nature," which "sind selbst Teil der ersten Natur [are themselves part of primary Nature]" (Sohn-Rethel 1989: 58).

The second nature "entbehrt … jedweder möglichen Wahrnehmbarkeit [is devoid of all possible perceptibility (or sense reality)]" (Sohn-Rethel: 57). It is the universe that "von Marx so genannten 'Wertgegenständlichkeit' ausmacht [constitutes Marx's so-called 'value objectivity']" and, as such, exists "außerhalb oder jenseits des gesamten Feldes von Naturstoff und Wahrnehmungsempirie [outside or beyond the entire sphere of natural matter and empirical perception]" and their continuous spatiotemporality (Sohn-Rethel 1989: 61). The second nature emerges out of the abstraction of the primary nature (material nature or sense reality), and consists of purely quantitative immaterial values and their social (i.e., differential) relations. For both Marx and Sohn-Rethel, terms such as "social" and "socialization" or "interpersonal" are the antipode of inherent natural qualities and the world of use.[4] Structural linguistics uses the terms "relational" and "differential" in the same way, that is, as designating the way in which void elements in a system obtain positive values only through their synchronic differential ("social") relations to the other elements in the same system.

Sohn-Rethel stresses that this abstraction of nature in capitalist economy is real: "While the concepts of natural science are thought abstractions, the economic concept of value is a real one," for "commodity abstraction … does not originate in men's minds but in their actions" in "the spatio-temporal sphere of human interrelations." This fact "does not give 'abstraction' a merely metaphorical meaning" but a "literal sense" (Sohn-Rethel 1989: 20).[5] Modern subjectivity is split between conscious person and unconscious action: "Im Warenaustausch fallen Handlung und Bewußtsein, Tun und Denken der Tauschenden auseinander und gehen verschiedene Wege. Nur die Handlung des Austauschs ist abstrakt vom Gebrauch, das Bewußtsein der Handelnden ist es nicht [In commodity exchange the action and the consciousness, the doing and the thinking, of people involved in the exchange fall apart and go separate ways. Only the action of the exchange is abstracted from use, the consciousness of the actors is not]" (Sohn-Rethel 1989: 30). This split is replicated in the distinction between "social" and "private": "Allein die Handlung ist … das Gesellschaftliche des Austauschs, während das Bewußtsein der Handelnden privat ist und blind für den gesellschaftlich-synthetischen Charakter ihrer Handlung [Only the act of exchange is social, whereas the consciousness of the actors is private and blind to the social-synthetic character of their act]" (Sohn-Rethel 1989: 58). While *I* (consciously) purchase an apple in order to eat (metabolize) it, *we* (unconsciously) enact an exchange of abstract values. This is the meaning of Marx's statement that, to repeat, "'[t]hey do this without being aware of it'" (cited in Sohn-Rethel 1989: 20). The state of being as abstract value is inaccessible to the consciousness of the very persons whose acts bring it about. In other words, primary nature (use, or the metabolic interaction with nature, and its linear temporality) enters the domain of social exchange, in the form of individual consciousness, at the same time as our collective unconscious – our manual (unconscious and abstractifying) acts of exchange – engages in the secondary nature (abstract value, and its synchronic differentiality). In short, *the split between consciousness and the unconscious occurs within the realm of exchange itself.*

Echoing the title of his major work, Sohn-Rethel famously arrives at the conclusion that "the fallacies of the epistemological and idealistic tradition are more effectively eliminated if one does not talk of 'the theory of knowledge' but the division of mental and manual labour instead" (Sohn-Rethel 1989: 21). This thesis has largely been received as referring to the division of labor between intellectual and manual activities *within the realm of production*. Yet, as we have seen, what Sohn-Rethel has presented throughout his exposition of real abstraction is a split *within the realm of exchange*: that between the labor of the hands and that of consciousness (the intellectual labor of the persons, which remains unconscious of the labor of their own hands). The cornerstone of Sohn-Rethel's materialist epistemology consists in the division, and in establishing the relation, between *unconscious manual labor* and *conscious intellectual labor within* the *sphere of exchange*. It is for this reason that Sohn-Rethel made exchange, not production, the ultimate horizon of analysis. His thesis is that abstract thought is constituted through unconscious actions within the realm of exchange, and that, consequently, idealist epistemology must be replaced by a *theory of collective consciousness (intellectual labor) and the collective unconscious (manual labor)*.

The canonical misreading of Sohn-Rethel's distinction between manual and intellectual labor misses one of the most important contributions of both Marx's and Sohn-Rethel's works, namely: the fundamental function of the unconscious in secular capitalist modernity, both on the socio-economical and the subjective levels.[6] *The unconscious emerges within the sphere of capitalist exchange, as a structural system of differential relations of value, which provides the blueprint of the categories of abstract thought*.

In fact, Sohn-Rethel explicitly ascribes to the division of labor within production a non-essential and purely contingent relation to capitalist domination. It would seem, he writes, that the "Scheidung zwischen Kopf- und Handarbeit … ist von ähnlich unentbehrlicher Bedeutung für die bürgerliche Klassenherrschaft wie das Privateigentum an den Produktionsmitteln [the division between head and hand within production … has an importance for bourgeois class rule as vital as that of the private ownership of the means of production]." Yet, "[a]n der Entwicklung mancher der heutigen sozialistischen Länder läßt sich die Wahrheit ablesen, daß man das kapitalistische Eigentum abschaffen kann und doch den Klassengegensatz noch nicht los ist [one can recognize in the development of certain socialist countries today that in truth one can abolish property rights and still not be rid of class opposition]" (Sohn-Rethel 1989: 31–2). Therefore, "der Zusammenhang [the connection]" between class antagonism and the division of labor within production "ist ein rein kausaler und geschichtlicher [is purely causal and historical]." The two are "gänzlich disparat, d. h. es gibt zwischen ihnen, sei es im Ganzen oder in den Einzelheiten, keine Querverbindungen, die von dem einen auf das andere zu schließen erlauben [utterly disparate, that is, there exist no interconnections between them, either in whole or in part, that suggest that the one necessarily implies the other]" (Sohn-Rethel 1989: 31).

Sohn-Rethel's distinction between head and hand (consciousness and the unconscious) within the sphere of exchange has as little to do with the division of labor within production as Marx's distinction between material and immaterial has to do with chemistry. To exemplify this, let us read the following passage referring to Kant's *Critique of Pure Reason*:

> Wenn die Analyse ausschließlich mit den Begriffsformen der Geistesarbeit in der "reinen Mathematik" und "reinen Naturwissenschaft" beschäftigt ist … überhaupt mit ihrer "bloßen Möglichkeit" sowie ihrer Methode, so ist es klar, daß etwas draußen bleibt, nämlich die Handarbeit. Die Handarbeit schafft die Dinge, von denen die theoretische Vernunft nur die "Erscheinung" betrachtet, und ist von andersartigem Realitätscharakter, als er jemals dem Erkenntnisobjekt zukommen kann.
>
> [When analysis concerns itself exclusively with the concepts of intellectual labor in "pure mathematics" and "pure natural science" … and generally with their pure possibility and method, then it is clear that something is left out, namely: manual labor. Manual labor makes those things of which theoretical reason considers only the "appearance," so that its reality-character is too alien to become an object of cognition.]
>
> (Sohn-Rethel 1989: 1–2)

It would be inconsistent to read "manual labor" in this passage as referring to the proletarian domain of production. For, according to both Kant and Sohn-Rethel, theoretical or pure reason (*Vernunft*) relegates to the realm of phenomena (which is the realm of understanding – *Verstand*) also intellectual judgments, as long as they are based on empirical experience in time and space. Phenomena, which are always perceived in time and space, are the objects of understanding. Hence, any concrete particular experience, intellectual or manual, is a phenomenon and an object of understanding, not a cognitive object of theoretical reason. By contrast, the cognitive object of pure reason concerns the "absolute totality of all experience [which] is itself not experience" and, hence, not in time and space (Kant 1977: 70; §40). What is presupposed for the shift from the phenomenon to the cognitive object of theoretical reason is not intellectual labor, but the turn of focus from a particular experience (intellectual or manual) to the *totality* of such an experience. This is what Sohn-Rethel attempts to do, shifting his focus onto the totality of the experience of *all* cognition, including that which Kant's theoretical reason leaves outside because it considers "its reality-character [to be] too alien to become an object of cognition" – namely the unconscious, the knowledge unconsciously produced and performed by the people's acts in the field of socio-economic effectivity. For Kant, there is no room for things made by hand because in his scheme there is no room for the unconscious. Introducing manual labor as the unconscious is a necessary step for Sohn-Rethel in order to advance the thesis that abstract thought (Kant's *a priori*) is an effect of empirical reality (Kant's *a posteriori*). This does not mean – as naïve materialism would have it – that there is no *a priori*, but that the *a priori* is produced by the *a posteriori* as its own unconscious precondition. This is why the questions of historical materialism remain those of idealism:

> Wie ist reine Mathematik möglich? Wie ist reine Naturwissenschaft möglich? Wie sind synthetische Urteile a priori möglich? … *Daß* die "reine Naturwissenschaft" möglich ist, ist nicht zweifelhaft, denn sie ist Tatsache; folglich muß sich ergründen lassen, *wie* sie möglich ist. Das war die Argumentationsweise Kants, und dieselbe Argumentalion nötigt sich dem historischen Materialisten auf.
>
> [How is pure mathematics possible? How is natural science possible? How are synthetic *a priori* judgments possible? … *That* "pure natural science" is possible is indubitable; it is a fact. Accordingly, we must be able to show *how* it is possible. This was Kant's approach, and this remains the postulate of historical materialism.]
>
> (Sohn-Rethel 1989: 7)

Yet, Sohn-Rethel's responses to these same questions break with idealism, as they can be formulated only after having inserted the division between "hand" and "head" within the "head" itself.

The capitalist (mutual) abstractification of productive labor and value

Now, even as Sohn-Rethel rightly persists in that the hand–head division is an internal one within thought and exchange, he is wrong in assuming, contrary to Marx, that the genesis of real abstraction occurs exclusively within exchange and not in production:

> die Warenabstraktion, steht in keinem inhärenten Zusammenhang mit der zur Produktion der Waren erforderlichen Arbeit … [D]ie Warenabstraktion ist Tauschabstraktion, nicht Arbeitsabstraktion. Die Arbeitsabstraktion, welche in der kapitalistischen Warenproduktion in der Tat stattfindet, hat … ihren Ort im Produktionsprozeß, nicht im Austauschprozeß.
>
> [Commodity abstraction bears no inherent connection to the labor required for the production of commodities … Commodity abstraction is exchange abstraction, not labor abstraction. The abstraction of labor, which indeed takes place in the capitalist commodity production … occurs in the process of production, not in the process of exchange.]
>
> (Sohn-Rethel 1989: 49)

This is also why only the "value-creating labour" is termed "abstract human labour," in contrast to "concrete labour, which creates use-values" (Sohn-Rethel: 22), in spite of its possible abstraction (routinization, etc.) within the capitalist mode of production (e.g., its mechanization in the "mindless assembly line" or its "abstractification" resulting from computerization; see Reitter 2014, and Benz-Overhage 1982). The exclusivity of exchange as the source of abstraction (partly) explains Sohn-Rethel's concentration on (coined) money – "nur am gemünzten Geld die Realabstraktion überhaupt in Erscheinung treten kann [it is only with coined money that real abstraction can emerge]" (Sohn-Rethel 1989: 59). It also explains his thesis that "the critique of epistemology must be undertaken independently from that of political economy" (Sohn-Rethel 1989: 37) – the latter referring exclusively to the analysis of production.

Marx surpasses Sohn-Rethel in recognizing the replication of the split in exchange (thought) within production (realm of matter) itself. While for Sohn-Rethel only the exchange of commodities *qua* values confers on labor its abstract character retroactively, for Marx labor embodied in its product is abstracted already within capitalist production. Both Marx and Sohn-Rethel concur that:

> Weder ist die Arbeit von Haus aus abstrakt, noch ist ihre Abstraktion zur "abstrakt menschlichen Arbeit" ihr eigenes Werk. Die Arbeit abstraktifiziert sich nicht selber. Der Sitz der Abstraktion liegt außerhalb der Arbeit in der bestimmten gesellschaftlichen Verkehrsform des Austauschverhältnisses.
>
> [Labor is neither inherently abstract, nor is its abstraction to "abstract human labor" its own work. Labor does not abstractify itself. The site of its abstraction lies outside labor, in the specific social form of the exchange relation.]
>
> (Sohn-Rethel 1989: 16)

What Sohn-Rethel objects to is that "the inverse also holds for Marx, that the exchange relation does not abstractify itself either. It is abstracted, or rather, abstractified by labor," so that the "result of this relation is the commodity value" (Sohn-Rethel 1989: 16). While Sohn-Rethel maintains that only the abstractification of labor is the effect of abstract and abstractifying value, Marx maintains that *also* the value of the commodity is the effect of an already abstract and abstractifying labor. This to Sohn-Rethel means that, for Marx, "commodity value has the abstractifying exchange relation as its form" for a concrete historical epoch, but "abstractified labor as its substance" (Sohn-Rethel 1989: 16). That is, that the abstraction of labor is a transhistorical immutable fact and not the result of the specific form of capitalist exchange.

Such an argument would be politically dubious, for, so Sohn-Rethel reckons, if labor is transhistorically abstract, then one would end up raising social exploitation to a universal and transhistorical principle. Sohn-Rethel interprets the fact that Marx sees a continuum between "primitive bartering" and contemporary exchange – in that "human labor is always conceived as '*social* labor,' today as throughout all prehistory" (Sohn-Rethel: 178–9, emphasis mine) – as meaning that for Marx labor has always been abstract. From this he infers that "Marx zwischen dem Tauschverkehr, wie er der Ausbeutung vorausgegangen sein kann (!), und dem Tauschverkehr, wie er aus der Ausbeutung hervorgegangen ist, keinen grundsätzlichen Unterschied macht [Marx makes no fundamental distinction between exchange, as it could (!) have occurred prior to exploitation and the mode of exchange that resulted from exploitation]." As a result, "die Verdinglichung [the objectification]" that marks the capitalist mode of exploitation "scheint … bruchlos aus naturwüchsigen Verhältnissen hervorgegangen [appears as having been seamlessly derived from primordial relations]" (Sohn-Rethel 1989: 179). In short, Sohn-Rethel suspects Marx for having naturalized objectification and exploitation, and he thinks that the way to de-naturalize them is to turn to coined money, as a breaking point that for the first time in history realizes abstraction.

Yet, *Capital* makes clear that for Marx money does not amount to abstract value as a formal system. He indeed concurs with Aristotle that some form of value existed since the most primitive societies, as exchange owes to the natural state of "men having too much of this and not enough of that" (Marx 1990: 151, citing Aristotle 1992: 82; 1257a5). However, Marx also stresses that what is exchanged at that stage is quantities of use-value, and one can speak only of the value of material things, not of a value independent from its material substratum:

> In the direct exchange of products, each commodity is a direct means of exchange to its owner, and an equivalent to those who do not possess it, although only in so far as it has use-value for them. At this stage, therefore, the articles exchanged do not acquire a value-form independent of their own use-value, or of the individual needs of the exchangers.
>
> (Marx 1990: 182)

This is so even when coined money mediates in the exchange of these use-values, as Aristotle already knew: to say "5 beds = 1 house (κλῖναι πέντε ἀντί οἰκίας)" is indistinguishable from "5 beds = a certain amount of money (κλῖναι πέντε ἀντί … ὃσου αἱ πέντε κλῖναι" (Marx 1990: 151, citing Aristotle's *Nicomachean Ethics*, bk. V, ch. 5). The true metaphysical issue, as Aristotle already discerned, is that "[t]here can be no exchange … without equality, and no equality without commensurability (οὔτ'ἰσότης μὴ οὔσης συμμετρίας)." Therefore, the real question is how a "house should be qualitatively equated with [*either*] the bed" *or* with coined money – in both cases, the question is the same: what makes a house economically commensurable with anything else? Given this aporia Aristotle could only conclude that, "being distinct to the senses … it is, however, in reality, impossible (τῇ μὲν οὖν ἀληθείᾳ ἀδύνατον) that such unlike things can be commensurable," therefore, "this form of equation can only be … a makeshift for practical purposes" (Marx 1990: 151, citing throughout Aristotle's *Nicomachean Ethics*, bk. V, ch. 5). Aristotle is unable to infer that there is a "homogeneous element" or "common substance" shared by all material things, including coined money, and that this is value *qua* abstract human labor, because it is only in "the form of commodity-values" that "all labour is expressed as equal human labour and therefore as labour of equal quality" (Marx 1990: 152). Despite all the coins around him, Aristotle could not discover real abstraction due to "the historical limitations inherent in the society in which he lived," namely, a "society … founded on the labour of slaves … [and] the inequality of men and their labour-powers" (Marx 1990: 151–2). "[T]he equality and equivalence of all kinds of labour" presupposes that "the dominant social relation is the relation between men as possessors of commodities," and, in this sense, as equal (Marx 1990: 151–2).

In other words, what eludes Sohn-Rethel is that Marx argues that labor is *abstracted already within production – only* under the precondition that the labor in question is *waged* labor, *commodified* labor. However, this is something that *presupposes not coins but the existence of the capitalist mode of exchange and of abstract value* as such. The abstraction of labor, which is the precondition for the emergence of abstract value, itself presupposes the existence of this abstract value. *It is neither a pre-abstractified labor that abstractifies exchange, nor a pre-abstractified exchange that abstractifies labor – the two processes occur at the same time and presuppose each other.*

The causality between value and labor regarding their abstraction is invertible – and this without entailing that the exploitation in labor is inherent to labor. Sohn-Rethel reproaches Marx for letting both "naturwüchsige Kooperation und der verdinglichte Zusammenhang der Privateigentümer erscheinen der Substanz nach als dasselbe – als gesellschaftliche Arbeitszusammenhänge [natural or organic social cooperation and the objectified relation of private property owners appear the same in their substance – as social labor relations]" (Sohn-Rethel 1989: 178). Marx does indeed see both as social labor relations (society existed also before capitalism), except that in the first case they are *social* in the sense of Sohn-Rethel's *first nature* (i.e., social relations among humans that are mediated through nature), whereas in the second they are *social* in the sense of the *second nature* (i.e., purely abstract and differential). The commodification of labor and, hence, the emergence of capitalism, severed *for the first time in* history the second nature from the first. (Which is what enabled the dualist misconception of the separation between words and things; but Marx's point is that the two spheres share the same structures even after the autonomization of abstract value.)

Parmenides's coins do not accrue

It is true that the "philosophische Begriffsbildung verstandesmäßigen Denkens überhaupt, ihre formelle und historische Wurzel in der Realabstraktion der gesellschaftlichen Synthese vermittels Warentausch hat, d. h.

in der zweiten Natur [philosophical conceptualization of rational thought is formally and historically rooted in the real abstraction of social synthesis by means of commodity exchange, that is, in the second nature]" (Sohn-Rethel 1989: 60). Yet, much more than coins is required for the second nature to become independent from the first – which is the *principium specificum* of commodity exchange.

Coined money pertains to both natures, since the "ökonomische Funktion erfordert eine stoffliche Materie aus kostbaren Gebrauchsstoffen wie Gold und Silber [the functioning of economy requires a physical material made out of precious elements, such as gold and silver" (first nature), while it also "ist … durch abstrakte Immaterialität ihres Substrats ausgezeichnet, weil ja die Substantialität der Tauschhandlung für die Zeit der Transaktion von jeder stofflichen Gebrauchspraxis der Waren kompromißlos geschieden sein muß, um den Tausch möglich zu machen [is distinguished by the abstract immateriality of its substrate, since in order for the exchange to be possible, its substantiality must be uncompromisingly divorced from any material use of the commodities during the transaction]" (Sohn-Rethel 1989: 62–3). From this Sohn-Rethel infers "daß das Geld zurecht aus einem Material bestehen sollte, das … quantitativ von zeitloser Beständigkeit wäre [that money should consist of a material … of a quantitatively timeless character]," and since "solches Material gibt es aber in der ganzen Natur nicht [no such material exists in the entire nature]," he leaps to the conclusion that money "zeichnet … sich durch rein abstrakte Immaterialität aus [is characterized by purely abstract immateriality]" (Sohn-Rethel 1989: 63). Sohn-Rethel does not acknowledge the importance of the fact that, as he writes, the "emittierende Autorität … verbindet dies mit einer Garantieerklärung, daß die emittierten Münzen für den durch ihren Umlauf erlittenen Verschleiß kostenlos durch vollwertige ersetzt würden [issuing authority … guarantees that, due to the incurred wear during their circulation, minted coins will be replaced with [their nominal] full-value coins at no cost]" (Sohn-Rethel 1989: 63). Coined money involves abstraction, and this abstraction is "eine Realität … vom allerhöchsten denkbaren Objektivitätsgrad [a reality … of the highest conceivable degree of objectivity]" (Sohn-Rethel 1989: 61). Yet – as is evidenced in the issuing authorities' obligation to recover the coins' material erosion – coined money cannot sever the two natures to the point that the second ceases to depend on the first.

A further level of real abstraction is required for an economic system that would gradually loosen the tie between money and a fixed commodity (e.g., gold) up to the point of establishing a global "system of national fiat monies, with flexible exchange rates between the major currencies" (Sachs and Larrain 1993: 223; i.e., a monetary system of purely differential values, with no material convertibility), and, further, up to the point of employing fictitious capital. This autonomization of the second nature of value cannot find any cause in its prehistory and can instead posit its cause only retroactively, as an effect of its own emergence. The commodification of labor is presupposed for the emergence of a wholly independent system of value, which is itself presupposed for the commodification of labor. The problem of the causal generation of capital replicates the fundamental problem of secular thought: if God is not the creator (cause) of the world, then how was it created?

This question did not concern Parmenides, Sohn-Rethel's exemplary philosopher of coined money, according to whose ontology, "das Reale aller Dinge ist nicht ihre Sinneserscheinung, sondern ist einzig und allein das Eine, das ist, in seiner Sprache ausgedrückt: τό ὄν [the real of all things is not their sensory appearance, but rather solely the One, or put in his language: τό ὄν]," which is "ganz und in sich vollständig … unveränderlich, unteilbar und unbeweglich [whole and complete in itself … immutable, indivisible, and immovable]" (Sohn-Rethel 1989: 64–5). As Sohn-Rethel admits, "[d]er Gedanke dieses Begriffs ist eine offensichtliche Vereinseitigung und ontologische Verabsolutierung [this concept involves an obvious one-sidedness and ontological absolutization]" (Sohn-Rethel 1989: 65), as it degrades the other side of the coin, its material aspect, to a merely illusory "sensory appearance [*Sinneserscheinung*]," as the faulty appearance of the immutable One. At least part of Sohn-Rethel's reproach to Hegel's dialectic applies also to Parmenides: "Das Sein, mit dem das Denken eins, war nicht das raumzeitliche Sein der Dinge und Verhältnisse der tatsächlichen Geschichte und geschichtlichen Tatsachen, sondern es war … nichts als das Sein des Denkens selbst [The being with which thought was united was not the spatiotemporal being of things and relations of actual history … rather it was … nothing other than the being of thought itself]" (Sohn-Rethel 1989: 3). Abstraction cannot be real as long as the material world in which it occurs is considered to be inferior to the product of abstraction. Moreover, the secularization of the abstract itself requires explaining the genesis of not only the abstract but also the material, as it can no longer be attributed to a divine creator.

God, or substance, or labor-power

For Spinoza, "there is only one substance," which is "God, *or* Nature," and "[e]*xcept God, no substance can be or be conceived,*" so that "a substance cannot be produced by anything else," and is, therefore, "the cause of itself" (*Ethics* IV pref., IP14, IP14C1, IP7D). God or substance "*as such* is the power of making itself actual" (Lord 2010: 21) – the sheer *power or potentiality of self-actualization*. For this reason, "God is the immanent, not the transitive, cause of all things" (*Ethics* IP18). That is, unlike a creationist God, who is conceived as a cause preceding in time the created world, Spinoza's God is an "immanent" cause, a cause that is itself the effect of its own effects insofar as it does not exist but in its effects. By the same token, one cannot say which came first, God or the world – not unlike, as we have seen, the mutual abstractification of labor and value, each of which presupposes the other. For Sohn-Rethel, Marx's concept of "der abstract gesellschaftlichen Arbeit [abstract social labor]" is a "dem Hegelschen Erbe geschuldeten Fetischbegriff [concept of fetishism in the Hegelian tradition]" insofar as, although it "erkennt die Tatsache der Realabstraktion [recognizes the fact of real abstraction]," it "okkupiert genau den Platz, welcher der Realabstraktion aus der Kausalität der Tauschhandlung zukommt [occupies precisely the place accorded to real abstraction due to the causality of exchange]" (Sohn-Rethel 1971: 70). The reason why Sohn-Rethel thinks that Marx has inverted the true causality lies in an inability to conceive of retroactivity not as a mono-directional inversion of transitive causality but as immanent causality.

For Marx, "the use-value which the worker has to offer to the capitalist" is his "labour-power" or "labour-capacity, the aggregate of those … mental and physical capabilities … of a human being … which he sets in motion whenever he produces a use-value of any kind" (Marx 1993: 267; Marx 1990: 270). Since labor-power consists of *capabilities*, it "is not materialized in a product, does not exist apart from … [the laborer] at all, thus exists not really, but only in potentiality" (Marx 1993: 267). Labor-power must not be conflated with the "congealed" or abstract labor that is embodied in the commodity as the "value substance" (*Wertsubstanz*) that constitutes the unit for measuring the amount of value (*Wertgröße*) (Marx 2009: 49). Rather, labor-power is the sheer potentiality of actualizing itself as congealed labor within its product – it is the *power of self-actualization*. As Paolo Virno remarks, "[l]abor-power incarnates (literally) a fundamental category of philosophical thought: … the potential," something "which exists only as *possibility*." For the first time in history, labor "is bought and sold" as the most "exceptionally important commodity," thereby "tak[ing] on a pragmatic, empirical, socioeconomic dimension" (Virno 2004: 84, 82). Capitalist objectification concerns ultimately the objectification or *commodification of substance*, that is, the process through which labor-power is *forced to actualize itself* – whatever object of utility its product may be – *always already as abstract value*. The commodification of labor-power amounts to the transformation of the power of self-actualization into abstract labor – labor-time as the substance and unit of value. That labor-power is substance *qua* power-of-self-actualization is a transhistorical fact. By contrast, the commodification of this substance is its specific historical appropriation within capitalism, and it alone brings about real abstraction proper, that is, the autonomization of the "second nature."

Only the commodification of substance (labor-power) can yield surplus-value. The accumulation of surplus-value "cannot take place in the money itself, since … it does no more than realize … the price of the commodity it buys" and "the commodity is paid for at its full value," (C – M) (Marx 1990: 270). Therefore, the increase of value "must … take place in the commodity which is bought in the first act of circulation, M – C, but not in its value." It can "originate only in the actual use-value of the commodity [C], i.e. in its consumption." This "commodity," then, must be one "whose use-value possesses the peculiar property of being a source of value, whose actual consumption is … itself an objectification [*Vergegenständlichung*] of labour, hence a creation of value" (ibid., 270).

Surplus-value emerges because *potentiality's production and consumption overlap*, while the cost (wages) of the consumption (its purchase) of this labor is not equal with the price (exchange-value) of its product. Laborers do not labor twice, once to have their labor-power consumed by the one who bought it, and another time in order to produce a product. Yet, the price of their product is determined by the units of objectified (*vergegenständlicht*) abstract human labor within the autonomous differential relations of abstract value, whereas the cost at which laborers sell their labor-power is determined by the necessary "means of subsistence." These are themselves culturally specific, as "the extent of the so-called necessary requirements" and "the manner in which they are satisfied … depend on … the habits and expectations with which the class of free workers has been formed" (ibid., 275). As a result, and "[i]n contrast … with the case of other commodities, the determination of the value of labour-power contains a historical and moral element" (ibid., 275). Labor-power reveals the double sense of "consumption," as both purchasing and using up, the latter coinciding with labor-power's exhausted productivity. *Qua* purchasing, consumption is part of exchange; *qua* using up a material, it should be part of the first nature, alongside production. Using up labor-power, however, is *using up potentiality, not anything material*, so that to use up potentiality (labor-power) means to actualize it: I purchase labor *qua* productive power, say, for £10, and I sell it *qua* actualized, objectified abstract labor, for £12. *Labor-power's consumption* is its *actualization*.

The reason why Marx speaks of labor as "objectified" already within production is that labor-power is simultaneously productive and consumed (actualized as a material thing that, *in capitalism*, is always already the bearer of abstract value), so that the labor deposited in the product during production counts not only as use-value but also *directly as objectified abstract value*. In short, with capitalism, labor constitutes the unique instance in which *the realm of utility is penetrated by the realm of exchange*, so that abstract value overlaps with utility.[7]

When labor-power is commodified, abstract value becomes an autonomous system. For, as we know from the not-all set in set theory, precisely in order to become an autonomous system, abstract value must include within itself its exception or other – the spatiotemporal realm of production – while allowing it to continue to exist also as its other. This means that the system of abstract value must include within itself one element from the spatiotemporal realm of materiality, which, although outside the realm of exchange continues to function as a material commodity, yet within exchange functions as a pure value. Within the realm of production, labor-power functions as productive labor exercised on specific materials (hence, it is a use-value or material), while this same expenditure of labor functions as abstract value, as if it were always already within the realm of exchange.

Thus, capitalism consists of *three autonomous, yet interpenetrating, systems.* First, there is the primary nature (utility/production), which includes within itself its own exception (value) in the form of labor-power. Second, there is the second nature (value), which includes within itself materiality (manual act of exchange). Third, replicating both natures, there is thought. In terms of the second nature, thought is consciousness that includes within itself unconscious thought. In terms of the first nature, thought is again consciousness that includes within itself the potential – as that which ought to be, that is, ethics. This is why "the status of the unconscious … is ethical" and "pre-ontological," that is, "neither being, nor non-being, but the unrealized" (Lacan 1981: 33, 29–30).

With Sohn-Rethel, we understand that "the unconscious is structured like a language" (Lacan 1981: 20), like an autonomous system of abstract values. Then, with Marx and Spinoza, we understand that the unconscious is also structured as substance, the power of self-actualization *sub specie aeternitatis.* Because, as we saw in the preceding section, substance is an immanent cause – being itself the effect of its own effects – Sohn-Rethel's astute shift of emphasis from production to exchange as the ultimate frame of analysis has to be supplemented by the recognition of the retroactive effects of exchange on production.

The law of historical materialism

Capitalist exploitation – which presupposes the autonomization of the "second nature" – differs from the power relations that governed cooperative social labor under the dominion of the "first nature" insofar as in the latter the power of self-actualization was idealized. By contrast, in the former the power of self-actualization is commodified, which is to say, both objectified and fetishized (so that everything can function as a fetish). The idealism of secular philosophy that Sohn-Rethel critiques is itself a residue of the presecular idealization of the power of self-actualization (the monotheist conception of God) – where Hegel represents "absoluten Idealismus [absolute idealism]" and the "Gipfelpunkt des bürgerlichen Denkens [culmination of bourgeois thought]." Hegel's system "den Geist nicht nur zum Primat über die Handarbeit, sondern zur Alleinherrschaft ermächtigt [not only entitles the mind to primacy over manual labor but endows it with omnipotence]," since it reduces history to the actualization of that Spirit (Sohn-Rethel 1989: 20, 9). Sohn-Rethel and Hegel concur in that "die Natur erfährt ihre Fortsetzung in Form der Menschengeschichte dort, wo die Arbeit anfängt [nature experiences its continuation in the form of human history there, where labor begins]" (Sohn-Rethel 1989: 4). Whereas Hegel subsumes labor and all nature under Spirit, for Sohn-Rethel, "menschliche Geschichte Teil der Naturgeschichte ist, nämlich durchweg … von materiellen Notwendigkeiten beherrscht [human history is part of natural history, namely it is … governed throughout by material necessities" (Sohn-Rethel 1989: 4). These "material necessities," however, far exceed notions of a naïve materialism that wants to know nothing of spirits. In archaic societies, for instance, it is because the material on which people worked was itself inhabited by spirits that they would explain everything through those same spirits. If with Hegel the spirits are replaced with the Spirit, this owes again to the historically specific material conditions of both labor and thought, since the two are intertwined. The material conditions of labor and thought are always each other's incubators, whatever the level and form of abstraction may be.

As Sohn-Rethel stresses, the law of value that is intertwined with objectification and alienation is specific to capitalism; it is a historical law. Yet, Sohn-Rethel's primary thesis that, "[v]om materialistischen Standpunkt aus stellt sich das reine Denken … ist der Einwirkung der gesellschaftlichen Realabstraktion der Tauschhandlung geschuldet [from the materialist perspective … pure thought is a consequence of the impact of the social real abstraction of exchange]" (Sohn-Rethel 1989: 20–1), follows from a transhistorical law: the form of thought in any historical society corresponds to the mode of real abstraction occurring in that society's economy. Greek antiquity expresses the degree of real abstraction introduced by coined money – an abstraction with the one foot still in matter – whereas the philosophy of secular capitalist modernity expresses real abstraction during the gradual autonomization of value. In short, the dominance of the "Wertgesetz," the law of value (subjective genitive) is indeed transhistorical, but the form of value and, hence, the "Wertgesetz," the law of value (objective genitive), is historical (Sohn-Rethel 1989: 5).

Sohn-Rethel's methodology: commodity fetishism

Sohn-Rethel is the first to spell out the methodology that follows from Marx's theory of commodity fetishism – the ground of Sohn-Rethel's materialist epistemontology. He grasped that Marx's "theory of fetishism" entails, as we have seen, "that there is no theory of objectivity without a theory of subjectivity" (Balibar 2007: 56, 64–5). By discerning that abstraction occurs within social objectivity, Marx pointed to the socio-objective genesis and formation of the subject's abstract thought. Against the tradition of idealist transcendentalism, Marx's theory of commodity fetishism means, to repeat Balibar's words, that "the constitution of the world is not … the work of a subject, but a genesis of subjectivity (*a* form of determinate historical subjectivity) as part (and counterpart) of the social world of objectivity … [or] 'nature'" (Balibar 2007: 65–7). In our nature, things are both material objects and representations (value), which is why a materialist epistemology is effectively an *epistemontology*.

The relation between Kant and Sohn-Rethel reflects the shift from the State to the Market, which, as we have seen, corresponds to the politico-epistemological shift from ideology to commodity fetishism. While ideology is marked by a dualism between immanence and transcendence, fetishism reflects a society in which power is immanent in the constitution of the world of subjects and objects. The dualist political manifestation of the real abstraction as State and ideology expectedly fostered dualist and idealist philosophies (and vice versa), whether of the Kantian or the Hegelian type. By contrast, Sohn-Rethel provides the theoretical framework for analyzing the era governed by the market and fetishism. Accordingly, the motto of materialist epistemontology is: "Ich vertrete … die These von der gesellschaftlichen Entstehung des reinen Verstandes [I represent the thesis of the social genesis of pure understanding]" (Sohn-Rethel 1989: 21). Since only a monist-materialist conception of being escapes the pitfall of idealizing either the word or the thing, the motto must continue – "… and of ontology."

Notes

1 This chapter is a modified version of my article published in the special issue on Sohn-Rethel of *History of Human Sciences* (see Kordela 2016), published by SAGE Publishing (all rights reserved; http://online.sagepub.com).

2 It is in this sense that "[t]he real abstraction of capitalist society is not a logical abstraction" that ignores "differences" – a kind of intellectual distillation of the general from the concrete – "but rather an abstraction … born from difference, from … [a] specific social determinateness … capable of articulating an entire society" (Finelli 1987: 127; as translated in Alberto Toscano 2008: 275–6). In other words, a structure "is not quantitative, but topological and relational," whereby "the sites" and their differential relations "prevail over whatever occupies them" (Deleuze 2004: 174). We shall examine in more detail structure and structuralism in the next chapter.

3 Unless otherwise noted, all references to Sohn-Rethel are from Sohn-Rethel 1978. All references to Sohn-Rethel 1989 and Sohn-Rethel 1971 are my translations.

4 The "production of commodities" entails "that the specific social character of private labours carried on independently of each other consists in their equality as human labour," something which, "in the product, assumes the form of the existence of value" (Marx 1990: 167). Albeit materially (qualitatively) different, the various kinds of labor are reduced through their socialization in capitalism to their common element and thereby become qualitatively equal: "the social character of the equality of the various kinds of labour is reflected in the form of the common character, as values, possessed by these materially different things, the products of labour" (Marx 1990: 166).

5 Note that this does not simply mean that "during the act of exchange, individuals proceed *as if* the commodity" were an exchange-value, "although on the level of their 'consciousness'" they ""know very well"" that "commodities [are] material objects … of particular … 'use-value'" (Žižek 1989: 18). The objective

dimension of value abstraction indicates the inverse: "the consciousness of [the] agents is taken up … with the empirical appearance of things which pertain to their use"; "we must be careful not to apply [abstraction] to the consciousness of the exchange agents," which is "occupied with the use of the commodity they see, but occupied in their imagination only" (Sohn-Rethel 1989: 26–7). In the agents' imagination commodities appear *as if* they were use-values, when they really (objectively) are abstract values. It is around this lack of positively given materiality that the network of exchanges is organized. The mirage of commodity fetishism is double, with the *as if* on the side of either use or of value, depending on the perspective. Therefore, "in Marxism a fetish conceals [either] the positive network of social relations" (conscious thought), or, as "in Freud," "the lack … around which the symbolic network is articulated" (unconscious) (Žižek 1989: 49).

6 This false reduction of the entire realm of material spatiotemporality (use as production/consumption *and* the conscious intellectual labor (*Geistarbeit*) of persons within exchange) to the realm of manual labor within production, along with the concomitant equation of the entire sphere of exchange (conscious and unconscious) and of intellectual labor within production with abstraction – all this is widely evidenced in contemporary theories of real abstraction. According to Alberto Toscano, in the relevant current Italian and English literature there is a "juxtaposition of a commodity-centered and a labor-centered take on real abstraction," with an alignment, on the one hand, of "commodity-exchange," "epistemology," and "intellectual labor," and, on the other hand, "political economy," manual labor," and a "labor-centered" approach that focuses on "labor without qualities" (see Toscano 2008). However, according to Sohn-Rethel, "labor without qualities" is abstract labor as such, that is, labor-time worth a specific exchange-value, and as such, it is part and parcel of commodity-exchange – and hence of epistemology. What Toscano's classification of contemporary relevant literature evidences is that any reference to labor indiscriminatingly subsumes it under production and political economy. This is true unless the labor is "intellectual labor," in which case it pertains to an equally indiscriminatingly conceived homogeneous sphere of exchange and, hence, to epistemology. The internal split of the sphere of exchange (between conscious and unconscious aspects) that Sohn-Rethel foregrounds is, thus, reduced to the external opposition between two misconstrued spheres.

7 Among others, Michael Hardt and Antonio Negri argue that "the computerization of production" with its "immaterial labor" eliminates the "heterogeneity of concrete labor," as all forms of labor "involve … manipulation of symbols and information," so that "labor tends toward … abstract labor" (Hardt and Negri 2000: 292). First, whether it uses weaving machines or computers, labor as productive power is sheer potentiality, and, as such, neither material nor immaterial, but virtual. Second, taken as labor objectified in the product, labor has throughout capitalism been "abstract," and informatized capitalism has not changed this. The actual shift occurring through the computerization of production consists in the colonization of the means of production by the abstract symbols of "second nature." This phenomenon deserves study, but under the following double caveat. First, that the raw material required for these abstract symbols to function as means of production remain material machines. Second, that (Marx's/Sohn-Rethel's) economic materiality and immateriality or abstraction must not be conflated with the physico-chemical eponymous distinction. The physico-chemical consistency of use-value and consciousness is not necessarily material, just as, economically, information or language taken as use-value is material.

This purely relational or contextual determination of (im)materiality indicates that in capitalism, as Virno puts it, "[d]irect perception and the most spontaneous action come *last*," that is, after (unconscious) "abstract thought" has determined the very reality of which it is the effect (Virno 2001: 171). "This is the historical situation that comes about once the split between hand and mind manifests its *irreversibility*; when the *autonomy* of abstract intellect conditions and regulates the social productive process" (ibid., 171). In advanced capitalism, abstract thought is integrated in production and takes over control, since – and this is the point of commodity fetishism – "the products do not obey their producers, but rather vice versa: the producers act according to the products" (Sohn-Rethel 1989: 25).

I am addressing possible effects of the informatization of production in my work on biopolitics (including in Kordela 2013); see also Virno 2004 and Lorenzo Cillario 1996, although, to my understanding, both partake in the sliding between the two definitions of immateriality, thereby reducing computerized production to thought – be it Virno's "general intellect" of the multitude, or Cillario's "cognitive capital." This way one loses sight of the distinction between conscious and unconscious thought, or in Toscano's words, "of the radicality of the thesis put forward by Sohn-Rethel and paraphrased by Žižek – to wit, that under conditions of capitalism, thought is, in the final analysis, external to thought" (Toscano 2008: 284; see also Žižek 1989: 9–16).

References

Aristotle. (1992) *The Politics*, T.A. Sinclair (trans.), Trevor J. Saunders (rev.), London: Penguin Books.

Balibar, E. (2007) *The Philosophy of Marx*, Chris Turner and Gregory Elliott (trans.), New York: Verso.

Benz-Overhage, K. (1982) *Neue Technologien und alternative Arbeitsgestaltung: Auswirkungen des Computereinsatzes in der industriellen Produktion* [New Technologies and Alternative Work Design: Effects of Computer Use in Industrial Production], Frankfurt: Campus.

Cillario, L. (1996) *L'economia degli spettri: Forme del capitalismo contemporaneo* [The Economy of Specters: Forms of Contemporary Capitalism], Rome: Manifestolibri.

Deleuze, G. (2004) "How Do We Recognize Structuralism?," in *Desert Islands and Other Texts 1953–1974*, Melissa McMahon and Charles J. Stivale (trans.), David Lapoujade (ed.), Los Angeles, CA: Semiotext(e), pp. 170–192.

Finelli, R. (1987) *Astrazione e dialettica dal romanticismo al capitalismo (saggio su Marx)* [Abstraction and Dialectics from Romanticism to Capitalism (Essay on Marx)], Rome: Bulzoni.

Hardt, M. and A. Negri (2000) *Empire*, Cambridge, MA: Harvard University Press.

Hegel, G.W.F. (1977) *Phenomenology of Spirit*, A.V. Miller (trans.), Oxford: Oxford University Press.

Kant, I. (1977) *Prolegomena to Any Future Metaphysics That Will Be Able to Come Forward as Science*, James Ellington (trans.), Indianapolis, IN: Hacket.

Kordela, A.K. (2013) *Being, Time, Bios: Capitalism and Ontology*, Albany, NY: SUNY Press.

Kordela, A.K. (2016) "Materialist Epistemontology: Sohn-Rethel with Marx and Spinoza," *History of Human Sciences*, 29(2): 113–129.

Lacan, J. (1981) *The Seminar of Jacques Lacan: Book XI: The Four Fundamental Concepts of Psychoanalysis*, Jacques-Alain Miller (ed.), Alan Sheridan (trans.), New York: W.W. Norton.

Lord, B. (2010) *Spinoza's Ethics*, Bloomington: Indiana University Press.

Marx, K. (1990) *Capital: A Critique of Political Economy (Volume 1)*, Ben Fowkes and David Fernbach (trans.), New York: Penguin.

Marx, K. (1993) *Grundrisse: Foundations of the Critique of Political Economy (Rough Draft)*, M. Nicolaus (trans.), London: Penguin Books.

Marx, K. (2009) *Das Kapital: Kritik der politischen Ökonomie* [Capital: A Critique of Political Economy]. Cologne: Anaconda.

Reitter, K. (2014) "Alfred-Sohn-Rethel und die 'erweiterte Warenabstraktion'" (Linksnet) www.linksnet.de/de/artikel/20805.

Sachs, J.D. and F.B. Larrain (1993) *Macroeconomics for Global Economies*, Upper Saddle River, NJ: Prentice Hall.

Sohn-Rethel, A. (1971) *Materialistische Erkenntniskritik und Vergesellschaftung der Arbeit*, Berlin: Merve Verlag.

Sohn-Rethel, A. (1978) *Intellectual and Manual Labor: A Critique of Epistemology*, J. Young and P. Walton (eds), M. Sohn-Rethel (trans.), London: Macmillan.

Sohn-Rethel, A. (1989) *Geistige und körperliche Arbeit: zur Epistemologie der abendländischen Geschichte*, Weinheim: VCH, Acta Humaniora.

Spinoza, B. (1985) *The Collected Works of Spinoza*, Edwin Curley (trans.), Princeton, NJ: Princeton University Press.

Toscano, A. (2008) "The Open Secret of Real Abstraction," *Rethinking Marxism*, 20(2) (April): 273–287.

Virno, P. (2001) "The Two Masks of Materialism," Alberto Toscano (trans.), *Pli: The Warwick Journal of Philosophy*: 12.

Virno, P. (2004) *A Grammar of the Multitude: For an Analysis of Contemporary Forms of Life*, I. Bertoletti, J. Cascaito, and A. Casson (trans.), New York: Semiotext(e).

Žižek, S. (1989) *The Sublime Object of Ideology*, London: Verso.

3 Psychoanalysis and structuralism

> But, as for knowing who is responsible for [fantasy as] the setting [for desire] … the psychoanalyst [cannot] rely on … his science, nor on the support of myth. He must also become a philosopher.
>
> (Laplanche and Pontalis 2003: 133)[1]

In this chapter, I turn to Gilles Deleuze for his systematic and extensive attempts to define structuralism, particularly in a series of works in the late 1960s and early 1970s. These works provide support to the thesis that psychoanalysis and structuralism are so intertwined as to be parts of the same movement of thought. To this end, I begin, in a rather provocative manner, with the following double statement: the broadest term that can express the intrinsically psychoanalytic nature of Gilles Deleuze's thought is structuralism. Whether adopting psychoanalysis, appreciatively critiquing it, or even vehemently attacking it, structuralism is what fascinates Deleuze (not unlike Jacques Lacan) in Freud's work. In fact, it is not unlikely that Deleuze would have remained rather immune to Freud's attractions if, by the 1960s, and primarily through Lacan's intervention, psychoanalysis had not developed into an arena for probing structuralist thought. If nothing else, Lacan and Deleuze shared one passion: to explore and develop structuralism's potential for revolutionizing thought.[2]

Few other names, though, deserve credit regarding Deleuze's devotion to structuralist thought. Beyond Deleuze's profusely avowed debt to Jean-Paul Sartre, in the present context four others of his more or less contemporary thinkers warrant prominent reference. First, Louis Althusser, for having bolstered Deleuze's commitment to structuralism (which for him is another word for "theory") as an absolute condition of scientificity (and this, in spite of all his reservations regarding the actual practices of the majority of structuralists).[3] Second and third, Jean Laplanche and J.B. Pontalis, for having, in their 1964 article on the origin of fantasy (and the fantasy of origins), to which Deleuze refers repeatedly in the late 1960s, discerned structuralism as the condition of psychoanalysis' scientificity, and for having read Freud's long itinerary from his "seduction theory" in the early 1890s to his work on the "primal fantasy" and, finally, "auto-erotism" in the late

1910s – which coincides with his attempt to establish and define fantasy as the object of psychoanalysis – as a search for "structure."[4]

The ultimate creditor for Deleuze's structuralist/psychoanalytic proclivities, not counted among the four of his contemporary companions, remains, of course, his "'prince' of philosophers," Baruch Spinoza, whose non-anthropomorphic and monistic account of substance will always already have laid the ground of structuralist thought (Deleuze 1990: 60). Thus, this brief homage to Deleuze's philosophical friends must conclude with, fourth, Alexandre Kojève, the name of the person who identified Spinoza's thought as structural, that is, as "a *total*, or 'systematic,' or 'circular' Knowledge," incapable of explaining how "an *eternal* Knowledge could absorb everything that is in Time," and, for this reason, it, "obviously, is absurd" (Kojève 1980: 122). This quartet could represent the impetus for Deleuze's life-long, almost compulsive, reconstitution of the *object* and reconceptualization of *time* – the two central elements whose emancipation from traditional philosophical premises was required for the formation of structuralism as a systematic and self-conscious mode of thought.

Indeed, both Spinoza's system and structuralism, as well as psychoanalysis, appear utterly absurd from the perspective of experience or, as Deleuze would say, of representation, which is organized on the basis of linear time (the succession past-present-future) and the distinction between reality and non-reality, along with its corollaries: the true and the false, the objective and the subjective. These systems presuppose a different conception of temporality (and hence causality), as well as the collapse of all distinctions predicated in the reality/object – imaginary/subject divide (a collapse visualized in Lacan's formula for the subject – "$ ◊ a" – which includes the object: "a"; Lacan 1998: 303). As Deleuze writes in "How Do We Recognize Structuralism?" (written in 1967 and published in 1973), while "classical philosophy" had "conditioned" thought "to a certain distinction or correlation between the real and the imaginary," the "first criterion of structuralism … is the discovery and recognition of a third order … a symbolic order, irreducible to the orders of the real and the imaginary, and deeper than they are," which is also to say, irreducible to "a sensible form" or "a figure of the imagination" or "an intelligible essence" (Deleuze 2004: 171, 173). This is why the long, yet dense, arch from Spinoza to structuralism could not grow to something more than "absurd" without a break with "classical philosophy." However, as in every break, the new is neither sanctioned nor certain of itself.

To gain any credibility whatsoever, such a system has to account for the discrepancy between its own counterintuitive schemes and our intuitive experience of reality – which in the case of structuralism means precisely, to repeat Kojève's words, to explain how "an *eternal* Knowledge could absorb everything that is in Time." This is why Deleuze's universe is permeated through and through with a distinction between two aspects: the actual, which corresponds to our empirical representations, and the virtual, which expresses the transcendental conditions that enable the former – in psychoanalytic parlance, the ego and the unconscious. It is a matter, then, of conceiving the unconscious or the virtual as, following Freud's lead, "fantasy, the fundamental object of psychoanalysis," but in such a way that this object, fantasy, is not posited as the unreal antipode of the objects of reality (LP: 118). The virtual and the actual is of course a recapitulation of the Spinozian couple, attributes and modes; but if Spinoza's telescopic view of the modes made the attributes look "absurd," Deleuze had to take his magnifying lens and zoom it toward their difference until it revealed itself in the form of repetition. It is this focus, and its intertwined compulsion to repeat, that distinguishes Deleuze's work from both Spinoza's and Lacan's, and confers on it its idiosyncratic mark, conceptually, methodologically, and stylistically.

This mark is intrinsically related to Deleuze's structuralist postulate that actual time – the succession of past, present, and future, in which movement and change take place – reveals itself on the virtual level as what he calls the "third synthesis" of time. By using this term Deleuze alludes to Spinoza's "third kind of knowledge," which we shall approach in the last chapter. The "third synthesis" refers to a form of time that is "empty and out of joint, with its rigorous formal and static order," and which "is precisely the death instinct" (Deleuze 1994a: 111). Having been introduced by Freud in his *Beyond the Pleasure Principle* as the compulsion to repeat (*Wiederholungszwang*), the death drive or the "pure and empty form of time" can emerge only through an actual repetition that not only collapses all empirical oppositions, such as reality-imaginary or object-subject, but eliminates "all content," including any "temporal content" (Deleuze 1994a: 86, 110). This radical eradication of concrete contents is the very task of repetition since, as everyone knows from "love's repetition," in repeating, "we realize that our sufferings do not depend on their object" (Deleuze 2000: 72). This is why, although the "phenomena" we repeat "are always unhappy and particular," "the phenomenon of repetition forms a general joy" (ibid., 72) – comparable to the Spinozian "Joy" of "*the third kind of knowledge*," extracted from the "intellectual Love of God," that is, "the idea of God as its [Joy's] cause … not insofar as we imagine him as [a] present" concrete entity, but "as eternal" (*Ethics* VP32D and P32C). Repetition is Deleuze's method for transcending any concrete content, as the foremost precondition of structure, and, thus, for enabling "the repetition of the future, as [the] eternal return" of the "new, complete novelty" (Deleuze 1994a: 90).

Object and time

In "How Do We Recognize Structuralism?" Deleuze presents seven distinct, yet interrelated and partly overlapping, criteria that thought must fulfill in order to be structuralist, all of which concern the constitution of the *object* and, albeit less directly, the constitution of *time* (Deleuze 2004:

170–92).[5] As mentioned above, the "first criterion of structuralism … is the discovery" of a "symbolic order" (Deleuze 2004: 171, 173). The symbolic, as a precondition for structure, is "a combinatory formula [*une combinatoire*]" of purely negative elements that "have neither extrinsic designation nor intrinsic signification," so that "the sites prevail over whatever occupies them" (Deleuze 2004: 173–4). By vacuuming the combinatory elements of their content, repetition provides the bridge from actuality to the virtual object and its "empty form of time," and thereby reveals itself as the very process of the constitution of the (virtual) *object* and (empty) *time*.

Furthermore, the "atomic elements" of the structure, obtained through repetition, must "account both for the formation of wholes and for the variation of parts," for the "whole structure" and for the fact that its "symbolic elements … are organized necessarily in series" (Deleuze 2004: 173, 182, 186). Last, but not least, if repetition is to account fully for the possibility of the emergence of structure, it must also lead to the "Third" "differentiating" and "eminently symbolic object," the "empty square" or "Object = x," which guards against the "reflecting[,] … doubling, and duplicating" role "of the imaginary" by "preventing the one [series] from imaginarily falling back on the other" (Deleuze 2004: 184–6). It is particularly this criterion that leads Deleuze to the question: "what is the meaning of this idea that virtual objects refer, in the last instance, to an element which is itself symbolic?" This is a question in which, Deleuze continues, "the whole psychoanalytic – or … amorous – game of repetition is at issue" (Deleuze 1994a: 103).

In pursuing this question, I will trace the parallels between Freud's actual series of repetition (his failures and revised attempts) toward the constitution of fantasy as the object of psychoanalysis and Deleuze's reconstruction of this itinerary in his own series of repetition in *Difference and Repetition*, as the logico-conceptual path required for the simultaneous constitution and fulfillment of the conditions of structure. Preventing each series of repetition – Freud's and Deleuze's – from falling back on the other, Laplanche and Pontalis's 1964 article on fantasy functions as the "Third" – which, as we shall see, corresponds to the moment of the present – insofar as it recapitulates Freud's *historical* itinerary (past) as a *logical* problem. Then, in the third (future) reenactment, Deleuze can take up the logical problem, already divested of all historical residue, and show that *logic* itself requires a double formulation, both in actual and virtual time. Thereby, Deleuze's relation to psychoanalysis is revealed as the thesis: psychoanalysis does not deserve to be called "theory" (which is also to say, structuralism) unless it treats the actual *historical* past as the manifestation in actual time of a *logical* problem that is simultaneously given in virtual time.

Freud's own past theoretical framework, which lasted from 1893 to 1897, bears the name "seduction theory." Its "guiding principle" remained "the search for chronology, going backwards into time towards the first real, verifiable elements," which made Freud a "prisoner of … theoretical alternatives," such as "internal-external, imaginary-real" (LP: 119). To leave behind the past requires, according to Deleuze, establishing that the "phenomena of the unconscious cannot be understood in the overly simple form of opposition" (Deleuze 1994a: 106). Far from representing apparent (i.e., actual) conflicts, such phenomena must, according to Laplanche and Pontalis, be "the result of more subtle differential mechanisms" that take place on the level of "a pre-subjective structure, beyond both the strict happening and the internal imagery" (LP: 118). It has to be shown that the "unconscious," as the terrain of fantasy, "is differential and iterative … serial, problematic and questioning," and not, as a "Hegelian Post-Kantianism" would want it (a view apparently shared by Freud at that point), "oppositional," which is only the principle of "consciousness" (Deleuze 1994a: 108). Nevertheless, Freud's "seduction theory" did offer, "if not the theory, at least an intuition of the structure," since "seduction appear[ed] as an almost universal datum, which … transcended both the event and … its protagonists" (LP: 118). A theoretically full-fledged account of this transcendental order, in which the concrete contents – "the condition and the agents" – of the structure "will themselves be annihilated," is what is presupposed for structure and, hence, what both Freud's and Deleuze's futures await (Deleuze 1994a: 111).

In the meantime, "in 1897," Freud "discard[ed] … the seduction theory" for the sake of the "Oedipus complex"; but he "conceived" the latter as a "biological" or "endogenous reality, sexuality, which is itself supposed to be in conflict with a normative, prohibitive external reality" (LP: 118). In this move, fantasy was once again reduced to "no more than the secondary expression of this reality," while chronology united forces with biology into a renewed unsurpassable stumbling block: "the intrusion of the fantasy … into the subject[,] cannot but occur to the organism, the little human being, at a point in time, by virtue of certain characteristics of his biological evolution" (LP: 118, 115). So, with the Oedipus complex we seem, at least momentarily, to "have lost the structure" for good (LP: 118).

Yet, if the Oedipus complex constitutes a veritable step forward with which Freud enters his present, it is because, in its futile search for historico-biological data, the theory of the Oedipus complex had in effect stumbled on the structualist concept of sign. For what appears as the "temporal characteristics of human sexuality," as "too early (birth) and too late (puberty)," is the narrativization of the logical relation between "too much and too little excitation" (LP: 114). Past and future turn out to be not instances spread out in diachrony, but rather two intensities – "too much" and "too little" – that form the "totality of time" or, borrowing Hölderlin's term, "the caesura, [of] the before and the after" (Deleuze 1994a: 89). What lies between the before and the after – what we call the "present" – is the "*symbolic image*" – an image that "must be called a *symbol* by virtue of the unequal parts which it subsumes and draws together." For "the sign" always consists of two unequal parts since it "describes both the object and its absence" (Deleuze 1994a: 89, emphasis mine; LP: 131).

The symbol or the present "is the unequal in itself" and, as such, equal to itself and to itself alone, since everything else, being by definition equal to itself, can be either "too much" or "too little" in comparison to the symbol (Deleuze 1994a: 89-90). In its vertiginous twist, the chronological quest of the Oedipus complex eventually thrusts us into a "time … defined not only by a formal and empty order but also by a totality and a series" (Deleuze 1994a: 89), or, rather, two series, since it is always the case that "'structure' puts into play [at least] two series" (Deleuze 2004: 183).

Discovered in Freud's own self-analysis, the Oedipus complex did to chronology what Kant had done to Descartes: by introducing between "the determination [I think] and the undetermined [I am] … the form of the determinable, namely time" as an empty form, Kant shuttered the Cartesian *cogito* "as though the *I* were fractured from one end to the other … by the pure and empty form of time" (Deleuze 1994a: 86). "Totality" and the "seriality of repetition" are the conditions of the empty form of time and its fractured *I*, "the man without name, without family, without qualities, without self or I, the 'plebeian' guardian of a secret, the already-Overman whose scattered members gravitate around the sublime image" of the sign (Deleuze 1994a: 90). If Sophocles can here meet Nietzsche and a sensibility that characterizes modernity since Shakespeare's time, it is because when the "Northern Prince says 'time is out of joint'" he effectively says that he himself, no less than "the Northern Philosopher," "should be Hamletian because he is Oedipal" (Deleuze 1994a: 88).

Yet, the future is not yet accomplished (*vollbracht*) for either of the two partners. The sheer invocation of the sign and, for that matter, the empty form of time and the fractured "I" do not suffice for structure to establish itself, just as the mere presence of two series does not suffice to prevent them from falling imaginarily back on one another. So far "sign" merely indicates the imaginary, the redoubling of the word effected by the fact that the sign conjures in the imagination the presence of the absent object, just as it renders the present object absent. It is true that "as soon as we see two in 'one,' as soon as we make doubles [*déboublons*], the imaginary appears in person," but this does not suffice to make the sign symbolic (i.e., structural) (Deleuze 2004: 172).

Nevertheless, the reconceptualization of the Oedipal chronology as varying degrees of intensity already makes evident that:

> it matters little whether or not the event itself occurs, or whether the act has been performed or not … past, present, and future are not distributed according to this temporal criterion. Oedipus has already carried out the act, Hamlet has not yet done so, but in either case the first part of the symbol is lived in the past, they are in the past … as long as they experience the image [sign] of the act as too big for them.
>
> (Deleuze 1994a: 89)

For in "effect, there is always a time at which the imagined act is supposed 'too big for me'," and this supposition "defines *a priori* the past" or the first time (Deleuze 1994a: 89). "The second time … is … the present of metamorphosis, a becoming equal to the act" or "a doubling of the self, and a projection of an ideal self in the image of the act" – here the sign becomes the double of the self as its ideal, just as "the hero becomes 'capable' of the act" (Deleuze 1994a: 89). Because "what the self has become equal to" – the sign – "is the unequal in itself," "the third time" emerges "in which the future appears" and "the event and the act … turn back against the self which has become their equal and smash it to pieces" (Deleuze 1994a: 89–90). This completes the bridge from the actual to the virtual. Inversely, seen from the opposite perspective, from the virtual to the actual, it follows that, "as regards time, the position of structuralism is quite clear: time is always a time of actualization," in which "the elements of virtual coexistence are carried out at diverse rhythms" that make up actual time (Deleuze 2004: 180).

So far, the concerted efforts of the seduction theory and the Oedipus complex have yielded (a) the transcendence of the actual event and agents, and (b) a reconceptualization of time as the simultaneous coexistence of two intensities (past and future) bound together by the present (sign) as the totality of time. If the future is, nevertheless, not yet accomplished for either partner, Freud or Deleuze, it is because something of a realist history, contingent and character-oriented, continued to stick to the formality, preventing time from becoming sufficiently static to allow for an excessive formlessness. Put otherwise, the agent annihilated remains so far a *self* that is an *a priori* given, whereby the emergence of both the subject and the object remains an occulted mystery. What, therefore, still remains to be shown is that the totality of time itself engenders the distinction between subject and object, at the same time that it collapses them. This deficiency required the next round of repetition.

The year 1917 rekindled hopes. Freud seemed to bring the "need for a theoretical foundation" of fantasy close to "a veritable transmutation" by "introduc[ing] a new concept … the Urphantasien, primal (or original) fantasy." These can be recovered "beneath the diversity of individual fables," and which would lead him to the notion of "phylogenesis" (LP: 121–2). With this move:

> once again a reality is postulated beneath the elaborations of fantasy, but a reality which, as Freud insists, has an autonomous and structural status with regard to the subject who is totally dependent on it … It is tempting to accept the "reality" which inspires the work of imagination according to its own laws, as a prefiguration of the "symbolic order" defined by Lévi-Strauss and Lacan … Beneath the pseudo-scientific mask of phylogenesis … Freud finds it necessary to postulate an organization made of signifiers anteceding the effect of the event and the

> signified as a whole. In this mythical pre-history of the species we see the need to create a pre-structure inaccessible to the subject.
> (LP: 122)

Yet, Laplanche and Pontalis caution, we must not overtake ourselves and assume too easily that the protagonists have yet been fully eradicated, and their hesitation anticipates the necessity for yet another round of repetition. In their words:

> However we should not be in a hurry to replace the phylogenic explanation by a structural type of explanation. The original fantasy is first and foremost fantasy: it lies beyond the history of the subject but nevertheless in history: a kind of language and a symbolic sequence, but loaded with elements of imagination; a structure, but activated by contingent elements. As such it is characterized by certain traits which make it difficult to assimilate to a purely transcendental schema.
> (LP: 123)

Freud's own intimidation before such a leap is betrayed in his dallying differentiation "between original fantasies and others, those that one might call secondary, whether conscious or unconscious" (LP: 127). Nevertheless, his characteristically discerning intuition leads him in the right direction: his distinguishing criterion concerns directly the protagonists. In secondary fantasies:

> the scenario is basically in the first person, and the subject's place clear and invariable. The organization is … weighted by the ego … But the original fantasy … is characterized by the absence of subjectivization, and the subject is present in the scene: the child, for instance, is one character amongst many in the fantasy "a child is beaten." Freud insisted on this visualization of the subject on the same level as the other protagonists.
> (LP: 128)

That is, the issue is not simply a matter of "recogniz[ing] the equivalence" between active and passive, beating and being beaten, or "eating and being eaten in the fantasy of incorporation." For "so long as there is some idea of a subject, even if playing a passive role," the protagonists persist and we cannot "reach the structure of deepest fantasy," as "a purely transcendental schema" (LP: 129, 122–3).

Hence, one more, ultimate, round – the repetition of the future itself – is still required. This is the circle of the ultimate fantasy, narcissism or auto-erotism, for only "the narcissistic ego" can account for the distinction between "virtual and real objects," out of which the division between subject and object will emerge, and through which we eventually can "enter the third synthesis of time" as a truly "pure and empty form" (Deleuze 1994a: 111). To understand those rather obscure pages in *Difference and Repetition*, in which Deleuze derives the empty form of time from the incubator of narcissism, we must first become familiar with the psychoanalytic understanding of this concept.

Above all, as Laplanche and Pontalis emphatically remark, narcissism does not operate "in the object-directed sense, as a first stage, enclosed within itself, from which the subject has to rejoin the world of objects" (LP: 131). On the contrary, as Freud stresses in the Three Essays on the Theory of Sexuality, "the drive becomes auto-erotic, only after the loss of the object" – something which presupposes "the existence of a primary object relationship" (LP: 132). Evidently, this primary relationship and its *ur*-lost object cannot be like any other object relation the subject will experience after the trials of auto-erotism. It is in his attempt to approach this primary object that Freud pens down the following remarkable thought: as long as "sexual satisfaction" is "linked with the taking of nourishment, the sexual instinct has a sexual object outside the infant's own body in the shape of his mother's breast"; "it is only later that the instinct loses that object, just at the time, perhaps, when the child is able to form a total idea of the person to whom the organ that is giving him satisfaction belongs" (Freud 1974: 222). With this passage, which is an "invaluable … indication that the very constitution of the auto-erotic fantasy implies not only the partial object (breast … [etc.]), but the mother as a total person, withdrawing as she becomes total," Freud will have grown, to repeat Deleuze's words, "equal to the act" that catapults his work into the future of structuralism (LP: 141–2, n. 38).

The groundbreaking implications of Freud's reference to totality are enhanced in Lacan's 1964 account of the introduction of sexuality in human life. What the human "being loses in sexuality," Lacan says, is not the "breast" but *totality*, in its most comprehensive sense, that is, consisting of the following. On the one hand, totality includes "the libido, *qua* pure life instinct … immortal … or irrepressible … simplified, indestructible life," "whose characteristic is not to exist, but which is nevertheless an organ." This indestructible life Lacan exemplifies in the "lamella," Lacan's zoologically inspired fable for the libido. On the other hand, totality includes "the locus of the Other, insofar as it is there that the first signifier emerges" (Lacan 1981: 197–8). The primary object, lost by default, is this undifferentiated totality – at once indestructible life and signifier, being and thought, object and subject – that "is subtracted from the living being by virtue of the fact that it is subject to the cycle of sexed reproduction." And "it is of this that all the forms of the *objet a*," the "breast … [and] all the other objects" that "can be enumerated[,] are merely its representatives, its figures" (Lacan 1981: 198).

Sexuality causes this loss because, strictly speaking, in the human being (the very being that is subject to the signifier) sexuality is always auto-erotic.

For being "objectless" – the distinctive characteristic of auto-erotism – indicates that the "origin" of auto-erotism is "the moment when sexuality, disengaged from any natural object, moves into the field of fantasy," where the object is redoubled as totality, "and by that very fact becomes sexuality" (LP: 132). For "the natural method of apprehending an object is split in two." On the one hand, apprehending it in terms of "non-sexual functions," as a need, such as "the taking of food"; and, on the other hand, apprehending it through the "sexual drive." For the latter, the "external object is abandoned" so that the drive's "aim and … source assume an autonomous existence with regard to feeding" and, consequently, its "prototype is not the act of sucking, but the enjoyment of going through the motions of sucking" – the "ideal … of auto-erotism is 'lips that kiss themselves,'" in a total self-satisfaction that lacks nothing (LP: 132–3). Paradoxically, it is only with this "apparently self-centered enjoyment" of auto-erotism that "all distinction between subject and object has been lost" (LP: 133). The collapse of this distinction, then, comes at the price of a totality that, originating in the redoubling (or splitting) of an *ur*-lost object, will henceforth be always half of itself.

Now we can understand why Deleuze writes that Lacan's "concept of the phallus" – that is, "the 'phallus,' understood as a symbolic organ," i.e., both as the locus of the Other and organ – "effectively comprises the … characteristics" of totality. The phallus is the (actually) impossible, yet (virtually) necessary object that "not only does … lack something in relation to the real object from which it is subtracted, [but] it lacks something in itself, since it is always half of itself, the other half being different as well as absent." It "testif[ies] to its own absence and to itself as past" by "being essentially displaced in relation to itself, being found only as lost, being possessed of an always fragmentary identity" (Deleuze 1994a: 102–3). Thus, the "symbolic phallus," as the archetype of the total object or of the overlap of libido and the Other, is "the always-displaced fragment …: the object = x" that confers on the structure its symbolic character by preventing the series of the past and the future from falling back on each other (Deleuze 1994a: 103).

By now we may discern in Deleuze's text Sartre's echoes, both conceptually and rhetorically. According to Sartre's phenomenology, in order to express the totality of being one must express both its appearance and its essence. Its essence transcends its appearance insofar as "the existent … cannot be reduced to a *finite* series of manifestations since each one of them is a relation to a subject constantly changing." Although "an *object* may disclose itself only through a single *Abschattung*" – in a single aspect, profile, or shading – "the sole fact of there being a subject implies the possibility of multiplying the points of view *on* that *Abschattung*," and "[t]his suffices to multiply to infinity the *Abschattung* under consideration" (Sartre 1992: 5). Hence, "the appearance, which is *finite*, indicates itself in its finitude, but at the same time in order to be grasped as an appearance-of-that-which-appears [essence], it requires that it be surpassed toward infinity" (Sartre 1992: 6). In other words:

> What appears in fact is only an *aspect* of the object, and the object is altogether *in* that aspect and altogether outside of it. It is altogether *within*, in that it manifests itself *in* that aspect; it shows itself as the structure of the appearance, which is at the same time the principle of the series. It is altogether outside, for the series itself will never appear nor can it appear.
>
> (Sartre 1992: 6)

The series itself can never appear, for this would require that the infinity of *Abschattungen* – "the being-which-does-not-appear" (Sartre 1992: 6) – appears, which is impossible. The totality of being or the "for-itself" is, therefore, the appearance or "the in-itself" *and* the series of appearances that can never appear. This:

> totality which runs after itself and refuses itself at the same time, which can find in itself no limit to its surpassing because it is its own surpassing and because it surpasses itself toward itself, can under no circumstances exist within the limits of an instant. There is never an instant at which we can assert that the for-itself *is*, precisely because the for-itself never is.
>
> (Sartre 1992: 211)

This is why the time of the "for-itself," which is the "the time of consciousness[,] is human reality which temporalizes itself as the totality which is to itself its own incompletion; it is nothingness slipping into a totality as a detotalizing ferment" (Sartre 1992: 211). Finally, in the time of consciousness, "the In-itself is what the For-itself was *before*," but "Present, Past, Future" occur "all at the same time," for "the For-itself dispersing its being in three dimensions is temporal due to the very fact that it nihilates itself" (Sartre 1992: 198, 202). This is why in the empty form of time, the pure past – the "past as the contemporary of the present" – is both the in-itself and the for-itself, the mythic moment in which the infinity of *Abschattungen*, as it were, still appears. Sexuality is the moment at which human reality temporalizes itself. Thus, the overlap of the lamella or libido and the locus of the Other condensed in the "symbolic phallus signifies no less the erotic mode of the pure past than the immemorial of sexuality" (Deleuze 1994a: 102–3).

Deleuze succinctly encapsulates the point once more – "the symbol is the always-displaced fragment, standing for a past which was never present: the object = x" – to raise then the question we encountered at the beginning of this chapter, concerning as much structuralism as psychoanalysis: "But what is the meaning of this idea that virtual objects refer, in the last instance, to an element which is itself symbolic?" (Deleuze 1994a: 103). He then embarks in an almost seven-page-long rumination on a non-realist conception (i.e., not in terms of the actual and its linear time or, in short, in terms of consciousness) of repetition and difference punctuated with philosophical and literary references that lead to a renewed occurrence of "the object = x … as the immanent limit of the series of virtuals." This limit demarcates "the series of the real" and the "series of the virtual" as "the successive presents of … coexistent series" (Deleuze 1994a: 109). Deleuze lingers here to indicate that if Freud so long persisted on realistic divisions and temporalities, and if for him "Eros" can only be "the opposing element … [to] Thanatos," this is only because it "is inevitable that the two references become confused, the pure past assuming thereby the status of a former present, albeit mythical, and reconstituting the illusion it was supposed to denounce, resuscitating the illusion of an original and a derived, of an identity in the origin and a resemblance in the derived" (Deleuze 1994a: 109). For realistic consciousness, Eros is the line in which "the series of the virtual" constitutes "a past which differs in kind from any present [actual]," precisely insofar as it is conceived as a "former" or dead present, without recognizing that if this conception is at all possible, it is because of the coexistence of the series of the past and present – "a power of difference" which "Eros borrows from Mnemosyne" (Deleuze 1994a: 109). In realist thought, just as the present is the death of the past, the empty form of time – Thanatos – is the death of Eros.

Thus, having tarried with this inevitable confusion at the root of Freud's realism, in the next paragraph narcissism can eventually enter the stage performing the movement that realism needs to emulate in order to overcome itself: "However, it is by interiorizing the difference between the two lines [Eros and Mnemosyne] … that the libido returns or flows back into the ego and the passive ego becomes entirely narcissistic" (Deleuze 1994a: 110). To stress the absolute character of the coexistence of the two series, the real or actual and the virtual, in the narcissistic circuit, as opposed to the preceding cycles of repetition, Deleuze performs a final ritornello that brings us back to the "fracture of the I" executed by the Kantian introduction of time as "pure and empty form … separated from its content." Here again it matters little whether the act was already or not yet committed, so that in the *a priori* category of time the "already" and the "not yet" retain a minimum of "temporal content" (Deleuze 1994a: 110). The unique value of the "narcissistic libido" lies in the fact that it "abstracts from *all* content," being "the phenomenon which corresponds to the empty form of time" as "the *spatial* phenomenon of that form in general," without reference to an "already" and a "not yet," not even as exchangeable notions (Deleuze 1994a: 110, emphasis mine).

This is so because, when the "order of before, during, and after marks the division of the narcissistic ego in time," the "whole of time is gathered in the image of the formidable action" – "the action = x" – "as this is simultaneously presented, forbidden and predicted by the superego" (Deleuze 1994a: 110). For, what is here called "temporal series" or "before, during, and after" in truth "designates the confrontation of the divided narcissistic ego with the whole of time or the image of the action," whose spatial configuration consists of three elements: the problem or lack, which is at once presented (before) and predicted (after) – this is too big for me – the prohibition (during) – it ought not to be too big – and the realization of the prediction, as the death of the above two instances (*Instanzen*) and the genesis of the radical novelty (Deleuze 1994a: 110). In Deleuze's words:

> The narcissistic ego repeats once in the form of the before or lack, in the form of the *Id* (this action is too big for me); a second time in the form of an infinite becoming-equal appropriate to the *ego ideal*; a third time, in the form of the after which realizes the prediction of the *superego* (the id and the ego, the condition and the agent, will themselves be annihilated)!
>
> (Deleuze 1994a: 110–1)

It is only now, after narcissism's complete annihilation of all protagonists, conditions, and their temporal residues, that the empty form of time can reveal itself as a pure "rigorous formal and static order" (Deleuze 1994a: 111).

Thus, with auto-erotism, the "third repetition" or "third time of the series" amounts to "the repetition of the future, as eternal return," in which the future emerges as a "new, complete novelty," by dint of the fact that it "constitutes the autonomy of the product, the independence of the work … which leaves nothing intact of the default [past] or the becoming-equal [present]" (Deleuze 1994a: 90). It is the triumph of the sign liberated from all attachments to any self, timid or arrogant. By being thus radically selfless, the "extreme formality [of the sign] is there only for an excessive formlessness (Hölderlin's *Unförmliche*)," just as "change" – and "time is the most radical form of change" – is what "does not change" (Deleuze 1994a: 91, 89).

Yet, the further point not to be missed is that if narcissism alone can annihilate all protagonists, conditions, and their temporal residues, it is because, by introducing the signifier, it animates the law (superego). Herein lies one of Deleuze's most decisive theses regarding psychoanalysis, namely, that the function of the law transcends its role of sustaining the *status quo* by being simultaneously the very condition of the emergence of the new. This means that "territorialities" circumscribed by any law are always already destined to be "shot through with lines of flight testifying to the presence within them of movements of deterritorialization and reterritorialization" (Deleuze and Guattari 1987: 55). Or, as Lacan puts it, "transgression … only takes place if it is supported by the oppositional principle, by the forms of the Law" (Lacan 1992: 177). Given that "the law … is revealed … as identical with an order of language" (Lacan 1977: 66), it is only expectable that the very moment that "the passive ego becomes narcissistic, the activity must be *thought*" (Deleuze 1994a: 110). The auto-erotic introduction of the sign is the "new, complete novelty" that emerges as the future of the narcissistic repetition, and which, as we already precipitated, will always already have demystified the fact that virtual objects refer to an element which is itself symbolic. It is for this reason that "the importance of the reorganization that takes place at this level, in opposition to the preceding stage … cannot be overstated" (Deleuze 1994a: 110).

Nevertheless, as I hope to have shown, one also cannot overstate the importance of the preceding cycles of repetition, by which I mean both Deleuze's first and second syntheses of time (performatively recapitulated within the third) and Freud's repetitions through the seduction theory and Oedipus complex up to auto-eroticism. For it is only by going through them that our two initial quests are fulfilled. These include: (a) the requirement of structurality, which postulates the elimination of conditions, protagonists, and temporality – something which cannot be executed unless the structure is determined by its internal limit of totality (object-x) and the series it engenders; and (b) the requirement that the structure (totality and series) nevertheless accounts for the realistic experience of the actual, with its linear time, conditions, and protagonists. Without the repetition of the past and the present, the repetition of the future could not reveal itself as a palindromic translation between the actual and the virtual, presupposing all actual agents in the very move that extinguishes them.

Drive, lack, desire

The above exposition also indicates that what is often perceived in Deleuze's work as a criticism of psychoanalysis is actually his enthusiastic and painstaking philosophical labor toward guarding psychoanalysis against its most insidious peril: the non-structuralist temptation of conceiving the subject as an individual agent of events in chronological time. Surrendering to or resisting this tendency is also decisive in grasping another central psychoanalytic concept: lack. Whether Deleuze's theory, which is often characterized as a philosophy of the "plenitude of life" that "disjoin[s] desire from negativity," constitutes a departure from or an amplifying reaffirmation of psychoanalysis, depends also on a structuralist conception of lack (Butler 1999: 212).[6]

To approach this point, let us return for a last time to narcissism, as the nexus of drive and desire. As the fatal denouement of the narcissistic prediction with "its crushing unity and … irreversible series" indicates, it "is by means of the death instinct that [the narcissistic ego] is reflected in the ego ideal and has a presentiment of its end in the superego, as though in two fragments of the fractured I" (Deleuze 1994a: 111). The inevitable result of the fact that in narcissism "the commandment" of the law "appeared" is that "through it I came to desire death" (Lacan 1992: 83). In narcissism, it is not only the subject and the object that merge but also death and the amorous game, so that "Thanatos" is "by no means the complement or antagonist of Eros" (Deleuze 1994a: 111). Rather:

> It is all in the same movement that there is a reflux of Eros on to the ego [whereby it becomes narcissistic], that the ego takes upon itself the disguises and displacements which characterize the objects in order to construct its own fatal affection ... and that the death instinct appears, indistinguishable from that pure form ... of that narcissistic libido.
>
> (Deleuze 1994a: 113)

The "apparently self-centered enjoyment" of auto-erotism obliterates "all distinctions" "between subject and object," Eros and Thanatos, pleasure principle and death drive, and so on (LP: 133). Here, I would emphatically object that there *are* distinctions, but they are not to be understood as oppositions or dualisms. Just as the death drive is "not ... the exception to the [pleasure] principle but ... its *foundation*," the drive is also the foundation of desire (Deleuze 1994b: 113). This is a clear distinction, without setting up an opposition. Need can serve as the blueprint for exemplifying this relation:

> A phenomenon such as need can be understood in terms of "lack," from the point of view of action and the active synthesis which it determines, but as extreme "satiety" or "fatigue" from the point of view of the passive synthesis by which it is conditioned.
>
> (Deleuze 1994b: 77)

Considered from the perspective of action, need, as much as desire, appears as a "lack" that produces (linear) time as a project, as in Hegel's conception of desire, which Kojève formulates as follows:

> Man essentially creates and destroys in terms of the idea that he forms of the Future. And the idea of the Future appears in the real present in the form of a Desire ... Action that arises from *this* Desire engenders History. Hence there is *Time* only where there is *History*.
>
> (Kojève 1980: 139)

This "dialectical understanding applies only to historical reality – that is, to the reality created by Work according to a Project" (Kojève 1980: 146). However, from the perspective of the virtual, as Jean-Paul Sartre has established, desire is lack as the pure past, that is, the lacked totality. In Sartre's words:

> A lack presupposes a trinity: that which is missing or the "lacking," that which misses what is lacking or the "existing," and a totality

> which has been broken by the lacking and which would be restored by the synthesis of the "lacking" and the "existing" – this is the "lacked."
>
> (Sartre 1992: 135)

The "lacked" restored is desire as excessive satiety. From the perspective of the virtual, "lack is appearance on the ground of a totality," which is why it does not matter "whether this totality has been originally given and is now broken … or whether it has never yet been realized" (Sartre 1992: 138). Given that on the actual level, too, "human desire" is "a Desire directed toward another Desire," and not any actual thing (Kojève 1980: 139) – a point in which Spinoza and Hegel concur – "desire finds the principle of its difference from need in the virtual object" (Deleuze 1994a: 106). Desire is the most direct index of the virtual (lacked totality) in the actual (while need does so only from the perspective of the virtual).

However, it is crucial to understand that when we say, repeating Sartre's words, that it matters not whether this totality has been originally given and is now broken or whether it has never yet been realized, we mean that "lack" in this sense refers to something that lies outside time. Because of this important aspect, and because of Sartre's general Hegelian undertones, it might be more helpful to distinguish the two conceptions of lack – on the level of the actual and linear time, as opposed to lack on the level of the virtual – through a direct juxtaposition between Hegel and Spinoza. From the point of view of the actual and of Hegel, lack is tantamount to negation or limitation; by contrast, from the perspective of the virtual, lack indexes the positive determination of something through its immanent cause.

To explain this point, let us turn to Pierre Macherey's juxtaposition between Hegel and Spinoza regarding specifically the issue of determination and the fact that Hegel misrepresented Spinoza in arguing that "*omnis determinatio est negatio* [all determination is negation]" (Macherey 2011: 113). To understand one crucial difference between Hegel and Spinoza – and the difference between actual and virtual lack – we need to introduce a distinction between negative and positive determination. In Macherey's words, "to determine something negatively is to represent it abstractly according to its limits, in separating it from God that acts within it" – i.e., ignoring substance as its immanent cause – "and attempting to adapt it to formal norms … forged by the imagination" (Macherey 2011: 141). When we do this to a thing, we "relate it … to that which it is not," including to "its possible disappearance," which is why "we present it as contingent." By contrast, "to determine something positively … is to perceive it … according to the immanent necessity that engenders it within substance, according to the law of causality that is the same one through which substance produces itself" – since it is in the individual things that "substance produces itself." In this case, we "envisage it from the point of view of eternity, insofar as it is eternal, that is, insofar as it cannot be destroyed, other than by an exterior cause (*E* IIIP4)" (Macherey 2011: 141).

For, being the effect of eternal substance, the essence of every singular thing is eternal, and only its actual existence is finite and appears contingent. That is, in contrast to substance, whose essence necessarily entails its existence, singular "things do not exist necessarily," and, therefore, "their existence and their essence are 'determined' in completely different manners." Their existence is determined according to a negative determination or actual lack, whereas their essence is determined according to a positive determination or virtual lack (while the two are expressions of one and the same determination). "This is why the fact that singular things do not exist in eternity" on the actual level "has no effect at all on the eternity of their essence," that is, on their virtual determination (Macherey 2011: 173). In other words, "the same things are determined from different points of view," from that of eternity or the virtual, and from that of linear time and the actual. We could call these two determinations the "internal" and the "external," respectively. In the first case, "a finite thing is determined according to its essence, following which it tends indefinitely to preserve its being; in the other case, it is determined according to its existence in the conditions that limit it" (Macherey 2011: 173).

If in Spinoza, and in psychoanalysis, "determination can be understood simultaneously in a positive and a negative sense, it is because this notion does away with the traditional opposition of positive and negative" (Macherey 2011: 146). This is not unlike the other traditional oppositions that structuralist/psychoanalytic logic has made obsolete.

Therefore, we can accept Sartre's conception of lack only insofar as by "lacked" we mean not a divisible totality – whose parts would be the existing and the lacking – but the specific immutable and eternal essence that a singular thing expresses in its singular existence. Simply put, the lacked of the crescent moon is the full moon neither because the waxing moon craves to become full nor because the waning moon misses the full moon, but because the crescent moon always *is* the full moon.

This conception of lack provides the matrix for understanding "the connection between fantasy and desire" – the two names for the object of the unconscious. By "locating the origin of fantasy in the auto-erotism" and the fact that the "origin of fantasy" coincides with the "first upsurgings of desire" (LP: 131), Freud and Deleuze have also shown that:

> Fantasy … is not the object of desire, but its setting. In fantasy the subject does not pursue the object or its sign: he appears caught up himself in the sequence of images. He forms no representation of the desired object, but is himself represented as participating in the scene … As a result, the subject, although always present in the fantasy, may be so in a desubjectivized form, that is to say, in the very syntax of the sequence in question.
>
> (LP: 131–3)

This is why "the unconscious desires, and only desires," but "as a questioning, problematising and searching force which operates in a different domain than that of [action-oriented] desire and satisfaction" (Deleuze 1994a: 106). The action-oriented desire of historical time "goes … from one actual form to another," whereas unconscious desire "goes from the virtual to the actual, that is, from structure to its actualizations" (Deleuze 2004: 180). Therefore, from "the position of structuralism … time" is "genesis," "from the virtual to the actual" (Deleuze 2004: 180).[7] The interval between the two is the space of structuralist thought.

Postscript on fantasy

If the "origin of fantasy" coincides with "the very first upsurgings of desire" it is because the unique peculiarity of both lies in their "hallucinatory satisfaction." For desire emerges when, "in the absence of a real object, the infant reproduces the experience of the original satisfaction in a hallucinated form," namely, in the form of the sign, which will make out of the infant a human subject (LP: 131–3). Freud's and Deleuze's searches for the origin of fantasy and/or structure show us that this "origin" is in truth the "fiction" or "myth of origin" of all four: the drive, desire, sign, and ultimately the subject itself (LP: 131). It is:

> an analytic "construction" … which tries to cover the moment of separation between before and after, whilst still containing both: a mythical moment of disjunction between the pacification of need (Befriedigung) and the fulfillment of desire (Wunscherfüllung), between the two stages represented by real experience and its hallucinatory revival, between the object that satisfies and the sign which describes both the object and its absence.
>
> (LP: 131)

The primal fantasy of auto-eroticism, the very stage of the dissolution of the subject and the object, coincides with the introduction of the sign, the very entrance of the subject in the locus of the Other. In short, *the dissolution of the subject is the very origin of the subject*. And this short-circuit is accompanied by its corollary temporal loop, as retroactivity (Nachträglichkeit) and historical time coincide. In Laplanche and Pontalis's succinct formulation:

> [T]he original fantasies also indicate this postulate of retroactivity: they relate to the origins. Like myths, they claim to provide a representation of, and a solution to, the major enigmas … Whatever appears to the subject as something needing an explanation or theory, is dramatized as a moment of emergence, the beginning of history.

> Fantasies of origins: the primal scene pictures the origin of the individual; fantasies of seduction, the origin and upsurge of sexuality; fantasies of castration, the origin of the difference between the sexes …
>
> There is convergence of theme, of structure, and no doubt also of function: … through the scenarios constructed, the varied quests for origins, we are offered in the field of fantasy[] the origin of the subject himself.
>
> (LP: 124)

Conversely, the postulate of retroactivity – the principle of the virtual and of original fantasies – more often than not requires the narrative form of a myth to make the logic of retroactivity itself known on the actual level. I hope the mythological itinerary dramatized in this chapter, and shared by two co-travelers who could only have met virtually, has offered, not a theory, but some explanation as to why psychoanalysis and structuralism constitute one and the same line of thought. Now it is time to repeat, spelling out the new: "through the scenarios constructed … we are offered in the field of fantasy[] the origin of the subject himself" – as its own cause (LP: 124). This is the (atheist) Joy in which structuralism/psychoanalysis never ceases to indulge.

Notes

1 References to this text will henceforth be indicated with the abbreviation "LP."

2 As an aside, Deleuze's last interview of his life, with Didier Eribon, succinctly indexes the transference between the two thinkers (Deleuze 1995). For a detailed account of Althusser's critique of Deleuze's account of structuralism, which is mentioned also in the first chapter here, see Stolze 1998.

3 This equation owes to Deleuze's endorsement that "no one has better determined the status of the structure as identical to the 'Theory' itself than Louis Althusser" (Deleuze 2004: 173). In fact, Deleuze continues, "the symbolic must be understood as the production of the original and specific theoretical object" (ibid., 173). Deleuze added this statement as a consequence of the letter he received from Althusser (dated 29 February 1968), to whom Deleuze had sent earlier in the same month the first draft of his essay on structuralism. As Ted Stolze writes in his careful analysis of this correspondence, Althusser stressed the point that "structuralism can first of all be designated in terms of '*what it rejects*' –a break with the 'real' object, whether sensible, historical, or empirical – in order to constitute a distinct 'theoretical' object. This was, [Althusser] says, already true of Marx's break with the real, historicist, and empiricist object of history that was in fact the 'ideological object of the philosophies of history'" (Stolze 1998: 56). Structuralism is the continuation of this Marxian epistemology, for, Althusser continues: "[B]ehind the claim of 'structuralism' [is] this simple fact: a certain number of disciplines of the Human Sciences have discovered, (more or less) blindly" – the "only one to know it is doubtless Lacan" – "that they could only exist as *sciences* provided that they break with historicism, that is, with the *empiricist* ideology of their 'object.' They have 'discovered' the necessity of *theory* as an absolute condition of their scientific

existence" (Stolze 1998: 57). This point is of course further elaborated in Althusser and Balibar 2009, which is further discussed in the sixth chapter here.

4 Undoubtedly, Edward P. Kazarian hit the bull's eye when, in a passing footnote, he spotlights this 1964 article to remark that for the major shift that occurred in Deleuze's thought between 1961 and "some time after this, but before 1967" – notably, his reevaluation of Freud, the concomitant abandonment of "his forceful endorsement of Jung," and the effects of his exposure to the "direction of 'structure' in a sense that Deleuze will [henceforth] adopt" – "it seems that some of the 'credit' for all this should be given to Laplanche and Pontalis" (Kazarian 2010: 106, n. 17). I would add that the impact of Laplanche and Pontalis's article goes even further by setting the tempo for the scansions of repetition out of which the new can emerge. This is not only regarding repetition as one of Deleuze's most central theoretical concepts but also as one of the most defining marks of his entire work, including stylistically.

By this I do not mean that the centrality of repetition in Deleuze's thought is a contingent byproduct of the stylistic idiosyncrasies of his pen but, rather, that it is the performative manifestation of a concept that defines as much his thought as psychoanalysis (*Wiederholungszwang*), precisely insofar as both are structuralist. For, as Deleuze writes, although the "phenomena" we repeat "are always unhappy and particular," nevertheless "the idea extracted from them is general, and joyous" so that "the phenomenon of repetition forms a general joy" – comparable to the Spinozian "Joy" of "*the third kind of knowledge*," extracted from the "intellectual Love of God," that is, "the idea of God as its [Joy's] cause … not insofar as we imagine him as present … but … as eternal" (*Ethics* VP32D and C); and if this is so, it is only because, as everyone knows from "love's repetition," in repeating "we realize that our sufferings do not depend on their object" (Deleuze 2000: 72). Transcending the concrete object of experience is the primary precondition of structure, and the method for obtaining this is repetition.

Regarding Deleuze's trademarked, seemingly indefinitely extendable, series of examples – ranging from literature and cinematography to geology, mineralogy, military science, and so on – Eleanor Kaufman poignantly argues that all this is not offered as the bridge to help us "descend from the abstract to the concrete." Quite the contrary, Kaufman continues, "what we witness" in this "propagation of the chain of examples" is "the model devolving into the manic and interminable chain of concrete instantiations that in the very energy of their metonymic deferral take on a still higher level of abstraction," mesmerized by, again in Deleuze's words, the "law of progression by which we accede to a consciousness which transmutes our sufferings into joy," the "joy of repetition understood, or of the comprehension of its law" (Kaufman 2012: 455; Deleuze 2000: 72). Yet, as we shall see in the last chapter, structure is only the first step toward the joy that repetition can offer us. It is the step accomplished by reason (the second kind of knowledge, in Spinoza), but intuition (the third kind of knowledge) makes a step beyond universal structures into singular essences.

5 These are: "The Symbolic," "Local or Positional," "The Differential and the Singular," "The Differentiator, Differentiation," "Serial," "The Empty Square," "From the Subject to Practice" (Deleuze 2004: 170–92).

6 See also Olkowski 1999.

7 Let us here recall from the first chapter what Deleuze distinguishes as two kinds of eternity, which I differentiate by calling the one (pertaining to reason) synchrony, and the other (pertaining to intuition) eternity. The fact that, for structuralism, time is genesis from the virtual to the actual means that eternity manifests itself on the actual/modal level within time/duration. Eternity can be

grasped through the third kind of knowledge (intuition) as the singular essence of a mode, or through the second kind of knowledge (reason) as a universal structure, that is, in terms of synchrony (we shall return to this in the last chapter).

References

Althusser, L. and E. Balibar (2009) *Reading Capital*, Ben Brewster (trans.), New York: Verso.

Butler, J. (1999) *Gender Trouble: Feminism and the Subversion of Identity*, London: Routledge.

Deleuze, G. (1990) *Expressionism in Philosophy: Spinoza*, Martin Joughin (trans.), Cambridge: Zone Books.

Deleuze, G. (1994a) *Difference and Repetition*, Paul Patton (trans.), New York: Columbia University Press.

Deleuze, G. (1994b) *Masochism: Coldness and Cruelty*, Jean McNeil and Aude Willm (trans.), New York: Zone Books.

Deleuze, G. (1995) "Le 'Je me souviens' de Gilles Deleuze," interview with Didier Eribon, *Le Nouvel Observateur*1619 (16–22 November): 50–51.

Deleuze, G. (2000) *Proust and Signs: The Complete Text*, Richard Howard (trans.), Minneapolis: University of Minnesota Press.

Deleuze, G. (2004) "How Do We Recognize Structuralism?," in *Desert Islands and Other Texts*, Melissa McMahon and Charles J. Stivale (trans.), David Lapoujade (ed.), Los Angeles, CA: Semiotext(e), pp. 170–192.

Deleuze, G. and Guattari, F. (1987) *A Thousand Plateaus: Capitalism and Schizophrenia*, Brian Massumi (trans.), Minneapolis: University of Minnesota Press.

Freud, S. (1974) "Three Essays on the Theory of Sexuality," in *The Standard Edition of the Complete Works of Sigmund Freud* (vol. 7), James Strachey et al. (eds), London: The Hogarth Press and the Institute of Psychoanalysis.

Kaufman, E. (2012) *Deleuze, the Dark Precursor: Dialectic, Structure, Being*, Baltimore, MD: Johns Hopkins University Press.

Kazarian, E.P. (2010) "The Revolutionary Unconscious: Deleuze and Masoch," *Substance*, 122, 39(2): 91–106.

Kojève, A. (1980) *Introduction to the Reading of Hegel: Lectures on the Phenomenology of Spirit*, Allan Bloom (ed.), Ithaca, NY: Cornell University Press.

Lacan, J. (1977) *Écrits: A Selection*, Bruce Fink (trans.), New York: W.W. Norton & Co.

Lacan, J. (1981) *Book XI: The Four Fundamental Concepts of Psychoanalysis*, Jacques-Alain Miller (ed.), Alan Sheridan (trans.), New York: W.W. Norton.

Lacan, J. (1992) *The Seminar of Jacques Lacan: Book VII: The Ethics of Psychoanalysis, 1959–1960*, Dennis Porter (trans.), Jacques-Alain Miller (ed.), New York: W.W. Norton & Co.

Lacan, J. (1998) *Le séminaire de Jacques Lacan: Livre V: Les formations de l'inconscient, 1957–1958*, Jacques-Alain Miller (ed.), Paris: Seuil.

Laplanche, J. and J.B. Pontalis (2003 [1964]) "Fantasy and the Origins of Sexuality," in *Unconscious Fantasy*, Riccardo Steiner (ed.), London: Karnac.

Macherey, P. (2011) *Hegel or Spinoza*, Susan M. Ruddick (trans.), Minneapolis: University of Minnesota Press.

Olkowski, D. (1999) *Deleuze and the Ruins of Representation*, Berkeley: University of California Press.

Sartre, J.-P. (1992) *Being and Nothingness: An Essay on Phenomenological Ontology*, Hazel E. Barnes (trans.), New York: Washington Square Press.

Spinoza, B. (1985) *The Collected Works of Spinoza*, Edwin Curley (trans.), Princeton, NJ: Princeton University Press.

Stolze, T. (1998) "Deleuze and Althusser: Flirting with Structuralism," *Rethinking Marxism*, 10(3): 51–63.

4 Dialectics, or valences of structuralism

A work that claims for monist structuralism such an important role in the constitution of modern thought, cannot avoid raising the question: What is the relation between this monist structuralism and the Hegelian dialectic?

Fredric Jameson's *Valences of the Dialectic* (2009) offers one of the most pertinent ways to approach this question, as it argues that all structuralist (including post-structuralist) thought has, albeit without knowing it, always been dialectical. To be sure, by "dialectic," or rather "dialectics" (for, as he argues, there are many), Jameson envisions something quite different from what is traditionally understood under the term – i.e., the teleological plodding or march from thesis to antithesis to synthesis – and for which he reserves the name "pseudo-Hegelianism." At stake, Jameson argues, is a properly *postmodern* dialectical thought, which he sets out to define, explicate, and unfold in the same book.

Jameson's is a powerful and compelling thesis that not only deserves consideration but truly raises one of the most authentically philosophical questions which, launched out of postmodernity, has the potential to undermine retroactively centuries of epistemological and theoretical assumptions: *Is there a difference between dialectical and structuralist thoughts?*

Jameson's answer is: No – an answer with which, although initially appealing to me, when immersed in its extensive justification, I came, perhaps ironically, to disagree. Gradually I realized that what fascinated me was not so much the book's thesis, as the fact that out of each of its elaborate pages emerged, again and again and with inexorable persistence, this very same, irresistible, question: *Is there a difference between dialectics and structuralism?*[1]

Accordingly, what I present here is neither a summary of Jameson's impressive collection of engaging and timely essays, whose composition spans over nearly two decades and whose erudition presupposes many more, nor a dissection of Jameson's notorious style. Nor am I engaging with the viability of Jameson's suggestions and their implications for today's political practices.[2] None of the above is either an unworthy or an easy task to perform, but they are not intrinsic to my question, even as its answer may retroactively impact them. To address squarely this question, I focus instead on Jameson's conceptualization of structuralism as a postmodern dialectical mode of thought and then set it in dialogue with, and juxtapose it to, structuralism, as it was succinctly formulated in Deleuze's work in the 1960s. Through this encounter I will argue that, even after Jameson's overhaul of dialectical thought according to what he deems postmodern epistemological exigencies, an equation of dialectics and structuralism remains untenable – just as each of the two approaches maintains its unique value in articulating a distinct register of thought. After presenting the central criteria constituting postmodern dialectics and structuralism according to Jameson and Deleuze, respectively, I will exemplify the differences between the two modes of thought, and their respective realms, through an analysis of Franz Kafka's parable "Prometheus."

Dialectics

Drawing primarily on Vladimir Lenin, Georg Lukács, Theodor Adorno, and Slavoj Žižek, Jameson proposes three criteria as the most central principles of postmodern dialectical thought. The first involves a direct invocation of structuralism, postulating the need to:

> abstract an emptier mechanism from the stages of Hegelian logic, one formalistic enough to claim application to an impressive variety of material and disciplinary, social and ideological, contents. In fact, that was exactly what *structuralism* achieved with the *binary opposition*, and this is perhaps the moment to celebrate that breakthrough, with which, in my opinion, and unbeknownst to the structuralists themselves, dialectical thought was able to reinvent itself in our time.
>
> (Jameson 2009: 16–7)

By "binary opposition," Jameson refers to "Saussure's extraordinary formulation 'differences without positive terms,'" which radically subverted the "older Aristotelian common sense," according to which first there are "things and concepts as positive entities … with their own properties," and "only later [are these things or concepts] inserted into relationships and larger … structures" (Jameson 2009: 17). In identifying the "binary opposition" or the "differences without positive terms" as the fundamental structuralist principle, Jameson entirely concurs with Deleuze who has argued that: "Structuralism cannot be separated from a new transcendental philosophy, in which the sites prevail over whatever occupies them" (Deleuze 2004: 174). However, Jameson places at least equal emphasis on the fact that this principle is primordially dialectical, insofar as in Hegel, "identity begins to emerge as something that can only be distinguished from what is not" (Jameson 2009: 17). Hegel revealed in its fullest not only the

> constructional function of the negative, but also the appearance of difference as such, as something strangely inseparable from the identity from which it is supposed to be different [or, in Hegel's own words:] "the different is not confronted by *any* other but by *its* other … the other's *own* other."
>
> (Jameson 2009: 17–8; Hegel 1975: 172)

The second principle of postmodern dialectical thought, as the title of the chapter "Towards a Spatial Dialectic" indicates, is the replacement of time with space. Here Jameson opposes Alexandre Kojève's emphatic thesis that what differentiates Hegel from all philosophy ever since Parmenides is that for him "*Time* is the *Concept* itself" (Kojève 1980: 101).[3] In Hegel's own words from the "Preface" of the *Phenomenology of Spirit*: "*die Zeit … ist der daseiende Begriff selbst* [time … is the existent Concept itself]" (Hegel 1977: 27, translation modified; Hegel 1988: 34). It is no accident that Jameson programmatically avoids the *Phenomenology of Spirit* and focuses instead on Hegel's *Logic*. Logic, of course, lends itself more easily to a spatial or synchronic schematization.[4]

The spatialization of the dialectic is presupposed for the third principle, which is announced in the title of the second part of Jameson's book: "Hegel Without *Aufhebung*," that is, "the strict avoidance of the old pseudo-Hegelian caricature of the thesis/antithesis/synthesis" model, repetitively derided in Jameson's book (Jameson 2009: 19). Far from synthesis, Jameson argues, "the starting point for a dialectic" is "opposition," by which is meant neither a sheer dualist opposition nor simply the collapse of the opposites into identity, but a relation that sustains the tension between:

> on the one hand the identification of the opposites with each other, and on the other their greatest possible dissociation from [or "incommensurability" between] each other, while remaining within some minimal relationship which makes it possible to speak of both together as participating in an opposition in the first place.
>
> (Jameson 2009: 19, 24–5)

The model of thesis/antithesis/synthesis must be replaced by the relation between the incommensurables in identity. Hence Jameson's further postulate: "Here, then, powerful reasons must be invoked for positing any kind of relationship between the incommensurables, which is to say that some form of internal negation between the two must be theorized," so that the relation between the incommensurables in identity can be expressed (Jameson 2009: 25).

Now let us turn to a few of Jameson's concrete applications of these three principles.

The first example belongs to those that, in addition to attempting to exemplify the three cardinal principles of postmodern dialectics, also intend to demonstrate Jameson's further thesis that dialectical thought advances in a tripartite movement, familiar to many as a common Žižekian strategy. Jameson summarizes one of Adorno's versions in his essay "Sociology and Psychology," in which, having argued that the "separation of society and psyche is false consciousness," Adorno adds:

> But the basis of this false consciousness is not to be removed by a mere methodological dictum. People are incapable of recognizing themselves in society and society in themselves because they are alienated from each other and the totality … What compartmentalized disciplines project onto reality merely reflects back what has taken place in reality. False consciousness is also true: inner and outer life are torn apart. The truth of the whole sides with one-sidedness, not pluralistic synthesis: a psychology that turns its back on society and … concentrates on the individual … says more about the hapless state of society than … [a] "wholistic approach" or an inclusion of social "factors."
>
> (Jameson 2009: 55, citing Adorno 1968: 69–70)

Paraphrasing Adorno's point, Jameson spells out the three parts of the dialectical movement:

> we begin with the denunciation of [some] stupid old stereotype [e.g., individual versus society] … Still … that stupid first impression was not altogether wrong, … [for what we have is the following] tripartite movement …: stupid first impression as the appearance; ingenious correction in the name of some underlying reality or "essence" [in truth, there is no separation between individual and society]; but finally, after all, a return to the reality of the appearance. It was the appearance that was "true" after all [the separation between individual and society].
>
> (Jameson 2009: 57, second ellipsis Jameson's)

This example can serve as a central allegory about Jameson's own entire project. Indeed Jameson invites this reading of his book by employing the above words self-referentially:

> Here too, to be sure, we begin with the denunciation of that stupid old stereotype according to which Hegel works, according to a tripartite and cut-and-dried progression from thesis through antithesis to synthesis. [That was the first movement. Now the second movement:] But this is completely erroneous, as there are no real syntheses in Hegel and the dialectical operation is to be seen in an utterly different

> way (a variety of examples are adduced). [And now the third movement:] Still … that stupid first impression was not altogether wrong, there is a tripartite movement in the Hegelian dialectic, and in fact I have just illustrated it: stupid first impression … that was "true" after all.
>
> (Jameson 2009: 57, first ellipsis Jameson's)

In order for the allegory not to turn fatal for Jameson's own argument, its moral must be something other than what it purports to state. If the point were merely to reaffirm the truth of the starting point, then we should unqualifiedly endorse psychological individualism, just as we should not be misled by the underlying "essence" copiously presented in Jameson's book, but rather take the appearance, the so-called "pseudo-Hegelian" thesis/antithesis/synthesis model, as "true" after all. In the tripartite movement, alienation must reveal itself as something more than itself, as that which "reflects back what has [really] taken place in reality," just as "pseudo-Hegelianism" must be shown as not "completely erroneous," since, thanks to numerico-rhetorical symmetry, it reemerges, now as then, as tripartite. The dialectical tripartite movement consists in modifying the degree of truth and falsity within two opposite positions: the initial truth is shown to be entirely false through a second truth, but this second truth turns out itself to be false, though not entirely since it shows that the initial truth was after all the truth. In Jameson's words: "To be sure, this return to the … stupid first impression is accompanied by a new knowledge of the *errors* involved in the second moment, the moment of interpretation, but nonetheless still reaffirms the *truth* of the starting point" (Jameson 2009: 58, emphasis mine). Should this not entail that we should recognize so-called "pseudo-Hegelianism" as the true Hegelianism, while also acknowledging the second moment – the postmodern desire to obliterate synthesis and teleology and to shift from time to space – as the necessary error required for the first moment (pseudo-Hegelianism) to reemerge as true (Hegelianism)?

Whether this is or is not what follows from Jameson's argumentation, in the context of the relation between dialectics and structuralism it becomes imperative to compare this tripartite movement of postmodern dialectics to another ternary conceptualization of the relation between truth and the false – particularly as it lies in the background of both Hegel's philosophy and the French thinkers who took up structuralism in the mid-twentieth century, such as Jacques Lacan, Louis Althusser, and Deleuze. I mean, of course, Spinoza's monistic conceptualization of truth, according to which "*truth is the standard both of itself and of the false*" (*Ethics* IIP43S). It is crucial to note that in Spinoza the two sides in which truth manifests itself – the "itself" of truth, and its "false" – enjoy the same epistemological status, and it is only the "truth" that is the standard of both that enjoys a higher epistemological status. This means that Spinoza's ternary conception of truth cannot be equated with Jameson's dialectical "tripartite movement," since – in accord with Adorno's afore-cited words: "The truth of the whole sides with one-sidedness" – it decisively aims at privileging the one side in which truth manifests itself (i.e., the "itself" of truth, as opposed to the "false"). Herein lies the difference in structure or inflection or, to adopt Jameson's own term, the difference in, precisely, valence, between the dialectical and the monist/structuralist conceptions of truth.

In other words, Jameson's and Spinoza's conceptions of truth may appear as if they shared the same tripartite structure, but there is a profound difference between their positions, which, to a certain extent, can be likened to the difference behind the apparent similarity between Leibniz's and Spinoza's conceptions of the world. In Gotthold Ephraim Lessing's succinct account, "Leibniz seeks, by means of his [pre-established] harmony, to solve the problem of how two such different things as body and soul can be united"; Spinoza, by contrast, "expressly declares that body and soul are one and the same particular thing, which we merely conceive of at times under the attribute of thought and at times under the attribute of extension" (referring to *Ethics* IIP21 note). By analogy, we could say that, in Spinoza, truth is that particular thing that we conceive at times as truth and at times as false. "What kind of harmony," asks Lessing rhetorically, between body and soul or, for that matter, the "itself" of truth and its false, "can he have had in mind?" since "Spinoza ... sees no difference between them; he therefore sees ... no problem requiring resolution" (Lessing 2005: 33). To foreground both the similarity and the dissimilarity between Spinoza's and Leibniz's positions Lessing concludes his letter with a "simile" which partly applies also in our case:

> There are two savages, both of whom see their reflection in a mirror for the first time. They have got over their astonishment, and they now begin to philosophise on this phenomenon. The image in the mirror, they both say, makes exactly the same movements as a body makes, and it makes them in the same order. Consequently, they conclude, the sequence of movements of the image, and the sequence of movements of the body, must be explicable by one and the same cause.
>
> (Lessing 2005: 33–4)

As the editors remark in an attached footnote, "[t]he simile is clearly incomplete, but its implication is clear enough: the first savage will conclude that the two images are synchronised by an unseen cause (as in Leibniz's pre-established harmony), whereas the second will argue that the two images relate to one and the same body viewed from two different angles (as in Spinoza's monism). This in turn implies that Lessing finds Spinoza's account more convincing than that of Leibniz" (Lessing 2005: 34). By the same token, two philosophers may look at Jameson's and Spinoza's accounts of truth and infer that in both cases truth appears both as truth and as error. Yet in Jameson's case there are two distinct elements between which the functions of truth and error shift, as if by a pre-established harmony that guarantees this exchangeability of function between the two elements. By contrast, in Spinoza's case there is only one element and its two manifestations, whereby the shift of the truth-false functions can occur only between these two manifestations and is enabled by the fact that they are the manifestations of one and the same element. Thus, in Spinoza, the true truth is that which enables oppositions between (ostensible) truths and errors, whereas in dialectics everything is exhausted within such oppositions, which is why, to repeat Jameson's words, truth must be one-sided.

In Jameson's next exemplary case this dialectical predilection towards the one side, along with the concomitant disregard of the truth that is the standard of both sides, becomes more evident. This belongs to the group of examples that are indicative of what Jameson calls the "identity of bad opposites." Here, Jameson summarizes the thesis of one of his favorite references, Lukács, according to which the two modernist literary movements of naturalism and symbolism are in truth reducible to one and the same shared premise: "the experience of the external world as … dead and meaningless, lifeless and inert, without any internal dynamic of its own" – in short, as what in the Lukácsian nomenclature is called space (Jameson 2009: 30). Based on this common premise, naturalism "embraced" and "reproduced" "this world of lifeless extension" through "the additive process of description and mechanical enumeration," just as symbolism endowed the same "lifeless object with all kinds of superimposed and 'symbolic' meanings" (Jameson 2009: 30). Lukács then proceeds to locate the true "missing third term" – which was to reveal both naturalism and symbolism as "bad opposites" – in the further literary movement of realism and its method of "narration," as opposed to sheer "description." Narration, as understood by the "great realists," is a practice that is predicated on a "view of the outside world as historical process," that is, as time pregnant of meaning and intention, "a world of tendencies," a world that "is already an implicit narrative and thereby holds a narrative meaning within itself that does not have to be imposed from the outside by subjective fiat or by symbolist transformation" (Jameson 2009: 30). In Jameson's conclusion, the "single underlying flaw or ideological error" shared by both "bad opposites" (naturalism and symbolism) is their presupposed assumption that the world is not a historical process but inert space. There is, therefore, no "alleged moment of synthesis, in which the two … phenomena [naturalism and symbolism] are somehow reunited," for this "ideological error" – that the world is space – "precedes their separation rather than following and triumphantly overcoming it" (Jameson 2009: 31).

Granted, the "ideological error" – the presupposition of the world *qua* space – logically precedes the separation between naturalism and symbolism, but, we must object, it is now *realism* that triumphantly emerges to overcome them both, as their true synthesis, as the proper narrative form that sees the truth: that the world is a historical process, as opposed to "lifeless extension" or space. (I will not go into the possibility that this position seems to contradict Jameson's thesis that properly dialectical thought is spatial, and prefer instead to assume that Jameson means this as a historical argument, along the lines of: proper modernist dialectics is temporal; proper postmodern dialectics is spatial.) The crucial point is that in order to opt for either space or time, a slippage must occur from Saussure's formalist concept of *negative qua empty* topological space (as Deleuze would put it) to the *negative qua bad* – i.e., ideologically wrong, or evil – opposites, such as naturalism and symbolism in Lukács's example, against which realism emerges as a "positive value," not only in the sense of a positive topological space, but as a *good* – true or ideologically correct – value. One can take sides only between good and bad values, not between empty topological spaces.

What we witness in the process of the "bad opposites" is a surreptitious sliding from what aspires to be pure formalism to teleological moralism, so that the outcome of the process unapologetically contradicts Jameson's persistently stated intention to re-perform "that originary Saussurean paradox of a pure relationship 'without positive terms'" (Jameson 2009: 27). Only such a relationship could begin to qualify dialectical thought as structuralist and, by implication in Jameson's own argument, as adequate for comprehending the complexities of postmodernity. For, as Jameson emphatically admits, the aim of dialectics *cum* structuralism is "the qualification of negation in a situation in which there is nothing positive for the alleged negative to negate," so that the "reidentification of the two negatives does not give us any new and positive value, but only an enlarged target of critique at a higher and more comprehensive level" (Jameson 2009: 27, 31). Yet, the procedure of the identity of "bad opposites" on the ground of their initial moment of separation ultimately yields to realism as precisely a "positive value." Following Jameson's own prescription, we should acknowledge that realism constitutes itself on an enlarged target of critique at a higher level; that is, we would recognize that the conception of the world as a tendentious narrative and historical process is as much an "ideological error" as the assumption that the world is space.

Jameson, however, insists on side-taking, thereby bringing to the fore its arbitrariness. This becomes conspicuous through a direct comparison of the above examples (see Table 4.1), which reveals that dialectical thought bounces between two positions, the one being (arbitrarily) assumed to be true and the other false, and, depending on the concrete context, it opts either directly for the true (as in the example of realism, in which case all elements of the false are reduced to the "ideological error" of "bad opposites"), or for the false as the index of the true (as in the case of individualist psychology and Hegelianism itself).

Table 4.1 Dialectics in Adorno and Lukács

A. Example:		
	Adorno (individualist psychology)	
Truth (unrecognized)	False (mistaken for deeper truth)	Truth (recognized)
First appearance	Second appearance	Return to first appearance
Split between individual and society	Identity between individual and society	Split between individual and society
	Hegelianism	
Truth (unrecognized)	False (mistaken for deeper truth)	Truth (recognized)
Pseudo-Hegelianism (tripartite synthesis)	Arguments adduced	Postmodern Hegelianism (e.g., "tripartite movement," "bad opposites")
B. Example:		
	Lukács (Realism)	
False (ideological error)	False (bad opposites)	Truth (true, non-ideological alternative)
World = Space	Naturalism-Symbolism	World = Time : Realism

Why, in Lukács's case, choose realism and not naturalism or symbolism, which *qua* false consciousness should say more about the hapless state of a society incapable of seeing the truth of external reality as a historical process? Why choose individual psychology in Adorno's case but not pseudo-Hegelianism in Jameson's? Or is it, after all, the truth of postmodern Hegelianism with its "tripartite movement" and "bad opposites," indeed pseudo-Hegelianism?

Let us recall the passage in which Hegel advances his notorious thesis, meant to exemplify his entire argument about self-consciousness, that the "spirit is the bone," or, for that matter, penis:

> The depth which the Spirit brings forth from within – but only as far as its picture-thinking consciousness where it lets it remain – and the ignorance of this consciousness about what it really is saying, are the same conjunction of the high and the low which, in the living being, Nature naively expresses when it combines the organ of its highest fulfillment, the organ of generation, with the organ of urination. The

> infinite judgment, qua infinite, would be the fulfillment of life that comprehends itself; the consciousness of the infinite judgment that remains at the level of picture-thinking behaves as urination.
>
> (Hegel 1977: 210)

Now let us follow Žižek as he paraphrases Hegel's point in terms of the tripartite movement of postmodern dialectics:

> A close reading of this passage makes it clear that Hegel's point is NOT that, in contrast to the vulgar empiricist mind which sees only urination, the proper speculative attitude has to choose insemination. The paradox is that the direct choice of insemination is the infallible way to miss it: it is not possible to choose directly the "true meaning," i.e., one HAS to begin by making the "wrong" choice (of urination) – the true speculative meaning emerges only through the repeated reading, as the after-effect (or by-product) of the first, "wrong," reading.
>
> (Žižek 2006: 7)

It is not possible to choose directly spirit; rather, the choice must be mediated through the "'wrong' choice" of the contingent, natural, senseless entity (organ of urination), and only then does the "true speculative meaning" (organ of insemination – "i.e. precisely 'conception' as the biological anticipation of concept"; Žižek 2006: 7) – emerge. For:

> The dialectically overcome-entity is annulled in its contingent (stripped of sense, "senseless") aspect of natural, given ("immediate") entity, but it is preserved in its essential (and meaningful, significant) aspect; thus mediated by negation, it is sublimated or raised up to a more "comprehensive" and comprehensible mode of being than that of its immediate reality of pure and simple, positive and static given.

This last voice is not Žižek's but Kojève's, offering his definition of dialectical *Aufhebung* (*synthesis*, and its cognates, such as in the above passage: "overcome," "annulled" and "preserved," "mediated by negation," "sublimated," "raised up") (Kojève 1980: 15).

Whether in explicit synthesis or in implicit ("tripartite movement"), the good or higher side requires the bad or lower side as its intermediary "wrong" reading because, if it were read directly as the good side, it would have been missed. In short, it is always the case that "the spirit is a bone" – provided that it has always been decided which of the two (the spirit or the bone) is the truth (good) of both. (I leave aside the fact that, from Hegel to the postmodern dialectics, the decision remains idealist, i.e., that it is always the *spirit* that is what the bone is.)[5]

This dialectical one-sidedness can be discerned as lurking at the basis of the more explicitly political analyses offered in the essays under the

"Politics" part of Jameson's book, but it is cautiously counterbalanced by a sober, unassuming, and non-prophetic tone. While certain aspects of (capitalist) "evil" are diagnosed as "good" or "positive," Jameson grants them no more than the status of modest reminders of potential valences among others. Thus, Jameson's political analysis offers a compelling critique of standard Leftist moralizing or nostalgic sentiments, while also distancing itself from teleological – let alone, as some have claimed, "theurgical" – cosmic visions.[6] In other words, the success of Jameson's political analysis owes to its deviation from the very dialectical one-sidedness that he promotes throughout his exposition in the more theoretical part of the book.

This observation only reconfirms the need to distinguish between dialectics and structuralist thought, a distinction that we shall trace in more detail in the rest of this chapter. I should frame what follows by pointing out that by "distinction" I mean not that dialectics and structuralism are opposites bur rather that they are different, both in their logic and in their function. As intimated above, the crux of this difference lies in the fact that the dialectic's tripartite movement remains enclosed within two opposites, whether at the end they remain opposites or synthesize or turn out to coincide. In structuralism, by contrast, truth is that element which, when not considered, allows for the imaginary assumption of opposites, whatever their destiny may be. In fact, the function of these (ostensible) opposites – whether they coincide so as to let another, third alternative emerge as *the* truth, or whether the (false) one uses the other as its mediator so as eventually to emerge itself as the triumphant truth – is to hide this further, third, element. In other words, in structuralism the third element is no alternative to the other two. Rather, it is that which enables the appearance of alternatives or (bad) opposites. To clarify, let us engage Jameson's argument directly with structuralism.

Structuralism

In describing the logics of structure and sense, Deleuze provides a different articulation of the negative relation between the incommensurables in identity.

Deleuze would object to Jameson that the aforementioned dialectical models of analysis do not formulate a structure as their object, let alone constitute structuralist thought. For, whatever the configuration of truth and false in each case, they operate, like all traditional thought, on the basis of precisely the opposition between the "real" or "truth" and "imagination" or "false." By contrast, as we have seen, the break with tradition brought about by structuralism consists in "the discovery and recognition of a third order ...: that of the symbolic," a "structural object" beyond both "the word in its reality" and "images and concepts associated with words" (Deleuze 2004: 171). While "the real tends towards one [and] ... is one in its 'truth,'" "the imaginary appears" "[a]s soon as we see two in 'one,' as soon as we make doubles"; the "symbolic order," on the other hand, would correspond to the number "3," that is, something "irreducible to the orders of the real and the imaginary" (Deleuze 2004: 172–3). Structure, therefore, is neither "a *form*" nor "an *essence*," but, to repeat, "it is more a combinatory formula [*une combinatoire*]" of purely negative elements that "have neither extrinsic designation nor intrinsic signification" (Deleuze 2004: 173).[7]

Let us recapitulate some of Deleuze's seven criteria that allow us to recognize structuralism, or, conversely, the seven conditions that a mode of thought must fulfill in order to be called structuralist. Next to the symbolic, the second criterion coincides with the one that Jameson, via Saussure, singles out as the condition of structuralism, namely the "positional," or, to repeat, the fact that in a structure "the sites prevail over whatever occupies them," which is why the "scientific ambition of structuralism is not quantitative, but topological and relational" (Deleuze 2004: 174). In addition to the *symbolic* and the *positional*, two other criteria are most directly relevant to the present argument: the *serial*, and the *empty square or object-x*.

By seriality Deleuze refers to the fact that the "symbolic elements … taken in their differential relations, are organized necessarily in series," which may be "linguistic, economic," "social," and "biological," as in "Foucault's triple series" in his *Les Mots et les Choses* (*The Order of Things*) (Deleuze 2004: 182). "[E]very structure is serial," in fact, "multi-serial," and the "question" remains of knowing which series is "signifying, the others only being signified," a question to which we shall return below (Deleuze 2004: 182).

With the condition of seriality the further crucial question emerges, which will lead to the next criterion of structuralism: "what keeps [any] two series from simply reflecting one another" like mirror images or doubles of one another? For, if nothing does, then the "whole of the structure would … fall back into the state of a figure of imagination," whereby the one series would reflect the other like mirror images of one another, with the fatal consequence that one of the two would be mistaken for real or true (e.g., to refer to our earlier examples, realism, or, alienation), and the other as false (Deleuze 2004: 183). Deleuze's answer to his question is: the "empty square" or "object-x." This "object is eminently symbolic … because it belongs to no series" and, while it has no double, it "is nevertheless present in both," the signifying and the signified series (Deleuze 2004: 184). "Against the dual character of the imagination, the Third [or object-x] … essentially intervenes … [and] distributes series," "mak[ing] them communicate with each other, all the while preventing the one from imaginary falling back on the other" (Deleuze 2004: 185). As an example of this "object-x," Deleuze refers to the letter in Lacan's analysis of Poe's "The Purloined Letter" (Lacan 1966: 19–75).[8]

In *The Logic of Sense*, Deleuze turns to the two fundamental series whose relation any philosophy has always to define: the series of "things" and "propositions" or being and language (Deleuze 1990: 28). Sense is then defined as precisely that object-x which traverses both series, differentiating them in their identity and conferring on them their structurality, insofar as it circulates between them, without being "only one of the two terms of the duality" of things and propositions, but rather their "frontier" or the "articulation of the difference between" (Deleuze 1990: 28). However, the problem with sense, Deleuze continues, is the "*paradox of regress, or of indefinite proliferation*," the fact that every name available in language has a sense which can itself be stated only through a further name which, in turn, must have a sense which again requires a name to be named, and so on (Deleuze 1990: 28). However, although this regress is indefinite, its entire structure requires for its formulation only "a regress of two alternating terms: the name which denotes something and the name which denotes the sense of this name. This two-term regress is the minimal condition of indefinite proliferation" (Deleuze 1990: 30). More precisely, as Deleuze shows through his analysis of Lewis Carroll's "title of the song [the Knight] is going to sing to Alice," in *Alice's Adventures in Wonderland*, this regress of "two alternating terms," which stands for the whole indefinite regress of sense, can be represented by no fewer or more than "four" elements:

> (1) "the name of what … really is"; (2) "the name denoting this reality"; (3) "the sense of this name … which forms a new reality"; and (4) "the name which denotes this reality."
>
> (Deleuze 1990: 30)[9]

The tetradic itinerary of sense as the "frontier" between propositions or names and things or realities, passes, according to the aforementioned criterion of structure, through the two series: things or realities (#1 and #3), and propositions or names (#2 and #4).

To make this abstract scheme more concrete, let us return to Jameson/Lukács's literary genres, and read them this time through Deleuze's matrix: (1) the name of what really is the "external world as meaningless, lifeless extension" – space; (2) "the name denoting this reality" is naturalism and/or symbolism; (3) "the sense of this name … forms a new reality": the corollary/alternative reality of the above, the external world as "historical process" – time; and (4) "the name which denotes this reality" is "realism."

Now, as Deleuze proceeds to write, of these "two heterogeneous series," which constitute one of the "minimal conditions for a *structure* in general," one "shall be determined as 'signifying' and the other as 'signified'" (Deleuze 1990: 50). In other words, there must be a further element, beyond the two of each heterogeneous series, which, as we have seen, is required in order to prevent the one from imaginary falling back on the other, and does so by determining the one as signifying and the other as signified. In Deleuze's words: "The two heterogeneous series converge toward a paradoxical element which is their 'differentiator'" (Deleuze 1990: 50–1). "This element," Deleuze continues:

> belongs to no series; or rather, it belongs to both series at once and never ceases to circulate throughout them ... It appears in one of the series as an excess, but only on the condition that it would appear at the same time in the other as a lack. But if it is in excess in the one, it is so only as an empty square; and if it is lacking in the other, it is so only as a supernumerary pawn or an occupant without a compartment. It is both *word and object* at once ... It has the function of articulating the two series to one another, of reflecting them in one another, of making them communicate ... [And finally,] it has the function of ... determining as signifying the series in which it appears in excess, and, as signified, the series in which it appears correlatively as lacking, and, above all, of assuring the bestowal of sense in both signifying and signified series.
>
> (Deleuze 1990: 51)

This paradoxical element or differentiator, this object-x which is the condition for symbolic structure, and which "is both word = x and thing = x," is – as was intimated by the fact that sense is marked by the paradox of infinite regress, and as Deleuze reveals three chapters later – *nonsense* (Deleuze 1990: 66). In his words:

> Inside the series, each term has sense only by virtue of its position relative to every other term. But this relative position itself depends on the absolute position of each term relative to the instance=x. The latter is determined as nonsense and circulates endlessly throughout the series ... In short, sense is always an *effect* ... being always produced by the circulation of the element=x in the series of terms which it traverses.
>
> (Deleuze 1990: 70)[10]

Returning to our Lukácsian example, nonsense is the identity of the two incommensurables, time and space – hence, space-time – which circulates throughout the two pairs of the series of things and words, appearing in the one pair (series #1 and #2) as excess or empty square – space – and in the other (series #3 and #4) as lack or an occupant without a compartment – time. Thus, nonsense determines series #1 and #2 as signifying, and #3 and #4 as signified: the function of the first two series of things and words is to signify through their excess of space the next two series of things and words as lacking or supernumerary time. Thus is obtained, as an effect of nonsense, sense – and specifically in this case, the sense of dialectical thought in the modernist (Hegelian-Kojèvean-Lukácsian) tradition, for which the space of the world is there to signify it as a historical process. Time or historical process is what modernism takes to be its truth, space being the false underside of that truth. It takes only the inversion of the positions of excess and lack in the two pairs of the series (see Table 4.2) in order for the sense of a spatial or postmodern dialectic to emerge, for which the time of the world is there to signify it ultimately as meaningless and non-intentional or non-teleological space.

However, these two senses – the modernist and the postmodernist, according to Jameson – are only the two sides of one and the same coin – dialectics – which can only perceive one another in terms of truth and falsity, and hence of mutual exclusion. Structuralism, by contrast, aims at the relation of *any sense* whatsoever (true or false) to *nonsense*, and at sustaining their negative relation as the identity of incommensurables. This is precisely the point of Lacan's thesis, advanced in 1964, that "interpretation is not open to any meaning" and that the claim that "all interpretations are possible … is patently absurd," for "the effect of interpretation is to isolate in the subject a kernel … of *non-sense*"; the aim and sole proper function of interpretation is "to bring out irreducible *non-sensical* – composed of non-meanings – signifying elements" (Lacan 1981: 250). In other words, for structuralism, as Deleuze puts it, "sense and nonsense have a specific relation which cannot copy that of the true and the false, that is, which cannot be conceived on the basis of a relation of exclusion" (Deleuze 1990: 68). To conceive of truth and falsity as mutually exclusive, that is, as opposites, is to express them in their imaginary relation – as is the case in Lukács's treatment of space and time, and in his subsequent preference of time as truth, over the falsity of space. Yet, this is an imaginary relation that has not yet touched *nonsense*, that is, the truth that is the standard of both the imaginary true and the imaginary false.

In other words, the "relation between the incommensurables in identity" that Jameson is rightly after is not the relation between naturalism and symbolism, as the pseudo-incommensurables against the background of a realism that explains and theorizes their identity, but the relation between time and space in identity: space-time. These are the incommensurable

Table 4.2 Structure of Postmodern Dialectics

Jameson's spatial/postmodern dialectic via Deleuze:
(1) "the name of what … really is": World = Time
(2) "the name denoting this reality": Synthesis
(3) "the sense of this name … which forms a new reality": World = Space
(4) "the name which denotes this reality": Opposition/Spatial Dialectic

categories whose identity is neither explained nor theorized but purely *posited* as *nonsense* – as a supra- or ultra-sensical postulate decreed by the unifying term "the world," that is, by the mere fact that this world *can* be denoted either in terms of space, as in naturalism and symbolism, or in terms of time, as in realism.[11] Occasionally, it can be denoted in both terms, time and space, as is apparently for Deleuze the case of Lewis Carroll.

In the particular example from Jameson and Lukács, the truth or non-sense or the differentiator or the object-x, which is the standard of both imaginary truth and falsity, can be conceived in terms of space-time in the mathematics of general relativity or of curved space-time. In Euclidean geometry, for which space and time are in a relation of exclusion, the distance between two points is measured only in purely spatial terms, just as the separation of events taking place in time is measured only in temporal terms. By contrast, in space-time, point and event are taken as a "relation between the incommensurables in identity," so that the separation between two pointevents is measured by what is called the invariant interval between the two pointevents. This invariant interval (s^2) takes into account both the temporal and the spatial separation between the pointevents. Thus, the space-time interval between two pointevents is given through the formula: $s^2 = Dr^2 - c^2\, Dt^2$, where c stands for the speed of light, and *Dr* and *Dt* for the spatial and temporal differences between the two pointevents.

We could draw the analogy further and say that just as "spacetime intervals may be classified into three distinct types, based on whether the temporal separation or the spatial separation of the [pointevents] is greater: time-like, light-like, space-like,"[12] so, too, our perception of the world and its narrativization in literary, historiographical, or other forms, varies historically, at times leaning toward time-like narratives, and at other times toward space-like narratives. However, this proclivity toward either is an effect of our imaginary relation – which is not to say unreal but a relation determined by historico-cultural, ideological, etc., factors – to the truth/differentiator, namely, in this case, space-time.

Put differently, in this example, space and time, conceived as opposites, stand in an external and derivative relation to the truth that is their standard, that is, they presuppose this standard as their condition of possibility. They also stand in an imaginary relation to each other, which is why they can be exchanged (e.g., time, realism, and synthesis occupying the position of imaginary truth in modernism, and the position of the false in postmodernism). Nevertheless, as we have seen, the two, (imaginary) truth and false – the former constituting the signified, the latter the signifying series – do not relate in the same way to the truth that is their standard. The distinction between imaginary truth and error replicates the traditional opposition between being and appearance. The truth that is their standard, on the other hand, does not presuppose the imaginary truth and error – except in the sense that, to put it in Spinozian terms, substance can also be said to presuppose its modes insofar as substance is an immanent and not a transitive cause, and hence, it is itself the effect of its own effects. The truth as the standard has primacy over the imaginary truth and false in the same sense that substance, albeit immanent, has primacy over the modes. This truth includes within itself, to repeat Jameson's apt expression, the "relation between the incommensurables in identity," as its own internal relation that involves no duality or redoubling, as is the case of space-time, or of substance conceived as differential.

Kafka's valences

In addition to *Alice*, Kafka's work has been another exemplary literary vehicle for Deleuze to formulate his theory of sense as the effect of nonsense. In their 1975 book on Kafka (English translation in 1986), Deleuze and Félix Guattari employed the strategy of pursuing centrifugal explosive movements that, starting from any given monad, allow ever more series to proliferate and establish multiplicities of connections among singularities and lines of flight throughout the universe of both Kafka *and* sense and expression. Here I would like to pursue a kind of inverse path, one of centripetal implosion, with the aim of squeezing, as it were, the universe of sense within one single monad. The intended outcome being not, of course, the isolation of the monad but finding in the monad the expression of the whole universe of sense. All this with the proviso – as follows from the earlier reference to Leibniz in this chapter – that the relation between monad and universe is due not to some pre-established harmony but to the fact that the monad and the universe are manifestations of the same thing. The monad in question is Kafka's parable "Prometheus," written between 1917 and 1923.[13] Here is the text in the original and in English translation, with my interventions regarding the translation, in bold font in the German, and in brackets in the translation:

> Prometheus
>
> Von Prometheus berichten vier Sagen: Nach der ersten wurde er, weil er die Götter an die Menschen verraten hatte, am Kaukasus festgeschmiedet, und die Götter schickten Adler, die von seiner immer wachsenden Leber fraßen.
>
> Nach der zweiten drückte sich Prometheus im Schmerz von den zuhackenden Schnäbeln immer tiefer in den Felsen, bis er mit ihm eins wurde.
>
> Nach der dritten wurde in den Jahrtausenden sein Verrat vergessen, die Götter vergaßen, die Adler, er selbst.
>
> Nach der vierten wurde man **des grundlos Gewordenen** müde. Die Götter wurden müde, die Adler wurden müde, die Wunde schloß sich müde.

> Blieb das unerklärliche Felsgebirge. – Die Sage versucht das Unerklärliche zu erklären. Da sie aus einem Wahrheits**grund** kommt, muß sie wieder im Unerklärlichen enden.
>
> (Kafka 1970: 306)

> Prometheus
>
> There are four legends concerning Prometheus: According to the first he was clamped on a rock in the Caucasus for betraying the secrets of the gods to men, and the gods sent eagles to feed on his liver, which was perpetually renewed.
>
> According to the second, Prometheus, goaded by the pain of the tearing beaks, pressed himself deeper and deeper into the rock until he became one with it.
>
> According to the third his treachery was forgotten in the course of thousands of years, forgotten by the gods, the eagles, forgotten by himself.
>
> According to the fourth everyone grew weary of the meaningless affair [of what had become groundless]. The gods grew weary, the eagles grew weary, the wound closed wearily.
>
> There remained the inexplicable mass of rock. – The legend tried to explain the inexplicable. As it came out of a substratum [ground] of truth it had in turn to end in the inexplicable.
>
> (Kafka 1979: 152)

Each of the first four paragraphs summarizes a version of the legend of Prometheus, and the fifth paragraph functions as a coda that retroactively impacts the entire parable. Quite predictably, the first four paragraphs recapitulate the four positions required to formulate the paradox of the indefinite regress of sense. The key, however, lies in what one decides to see in the first paragraph.

One may decide to see in it a summary of the well-known version of the legend of Prometheus, according to which, having betrayed the secrets of the gods to humans, the gods subjected him to the perpetual punishment of having his ever-regenerated liver devoured by the eagles.

The distinctive quality of this first version is that it is presupposed for the other three. If in the second version Prometheus "pressed himself deeper and deeper into the rock until he became one with it," it is only because he was "goaded by the pain of the tearing beaks" that inflicted the punishment on him. Similarly, the fact that in the third, and with the passing of millennia, "his treachery was forgotten" by all the characters involved in this plot of transgression and punishment – "the gods, the eagles," and "himself" – only reaffirms the preexistent reality of this plot. In the fourth version, in which all "grew weary of the meaningless affair," the fact that his wound also "closed wearily" means that there was in the first place a wound – that is, a punishment and, hence, its cause, Prometheus's betrayal. Moreover, just as the coda could not be on any other position, the order of the four paragraphs is fixed: the first, as the presupposition of the rest, must come first, and it is only directly after it that the second can come; after the second it may initially appear that any of the other two could follow, but because Prometheus's treachery must first be forgotten for the affair to become meaningless, only the third can be in the third position. The persistence of the first version in the other three as their presupposition, as well as the ordinal sequence of the paragraphs, suffices to subsume all of them under one and the same series – a series of the legend of Prometheus. However, these conditions alone cannot establish this legendary quartet as *the* series of the legend of Prometheus, by which I mean not some random selection of four out of various other versions of the legend, but as the series of *all* possible versions in their potentially infinite regress. For this to be the case, this tetradic series itself must consist of two series, and it must represent formulaically all possible ways in which these two series can make sense.

Reading the English version, our view of the two series may become slightly obstructed, as a fundamental connection is weakened through the translation. What in the fourth paragraph appears as "everyone grew weary of the meaningless affair," in the original actually reads: "wurde man des grundlos Gewordenen müde [one grew weary of what had become groundless]." The forgotten treachery of the third paragraph becomes in the fourth the absence of ground. Meanwhile, as we read in the coda, the legend itself comes from a "Wahrheitsgrund [a ground of truth]" – a treachery, that is far from forgotten – and it is for this reason, the text tells us, that it must again end in the inexplicable: the "mass of rock." It follows that the two primary series in Kafka's edifice are the ground of truth or treachery, and the inexplicable or the mass of rock. These are the two incommensurable positions of sense with regard to the truth of causality: either there is a ground of truth, a cause, for everything *or* there is no cause for everything, so that it remains inexplicable.

Simultaneously, these two series are superimposed with, and inseparable from, another pair of incommensurables, a numerical one. For in the first paragraph, treachery introduces conflict or the Two – say, between men and gods or, to recall Adorno's example, individual and society. In the next paragraph, the mass of rock introduces union or the One: there is only one Being, as Prometheus becomes one with the rock. Between these two extremes, Two and One (conflict and union), move paragraphs three and four, which could be an indefinitely long series of paragraphs, as long as – as is indeed the case in paragraphs three and four – there are distinct beings (gods, eagles, Prometheus), *and* the cause and testimony of their conflict evanesce: the treachery is forgotten until the affair becomes groundless and the wound eventually closes. It is only after the closure of the wound that treachery and the mass of rock – the Two or the "ground of truth" out of which came the legend, and the One or the inexplicable – are left alone in the coda, in their union and incommensurability.

Whether in the realm of causality or in that of number, or, as Kant would put it, whether in the dynamic or the mathematic realm – and, as Kafka indicates, one is always in both – sense may produce indefinitely many and variable legends, all of which, however, articulate one and the same relation: the relation of the causal/dynamic and numerical/mathematic incommensurables in identity.[14]

As for the element-x circulating throughout the series of the Two and the One, this is the wound. In the first paragraph, the wound is the effect of fission (treachery), while in the second it is the cause for the union of being. In the third paragraph, it tacitly subsists, even as its cause, treachery, is forgotten. In the fourth, it finally closes wearily to give way to the eventual union of the incommensurables in the coda. The wound is the nonsense that allows for the emergence of sense – in all the nuances that sense can articulate the relation between One and Two. For in the universe of this monad, only the wound is both One and Two: a mass of flesh not unlike a mass of rock, and yet incommensurably unlike it, as it can emerge only out of a conflict – a clash between one mass and another – just as, for this same reason, it can, if it is truly unbearable, incite the wish to eliminate any distinct masses.

If the motto of the Hegelian dialectic is "the spirit is the bone" (the Two is One), then the maxim we can derive from Kafka's "Prometheus" is: the spirit *is* and is *not* the bone, and both theses are possible on account of *a third element*: the wound – including its closure, possibly also its exclusion. Thus we arrive at, to repeat Jameson's stated intention, "an enlarged target of critique at a higher and more comprehensive level." For now, new questions emerge, such as: Can the spirit *be and* be *not* the bone as long as the wound is not closed? And can a wound such as Prometheus's ever be closed? Which is also to ask: if structuralism is not a valence of the dialectic, is it possible that it is a valence of the Kantian antinomies? Or is it rather a valence of set theory? In short: In what of all possible modes of exclusion/inclusion does the third, nonsensical, term relate to the two series?[15]

Coda

A. Prometheus repeated

Now, let's start again, making this time the decision to see in the first paragraph of "Prometheus" a rift and an imbalance between several series of two heterogeneous series: humans and gods, immense debt and excessive punishment, ever-growing human liver and god-sent liver-devouring eagles. What appears as lacking in the one series appears as excess or supernumerary in the other series – *already in the first paragraph*. By making this decision we know from the outset that the primary sense, the being or reality of what the legend of Prometheus *really is* is lack/excess, that is, nonsense or the identity of the incommensurables: lack and excess as immanent to each other.

The second paragraph offers us the name denoting the first reality: sheer immanence, the total identity of Prometheus and the rock as a result of unbearable excessive pain. The excessive pain inflicted on Prometheus is the means for making up for his debt, that is, for eliminating the initial imbalance or rift between lack and excess in the two heterogeneous series of the first reality. However, it evidently fails to do so, as his pain can only remind Prometheus and the world of his debt. Thus, the incommensurability between excess and lack remains but the fusion with the rock introduces a radical indistinction of beings, so that it cannot be said which being is the bearer of each (excess or lack) or, what amounts to the same, each being is the bearer of both. This coincidence of both in each and every being amounts to the plenitude of Being. This is how the rift in Being of the first reality comes to be denoted by the name "One" or "plenitude of Being" in the second paragraph.

If the second version of the myth consolidates (the rift between) lack and excess in the plenitude of Being, the third version does away with both by means of a total lack of memory: everyone forgot. Forgot what? Prometheus's treachery – that is, the very cause of the identity of the incommensurables: excess and lack. Thus, we have arrived at a new reality: the oblivion of the cause. However, that the cause has been forgotten does not mean that its effects are eliminated; on the contrary, as Lacan reminds us: "the effects are successful only in the absence of cause" (Lacan 1981: 128). Their groundlessness is the necessary condition for effects to be successful.

Nevertheless, despite the efficacy of the effects, one can always become weary of what has become "groundless." Just as the first reality found its name in the second legend through excess pain, here too the name of the second reality – oblivion of cause – is given in the fourth paragraph through another feeling in excess: weariness (in the face of the groundlessness of the effects).

The word "groundless" appears not just as a logical consequence of what has come before but as the bridge to what is coming now: the coda, where we read that the legend "comes from a *ground* of truth."

A brief parenthesis is due here to remark that the fifth paragraph forms unmistakably a coda for various reasons. The first reason, least persuasive because speculative (as it assumes that Kafka was a structuralist), is what Deleuze told us: four elements are involved in the expression and denotation of sense. Second, what Kafka told us: "There are four [not five] legends concerning Prometheus." Third, the punctuation and grammar of the paragraph: the greater part of the coda is marked as such by both the long dash and the shift to the present tense, which appears only once more, in the very first sentence of the first paragraph, which announces the existence of four legends – "There are four legends concerning Prometheus" – and which is thus also set apart from the four paragraphs containing the four legends. Finally, while the story introduces "four legends," in plural, in the coda we have one legend: "The legend." This can be read in at least three complementary ways: (a) what follows after "The legend" is true of not only Prometheus's legend but *the* (any) legend in general; (b) the four legends are in truth four versions of one and the same legend, in the Lévi-Straussian sense, according to which all versions of the myth – say from the Homeric and Sophoclean versions of *Oedipus*, to Freud's version and beyond – are equally authentic versions of one and the same myth;[16] and (c) the four legends are in truth one legend, insofar as they constitute a conceptual continuum in which the fourth presupposes the third, etc. (as we already have seen to be the case).

Having now all this in mind, we return to observe that as the coda invokes the "ground of truth" as the origin of the legend, it refers us back to the first legend: the reality of the identity of the incommensurables, lack and excess – now reappearing as the excess and lack of cause: the "ground of truth" and the "inexplicable" "mass of rock." The coda recuperates the first reality to reveal that beyond any heterogeneous series constituting a legend, and in which lack and excess may appear in any concrete (and imaginary) form – ranging from moral debt and punishment to the ground of truth and the inexplicable – the ultimate two heterogeneous series of any legend, and of any sense, are those constituted by the object-x, nonsense, the identity of incommensurables. This object-x can appear in the one series as excess, in the other as lack of any thing whatever. If one is a skilled writer, one can always find some thing that nicely fits as the frontier between them, sounding more sensical than it really is, such as "Prometheus's wound," or Jameson's and Deleuze's "identity of incommensurables."

B. Hegel repeated

In this case, it may therefore be said that it was the "appearance," the "first reality" or "impression" – the first paragraph – that "was 'true' after all." Under the condition, of course, that this first reality stands – as was from the outset stated in this coda – neither for excess nor for lack, but for both, in their negative relation of incommensurability and identity. If the dialectic succeeds in performing this variant – in which the first "false" or "naïve" impression is one with its negative, the second "true" or "deeper" impression – then it may be argued that it forms a valence of structuralist thought.

However, "valence" indicates both same origin with and distinction from that of which it is a valence. The crucial thing, in other words, is that structuralism and dialectics are neither true opposites nor "bad opposites," that is, one another's mirror images to which indeed applies Hegel's afore-cited and most succinct description: "the different is not confronted by *any* other but by *its* other … the other's *own* other" (Hegel 1975: 172). It is because of the absence of a third element in Hegel's thought – the fervor for the *coincidentia oppositorum*, this direct and "immediate coincidence of the opposite poles," as Žižek has recurrently pointed out, in which "each pole passes immediately into each opposite; each is already in itself its own opposite" – that his work offers the most realistic staging of the imaginary relation (Žižek 1989: 172).[17]

However, Hegel's immersion in the imaginary relation does not necessarily deprive him of the possibility of a distance that would allow him to manipulate the coincidence of opposites in full consciousness of its imaginary character. By this I mean that it is not unlikely that Hegel gave a picture of the world and history modeled on the imaginary coincidence of opposites, having concluded that, since in modern thought the imaginary is an indispensable function, the most appealing philosophical (and, for that matter, political) systems are those that offer as solutions the most appealing reveries. This possibility is indicated in the commentary accompanying his famous thesis that "the supersensible is therefore *appearance qua appearance*" (Hegel 1977: 89; §147). In order that in the "supersensible" or "inner world," in that "void" which is "*empty in itself*," both "devoid of *objective* Things" and "also void of all spiritual relationships and distinctions of consciousness" – "in order, then, that in this *complete void* … there may yet be something, we must fill it up with reveries, *appearances*, produced by consciousness itself" (Hegel 1977: 88–9; §146). However, can such filling be philosophically honest or existentially fair? Whatever the answer to this question may be, Hegel is convinced that the absolute void itself "would have to be content with being treated so badly for it would not deserve anything better, since even reveries are better than its own emptiness" (Hegel 1977: 89; §146). "The inner world, or supersensible beyond," Hegel continues, "*comes from* the world of appearance," that is, from objectively given reality as it appears or is perceived, and, therefore, "appearance is its essence and, in fact, its filling" (Hegel 1977: 89; §147). The two opposite poles indeed coincide entirely: "the supersensible is the sensuous and the perceived" – *except* that now that the sensuous has coincided with the supersensible, it is "posited as it is *in truth*," which changes things drastically for "the *truth* of the sensuous and the perceived is to be *appearance*" – that is, not the sensuous world but reveries, produced by consciousness (Hegel 1977: 89; §147).

Hence, when in the next sentence Hegel famously concludes "the supersensible is therefore *appearance qua appearance*," he is saying that the supersensible is the sensuous world or *reality qua reverie*. This is why he adds:

> We completely misunderstand this if we think that the supersensible world is *therefore* the sensuous world, or the world as it exists for immediate sense-certainty and perception; for the world of appearance

> is, on the contrary, not the world of sense-knowledge and perception as a world that positively *is*, but this world posited as superseded, or as in truth an *inner world.* It is often said that the supersensible world is not appearance; but what is here understood by appearance is not appearance, but rather the *sensuous* world as itself the really actual.
>
> (Hegel 1977: 89; §147)

Hegel maintains here that the supersensible, the truth behind the appearance, is (this first, superficial) appearance, the sensuous world, but *only* insofar as it is taken as reverie – that is, redoubled, not unlike Zeuxis's painted curtain which Parrhasios mistakes for real and asks Zeuxis to remove so that he can see the actual painting. This is the function of the imaginary: to turn a fake curtain into reality, just as it can turn, at times, a time pregnant with meaning, and, at other times, space into the truth of the world. As Lacan put it, Hegel's radical advance beyond "a certain religious individualism which grounds the existence of the individual in his unique tête-à-tête with God" does not go beyond "showing that the reality … of each human being is in the being of the other" – the imaginary fantasy *par excellence* that leads to the master-slave dialectic, among other ideological schemes (Lacan 1991: 72). However, if this is the case, then we must admit that Hegel's laudable feat consists in unfolding the complexities of, precisely, the imaginary, and, in fact, in doing so with incredible systematic precision, both in fictional/narrative form – as in the master-slave dialectic or his historical accounts – and purely theoretical form – as in his abstract accounts of the constitution of self-consciousness. Since we can never be outside ideology and the imaginary, we will never "have gone beyond Hegel" (Lacan 1991: 71).

Yet, even as it is undoubtedly true that we live and breathe in such reveries, the imaginary function is not the limit of human experience nor is insight into the imaginary the profoundest truth we are capable of. This is why, although he devoted a considerable portion of his *Ethics* to it, Spinoza's ultimate concern was something else. For, as much as the imaginary, not unlike money, is what makes the world go round, it is nothing more than, as follows also from Hegel's above passage, the best defense we have against the murmur of the void – the nonsense – that haunts us from cradle to grave. As Lacan continues to say, because of his commitment to the imaginary relation Hegel had to remain anthropomorphic and "at the limit of anthropology" (Lacan 1991: 72). By contrast, "Freud got out of it" and "isn't a humanist" due to his "discovery … that man isn't entirely in man," but rather in the "machine" (Lacan 1991: 72–3). In this "metaphor of the human body as a machine … we see the manifestation of a certain beyond of the [imaginary] inter-human reference, which is in all strictness the symbolic beyond" (Lacan 1991: 76). This is why, if what we are after is structure, we must go beyond Hegel, even as we always are in Hegel.[18]

At a certain point Jameson acknowledges the symbolic beyond as the vast "socioeconomic" machinery of generally the "dynamics of history" and particularly "the capitalist mode of production" with its own "time" and its "inhuman periods of fatality and insurmountable misery" which are "out of sync with," and remain "incomprehensible" from, the perspective of "human" or "individual time" (Jameson 2009: 369–70). He also acknowledges that the human being in the face of such an inhuman symbolic beyond can only "hasten" to take recourse to the imaginary and "translate [this beyond] into the all-too human terms of success or failure" (Jameson 2009: 369–70). However, if the alienation of individual and society is as true as their identity, should we not conclude, with Freud, that the human individual itself is the very inhuman machinery that alone was capable of producing such a society? Thus, Jameson is right to conclude that "the only meaningful," at once philosophical and political, question is: "how can I recognize this forbiddingly foreign totality as my own doing," as "*completely invented by me*," and "its laws as my own projection and my own praxis?" (Jameson 2009: 608). Lest this project be yet another imaginary projection of all-too human laws, it is imperative that we acknowledge the inhuman structures of human beings. This is indeed our "peculiar existential and epistemological dilemma, comparable to the science-fictional one of beings inhabiting a cosmos" and selves "they do not have organs to perceive or identify" (Jameson 2009: 370).

"Perhaps," as Jameson suggests, "only [this] acknowledgment … is capable of generating some new ethic" (Jameson 2009: 370). Perhaps, though, the matrix of this ethic has been there since the inception of the socio-economic machine called capitalism, available yet still wanting the organs capable of perceiving it. Perhaps the symbolic beyond of capitalism has always lain in plain view, but not for the sensorium of the imaginary. Perhaps developing the adequate organs requires, after all, a tripartite historical movement, not unlike the one described by Jameson:

> [P]erhaps it was as historically important as it was necessary for human society to have gone through the experience of consumerism as a way of life, if only in order more consciously later on to choose something radically different in its place.
>
> (Jameson 2009: 382)

The epistemological dominance of the imaginary in the last two centuries may parallel the history of consumerism. Hegel then would, after all, always have been right both to see in Spinoza the first properly secular philosopher and his own precursor *and* to "misread" him. For Hegel's misreading was of course necessary so that he could develop his own theory,[19] but not *just as a betrayal of Spinozism* – even as history appears to verify this position. I think our lesson from history should rather be that Hegel's necessarily *correct* misreading required for the formulation of the imaginary as that valence of the symbolic necessitated, logically and historically, for thought to point to the real.

Notes

1 This book is possibly a culmination in Jameson's endeavor to raise and address this question, but certainly not his first such attempt. See, for instance, Jameson 2006 – whose final statement – "(*to be continued*)" – frames it as a prelude to his later book.

2 For extant reviews addressing these topics see, for instance, Brown 2009; Eagleton 2009; Fischer 2010.

3 According to Kojève, Western philosophy can be classified in four basic types. First, the Parmenidean-Spinozian line, for which substance, or what Hegel would call the Concept (*Begriff*), *is Eternity.* Second, Hegel, for whom the Concept is Time. Third, a type of philosophy divided into the three subcategories represented by Plato, Aristotle, and Kant or the Judeo-Christian tradition, for all of which the Concept is *eternal*, i.e., "it 'participates' in Eternity … but Eternity itself is something other than the concept." And, fourth, the line of skepticism or relativism, which strictly speaking does not deserve the name "philosophy," as it is predicated on a "*vulgar denial*" of the Concept, since it reduces it to the *temporal* (not to Time, but to that which participates in time), so that the Concept "is just as temporal as any other thing existing in Time," thus preventing the possibility of "a true or genuine Knowledge" (Kojève 1980: 101–2, 116).

4 As for Kojève, his name appears only once in Jameson's entire book, in a passing reference to the master-slave dialectic (Jameson 2009: 100).

5 For a succinct analysis of this (here only peripherally mentioned) point, in relation to the "negative" anti-materialist spirit of Christianity, as well as for an astute presentation of the dialectical logic as the matrix of both the Christian and the postmodern modes of ideological interpellation, see Pfaller 1998.

6 I am referring here to Hardt and Negri's thesis that "the teleology of the multitude," which consists in "a material affirmation of liberation," "is theurgical" (see Hardt and Negri 2000 – a reference that indicates that it is not only self-proclaimed dialecticians who are capable of dialectical thought (see Hardt and Negri 2000; I am not the first to have made this observation, but for the interested reader, I elaborate on the unacknowledged Hegelianism of *Empire* in Kordela 2007). In the chapter with the telling title "Utopia as Replication," Jameson makes an explicit brief reference to Hardt and Negri's work to turn then to Paolo Virno's criticism, where he finds a more fecund ground for his conceptualization of Utopia as a valence of the present or as "an alternate world," neither "after" nor "before this one," a world "contiguous with ours but without any connection or access to it" (Jameson 2009: 410–34, 612; see Virno 2004). In a different context and approach, while again criticizing Jameson (and partly Deleuze), I arrive at a conception of a temporality that entails Utopia as precisely an alternate world, yet simultaneous, with ours (see Kordela 2006, but also Kordela 2013).

7 This is part of what bestows on structuralism its theoretical or scientific character. See also note 3 in the third chapter.

8 For an English translation see Lacan 1988.

9 Note that Deleuze prefaces this part of his exposition of sense by inviting us to "agree to think of a proposition as a name" (Deleuze 1990: 28).

10 Note that, due to the "paradoxical" fact "that it is at once word and thing," nonsense – unlike "the normal law governing all names endowed with sense," according to which "their [expressed] sense may be denoted only by another

name" – is "a word that denotes exactly what it expresses and expresses what it denotes. It expresses its *denotatum* and designates its own sense. It is therefore completely abnormal ... The name saying its own sense can only be *nonsense*" (Deleuze 1990: 67). By the same token, the moment one denotes the sense of nonsense by means of other names, one turns it into sense – which is what is inevitably done, at least to some extent, here as much as in Deleuze and all structuralism, at the very moment when one says, for instance, nonsense is the precondition of sense. However, this observation would deteriorate into a "bad play on words" if its aim were just to object that "nonsense has a sense, the sense being precisely that it hasn't any" (Deleuze 1990: 67–8). On the contrary, the reference to nonsense as an "abnormal" word-thing aims at establishing an irreducible relation between sense (the norm) and nonsense (the exception) that differs from the relation between the true and the false.

To explain this point, it will be helpful to make explicit the analogy between the problematic of sense (linguistic series) and another series, the economic. The paradox Deleuze is grappling with is no different from the paradox Marx discovered when attempting to grasp the logic of exchange-value in capitalism, which we could paraphrase according to our terms as follows. Inside the series of commodities, each commodity obtains an exchange-value only by virtue of its position relative to every other commodity. However, the series of commodities is marked by the paradox of infinite regress, the fact that each commodity's exchange-value can be defined through the exchange-value of another commodity, whose exchange-value must in turn be defined through the exchange-value of another commodity, and this ad infinitum. Thus, no commodity could obtain exchange-value through its relative position to other commodities unless the entire series did not itself depend on the absolute position of each commodity relative to the instance = x – nonsense, which in the series of economy is money. For money is marked by the at once paradoxical and nonsensical characteristic of being both the exception to the series of commodities – as the exclusive measure of the value of commodities, or a non-commodity insofar as its sole use-value *is* its exchange-value – and a member of the series – insofar as it itself is a commodity (see Marx 1990, particularly the chapter "The Value-Form, or Exchange-Value"). In Marx's words: if "gold confronts the other commodities as money [it is] only because it previously confronted them as a commodity," and nothing could have "won a monopoly" as the "universal equivalent" if it itself, "like all other commodities," had not "also functioned as an equivalent" (Marx 1990: 162–3). To ground his point, Marx offers examples of societies in which gold, furs, and other commodities or objects of utility were used as money, but we, in late capitalism, do not need such examples, as we know that even paper money occupies "exclusively the position of the equivalent form" while remaining a commodity sold by credit companies. As Kojin Karatani remarks, Marx's ingenuity consists in the fact that, while all other ("bourgeois") economists of his time treated money as a "barometer" (an absolute exception), he treated "capital itself, and therefore money itself, as a commodity" (Karatani 1995: 69–70). Marx's approach is not unlike "Cantor" who, in the context of the series of numbers, "treated infinity as a number," so that the set of all numbers (infinity) became a member of itself. In the economic series of capitalism, Marx, too, "identifies a paradox in which a class of the meta-level descends to the object level to occupy the same locus as the members; in other words, to become a member of itself," whereby capitalism becomes a "deconstructive" system with no "transcendental center" (Karatani 1995: 69–70). Deleuze helps us understand that structure is always "deconstructive," that is, it depends not on a "transcendental center" but on a nonsensical element, an element that is not a member of any series while circulating and being omnipresent in all series.

11 The same is true of the incommensurables "individual = society" and "individual versus society," in Adorno's example.

12 https://en.wikipedia.org/wiki/Introduction_to_the_mathematics_of_general_relativity#Curvilinear_coordinates_and_curved_spacetime.

13 Given the years of its composition, even when read as an allegory for sense, "Prometheus" may always carry with it undertones of an allegory for revolution. I also take the opportunity here to thank the students who discussed with me Kafka's short story in fall 2009, and particularly Ross Shields and Siarhei Biareishyk.

14 I am of course referring to Kant's "paradoxes" or "antinomies" of reason, into which reason necessarily falls when it examines the totality of experience (i.e., something that is never given to experience, as is also the case with the totality of sense or all possible legends of Prometheus). Reason can examine this totality either in terms of its limits in time and space or in terms of the causal relations that determine it. Kant calls the first aspect "mathematic," as it involves the addition of temporal or spatial parts, and the second "dynamic," as it examines the causal dynamism governing the totality. In both cases, reason can prove as true two antinomic conclusions, such as: the world has and has not a limit in time and space, or everything in the world is and is not determined by natural causality (see Kant 1998: 467–95: A420/B448–A461/B489).

15 Although addressing this question would be the ambition of another work, I indicate here that a response calls for an engagement with at least two models of thought. On the one hand, the Kantian antinomies, for which, unlike in Kafka, there is a categorical division between dynamic and mathematic matters, such that the "wound" (nonsensical element) would have to be not only closed but excluded (and possibly even foreclosed) in the dynamic realm, while in the mathematic realm it could not be closed. On the other hand, set theory and the various paradoxical sets it has identified. In an earlier footnote here, on the relation between the series of sense and the economic series, I indicated that structuralist thought is largely predicated on what is now largely known as the not-all set, which remains open insofar as its exclusion is a member of itself. Further questions arise here, such as: what is the exact difference between the not-all set and the antinomies, or are unintentional slippages from the one model to another possible, and what are the consequences? (I attempt to address some of these questions in Kordela 2007.)

16 A thesis advanced in Lévi-Strauss, *c.* 1974.

17 Not of the Real, for which Žižek occasionally seems to mistake this *coincidentia oppositorum*.

18 Spinoza's focus – notably in his *Ethics*, but also in passages in his political writings – on this machinic, purely structural or symbolic beyond rightly deserves the characterization non-anthropomorphic, not unlike some of Freud's work and certainly Lacan's. However, this tendency may lead to the misconception that for Spinoza the imaginary is something to be disregarded as purely false knowledge, that is, as non-knowledge whatsoever. This is arguably the case in some of Deleuze's readings of Spinoza, especially his reading of Spinoza's commentary on Adam's "fall" in his *Theologico-Political Treatise.* As I have argued elsewhere, the reduction of the imperative to action (including the ethical imperative) to an eternal truth, such as a mathematical law, is incompatible with Spinoza's principle that truth is the standard both of itself and the false (i.e., of the imaginary) (see Deleuze 1988; and Kordela 2007). In the same work I also show that Žižek's criticism of Spinoza's ethics as a reduction of deontology to ontology is in truth applicable only to Deleuze's aforementioned reading, and not to Spinoza (see Žižek 2004). For a much

more detailed elaboration on the function of the imaginary and fantasy in Spinoza, see Kordela with Bermas-Dawes 2017.

19 I am of course referring here to Pierre Macherey's position (see Macherey 2011). *A propos* Macherey, his thesis regarding Lacan's reading of Hegel concurs with the thesis advanced here, namely, that "if there is a dialectic of the subject [in Lacan], it is ... in so far as the subject is a subject for an other, or even, literally, subject of another which obscurely determines it more profoundly that itself," which is "realized paradigmatically in ... transference" (Macherey 1998: 63). This, by the way, is also Spinoza's principle regarding the imaginary relation, in which the subject is always affected by what it imagines that the affect of the other is. Moreover, Macherey pursues his search for the Hegelian dialectic further and finds it through the examination of foreclosure and psychosis, where Lacan mentions the term "'dialectic' ... to signify ... [the] relation of exclusion which ties the real and the symbolic into a circle which, even when it is broken, does not fail to constitute an insurmountable limit" (Macherey 1998: 73). Here "it could be said again that a hallucination is an *Aufhebung*, a negation of a negation, but on the condition of specifying that it is not in this sense that the effect of reality aroused by it could simultaneously reconcile subject and object through a recognition of their common belonging to a third moment – Consciousness or Spirit – which would surpass their opposition: on the contrary, it affirms that their duality is irreducible" (Macherey 1998: 73–4). Therefore, Lacan follows Hegel only in the context of the imaginary and transference, whereas regarding the overall "*rapprochement* of psychoanalysis and Hegelian philosophy on the basis of their common reference to a 'dialectic,'" Macherey concludes, "leads ... to a positing of divergence" (Macherey 1998: 74). Now, this dialectic without the third moment of a synthesis sounds closer to how Jameson envisions the postmodern dialectic, even as I claim that his attempt to practice it fails. The question is: even if one succeeded in realizing this dialectic of the insurmountable limit, should we consider this to be the ultimate horizon of knowledge?

References

Adorno, T. (1968) "Sociology and Psychology," *New Left Review*, 1(46) and 1(47).

Brown, N. (2009) "It's Dialectical," *Mediations*, 24(2): 151–163.

Deleuze, G. (1988) *Spinoza: Practical Philosophy*, Robert Hurley (trans.), San Francisco, CA: City Light Books.

Deleuze, G. (1990) *The Logic of Sense*, Mark Lester and Charles Stivale (trans.), Constantin V. Boudas (ed.), New York: Columbia University Press.

Deleuze, G. (2004) "How Do We Recognize Structuralism?," in *Desert Islands and Other Texts 1953–1974*, Melissa McMahon and Charles J. Stivale (trans.), David Lapoujade (ed.), Los Angeles, CA: Semiotext(e), pp. 170–192.

Deleuze, G. and F. Guattari (1986) *Kafka: Toward a Minor Literature*, Dona Polan (trans.), Minneapolis: University of Minnesota Press.

Eagleton, T. (2009) "Jameson and Form," *New Left Review*, 59 (September–October), 123–137.

Fischer, M. (2010) "Reading the Imperceptible Tremors of an Unimaginable Future," *Mute* (May). www.metamute.org/en/content/reading_the_imperceptible_tremors_of_an_unimaginable_future

Hardt, M. and A. Negri (2000) *Empire*, Cambridge, MA: Harvard University Press.

Hegel, G.W.F. (1975) *Hegel's Logic: Part One of the Encyclopedia of the Philosophical Sciences*, William Wallace (trans.), Oxford: Clarendon Press.

Hegel, G.W.F. (1977) *Phenomenology of Spirit*. A.V. Miller (trans.), Oxford: Oxford University Press.

Hegel, G.W.F. (1988) *Phänomenologie des Geistes*, Hans-Friedrich Wessels and Heinrich Clairmont (eds), Hamburg: Felix Meiner Verlag.

Jameson, F. (2006) "Lacan and the Dialectic: A Fragment," in *Lacan: The Silent Partners*, Slavoj Žižek (ed.), London: Verso, pp. 365–397.

Jameson, F. (2009) *Valences of the Dialectic*, New York: Verso.

Kafka, F. (1970) *Sämtliche Erzählungen*, Paul Raabe (ed.), Frankfurt: Fischer Verlag.

Kafka, F. (1979) *The Basic Kafka*, New York: Pocket Books.

Kant, I. (1998) *Critique of Pure Reason*, Paul Guyer and Allen Wood (trans., eds), Cambridge: Cambridge University Press.

Karatani, K. (1995) *Architecture as Metaphor: Language, Number, Money*, Sabu Kohso (trans.), Michael Speaks (ed.), Cambridge, MA: MIT Press.

Kojève, A. (1980) *Introduction to the Reading of Hegel: Lectures on the Phenomenology of Spirit*, Allan Bloom (ed.), Ithaca, NY: Cornell University Press.

Kordela, A.K. (2006) "Capital: At Least it Kills Time," *Rethinking Marxism*, 18(4): 539–563.

Kordela, A.K. (2007) *$urplus*, Charles Shepherdson (ed.), Albany, NY: SUNY Press.

Kordela, A.K. (2013) *Being, Time, Bios: Capitalism and Ontology*, Albany, NY: SUNY Press.

Kordela, A.K. and Bermas-Dawes, J. (2017) "Spinoza's Immanent Sovereignty: Fantasy and the Decision of Interpretation," in *Spinoza's Authority: Resistance and Power, Volume 2: On the Treatises*, Kiarina Kordela and Dimitri Vardoulakis (eds), New York: Bloomsbury.

Lacan, J. (1966) *Écrits 1*, Paris: Éditions du Seuil.

Lacan, J. (1981) *The Seminar of Jacques Lacan: Book XI: The Four Fundamental Concepts of Psychoanalysis*, Jacques-Alain Miller (ed.), Alan Sheridan (trans.), New York: W.W. Norton.

Lacan, J. (1988) "Seminar on the Purloined Letter," Jeffrey Mehlman (trans.), in John P. Muller and William J. Richardson, *The Purloined Poe: Lacan, Derrida, and Psychoanalytic Reading*, Baltimore, MD: Johns Hopkins University Press, pp. 28–54.

Lacan, J. (1991) *The Seminar of Jacques Lacan: Book II: The Ego in Freud's Theory and in the Technique of Psychoanalysis, 1945–1955*, Sylvana Tomaselli (trans.), Jacques-Alain Miller (ed.), New York: W.W. Norton & Co.

Lessing, G.E. (2005) "Spinoza only put Leibniz on the track of [his theory of] pre-established harmony ([Letter] To Moses Mendelssohn)," in *Lessing: Philosophical and Theological Writings*, Robert Nisbett and Hugh Barr (eds), Cambridge: Cambridge University Press.

Lévi-Strauss, C. (1974) "Structural Study of the Myth," *Structural Anthropology*, Claire Jacobson and Brooke Grundfest Schoepf (trans.), New York: Basic Books.

Macherey, P. (1998) "The Hegelian Lure: Lacan as Reader of Hegel," in *In a Materialist Way: Selected Essays by Pierre Macherey*, Ted Stolze (trans.), Warren Montag (ed.), London: Verso.

Macherey, P. (2011) *Hegel or Spinoza*, Susan M. Ruddick (trans.), Minneapolis: University of Minnesota Press.

Marx, K. (1990) *Capital: A Critique of Political Economy (Volume 1)*, Ben Fowkes and David Fernbach (trans.), New York: Penguin.

Pfaller, R. (1998) "Negation and its reliabilities: An empty subject for ideology?" in *Cogito and the Unconscious*, Slavoj Žižek (ed.), Durham, NC: Duke University Press, pp. 225–246.

Spinoza, B. (1985) *The Collected Works of Spinoza*, Edwin Curley (trans.), Princeton, NJ: Princeton University Press.

Stolze, T. (1998) "Deleuze and Althusser: Flirting with Structuralism," *Rethinking Marxism*, 10(3): 51–63.

Virno, P. (2004) *A Grammar of the Multitude: For an Analysis of Contemporary Forms of Life*, Isabella Bertoletti, James Cascaito, and Andrea Casson (trans.), New York: Semiotext(e).

Žižek, S. (1989) *The Sublime Object of Ideology*, New York: Verso.

Žižek, S. (2004) *Organs Without Bodies: Deleuze and Consequences*, New York: Routledge.

Žižek, S. (2006) "The Antinomies of Tolerant Reason," in *A Glance into the Archives of Islam*, www.lacan.com/zizarchives.htm#_ftn7.

5 Value

The aesthetic itinerary from content to structure[1]

In this chapter I would like to pursue a brief intellectual history of the concept of value in modern Western aesthetics, which, as we shall see, is also marked by the same movement toward formalization and, eventually, structuralism.

Of all aesthetic concepts, value is one that brings to the foreground art's interconnection with, or non-autonomy from, or, even more precisely, structural and conceptual homology with, the other fundamental constituents of human life and society. These include, most conspicuously, economy and ethics, but ultimately discourse in its entirety as the conglomeration of all products of thought and practice, and their modes of representation. There are aesthetic, economic, ethical, scientific, social, and cultural values, with innumerous subsets of values within them; one could hardly find a domain of human life that is not inscribed by value. Of all these values, the aesthetic and the economic are historically the most recent, gradually emerging in what came to constitute the secular capitalist modern era; and the parallel histories of aesthetics and economics share also the modern trajectory of a concomitant, and homologous, development in both ethics and the discursive modes of representation.

Four continuous, yet distinct, movements can be discerned in this quadruple development: first, what we could call the moment of "ideal content," which, strictly speaking, is something between a residue of the past and an incubator of modern value, and, in its various modulations, lasts until Immanuel Kant's intervention; second, the paradigm of "abstractism" or "formalization," which constitutes a veritable break and traverses the era of the Enlightenment; third, the movement of "structuralism," inaugurated in Romanticism as a decisive advancement of the preceding; and, fourth, the moment of "performative self-referentiality," a consequence of the third, already intimated in Nietzsche and practically simultaneously formulated by Martin Heidegger and Walter Benjamin.

The common quest in the works of the pioneers of aesthetic theory in the second half of the eighteenth century prior to Kant's *Critiques,* such as Alexander Gottlieb Baumgarten, Johann Joachim Winckelmann, and Gotthold Ephraim Lessing, concerns the establishment of the ideal in relation to which to measure the aesthetic value of given works of art. These thinkers unapologetically propose their personal (and social-class) tastes and preferences, including concrete pieces of art, predominantly from Greco-Roman antiquity – Laocoön being a famous example – as the standards and ideals that contemporary artists should emulate in their themes and techniques. If I call this embryonic phase of aesthetic theory the movement of "ideal content," it is not because these theorists presuppose an ill-conceived opposition between form and content, while focusing on the latter; on the contrary, they are highly aware of the complexities involved in the cluster form-content, explicitly addressing them in their theories. Rather, I employ the term "content," retroactively, in the structuralist sense, as the filling that comes to occupy empty sites in a purely relational network (form). This formal network having not yet been conceived, all there is for the discourse of ideal content is exclusively content.

This initial state of discourse on aesthetics – or, rather, taste – is predicated on what was then called "allegory." Through works like Goethe's *Faust* and, eventually, Benjamin's work on *Trauerspiel*, this concept of "allegory" will, retroactively, come to mean what these later works define as "symbol" (see Benjamin 1977; and Flax 1983). That is, "concrete images and figures by which general concepts have been represented," and which, thanks to their pre-established and fixed signification, can, and should, be "conveniently classified, and so arranged as to instruct the artist in how to apply and interpret [them] in relation to possible individual cases" (Winckelmann 1985: 52–3). This is as much Winckelmann's definition of allegory as Benjamin's definition of symbol. Moreover, the movement of "ideal content" is exemplary of what Foucault calls "the *Classical episteme*," which is premised on its "relation to a knowledge of order," and is thus motivated by the desire for "taxinomia," classification, and encyclopedization (Foucault 1970: 71). For Winckelmann, the destiny and value of the entire artistic project are wholly dependent on the production of such catalogues, the absence of which is the source of all evil in the state of his contemporary arts. In his words: "Every painter … longs for some learned compendium he could consult, and from which he could extract significant and concrete signs to denote supra-sensory objects," and it is only "a more thorough study of allegory [that] might also purify our taste … and lend it sense and veracity" (Winckelmann 1985: 52–3). Predating its distinction from symbol, allegory is here a remnant of the dominant conceptualization of representational value "since the Stoics," according to which the sign is grounded on "similitudes that link the marks [significant] to the things [signified]," rendering this link "organic" (Foucault 1970: 42). Secular representation gradually collapses these "similitudes," after which "things and words were to be separated" – with Kant's severance of thing-in-itself and representation sealing this process – and signs would become arbitrary (Foucault 1970: 43).

The discourse of "ideal content" is, therefore, based on the triple premise: (a) that its object consists in defining good taste; (b) that this taste must be determined in reference to concrete ideals regarding both the artwork's topic ("content") and technical construction ("form"); and (c) that the presupposed contiguity of signs and their meaning relegates all human expression, including art, to the taxonomic archive – even as such presecular remnants begin to falter at that time (see Heeg 2000).

The gradual shift from the "organic" to the "arbitrary" conceptualization of semantic value corresponds to the economic shift from feudalism to "'mercantilism' [which] freed the value of money from … [its] intrinsic value of metal," so that "money (and even the metal …) receives its value" "from its form," the "image" imprinted on it, that is, "from its pure function as sign" (Foucault 1970: 175–7). Exchange-value as a differential system of purely immaterial abstract values will eventually find its systematic formulation in Marx, for whom there is "not an atom of matter" in "the objectivity of commodities as values," and "their objective character as values is" not natural but "purely social" (Marx 1990: 138–9).

Already in 1781, Kant expresses this tendency toward abstract relational form in his criticism of "the critique of taste," which consists of "putative rules or criteria [that] are merely empirical" and can "therefore never serve as *a priori* rules according to which our judgment of taste must be directed." Kant exhorts his contemporary "Germans" – who "are the only ones who now employ the word 'aesthetics' to designate that which others call the critique of taste" – either to "desist from the use of this term" or to form a radically new "transcendental aesthetic" that would consist of "nothing but empirical intuitions" from which, however, "we will … detach … everything that belongs to sensation, so that nothing remains except pure intuition and the mere form of appearances, which is the only thing that sensibility can make available *a priori*" (Kant 1998: 156–7; A21/B35, note, and A21–22/B36). The most immediate effect of this new tendency lies in the total degradation of technique as criterion of artistic value, since it pertains to the *a posteriori* empirical object of art. Johann Gottlieb Fichte illustrates the new trend about to change the *Zeitgeist* when he writes:

> People have often confused this facility of artistic technique with spirit itself. It is certainly the determining condition for the expression of spirit, and anyone who sets to work must already have acquired it; but it is not spirit … It is true that the lightest and most careless brushstroke executed by the genius will have a veneer of those ideas. But the mere technician will never with his highest skills produce anything but a mechanical work, which at the very most might induce one to marvel at its structure.
>
> (Fichte 1984a: 90)

However, this formalist move required further the separation of aesthetic value from use-value, anticipating Marx's separation of exchange-value from the "coarsely sensuous objectivity of ... physical objects" of utility (Marx 1990: 138). Through this movement, the modern concepts of aesthetic and economic values, and aesthetics and political economy as distinct fields, will emerge, as is succinctly illustrated in the shift from David Hume to Adam Smith.

In this context, I refer the reader to Howard Caygill's *Art of Judgement*, as well as John Guillory's chapter on Adam Smith in *Cultural Capital*, both of which provide excellent accounts of the itinerary of aesthetics and political economy, from their undifferentiated state in moral philosophy to their separation as distinct fields which required the mutual repression of one another and of their common origin. This common origin, moral philosophy, was the byproduct of the gradual emergence of civil society in the seventeenth and eighteenth centuries, as a formation whose rules and governance could no longer be derived either from divinity or from the state. The directly relevant point here is that the establishment of political economy and aesthetic theory as distinct fields presupposed the simultaneous emergence and separation of use-value and aesthetic value, a phenomenon which, by the mid-eighteenth century, was precipitated by the commodification of art.

Hume's utilitarianism stands with the one leg in the precapitalist past, insofar as "he could derive the sensation of beauty directly from the perception of utility ... as the source of 'approbation' or pleasure common to all made objects" (Guillory 1993: 308). There is not yet an essential distinction between works of art and objects of utility in Hume's continuum of "riches," all of which "have a direct reference to commodities, conveniences, and pleasures of life" (Hume 1975: 247). For Hume, "every work of art has also a certain end or purpose," but, having his other leg already in the world of the capitalist commodification of art, Hume does not find "the specification of the end [of art] ... as easy as in the case of 'tables [or] chairs'" (Guillory 1993: 309–10). In "order to maintain the reduction of beauty to utility," he introduces the "tenuous distinction between an immediate" utility, pertaining to objects of utility, and "a deferred utility," pertaining to artworks and resembling more "the pleasure of contemplating the beautiful objects of the rich man than it does the pleasure of possessing" them (Guillory 1993: 309–10).

Adam Smith's subsequent move, in his *Theory of Moral Sentiments* (1759), consists in interiorizing Hume's external distinction between artworks and the rest of commodities within the commodity in general, "between its being as means (its 'beauty') and its being as end (its 'use')." He did so by arguing that "the desire for the object exceeds the gratification supplied by its use," for, "if this were not the case, no economy would develop beyond the level of production requisite for satisfying the minimal needs of human existence" (Guillory 1993: 311). Thus, Smith establishes "aesthetic disposition" as the "invisible hand" or "motor of economic production" by finding "in the surplus 'beauty' of the commodity over its actual use the source of the social *surplus*, the explanation of 'wealth'" (Guillory 1993: 311–2). "Aesthetics and political economy were never closer than" in Smith's *Theory of Moral Sentiments*, "since they were *conjoined in the concept of the commodity*" as an object at once of utility and beauty (Guillory 1993: 315).

However, this conjunction of aesthetic and economic values could not last long because of the capitalist disequilibrium between production and consumption, which stubbornly belied moral philosophy's denial of the accumulation of surplus-value and its postulate that "the exchange-value of the commodity … was supposed to express *both* the labor entailed in the commodity's production *and* the desire provoked in the consumer for the 'use' of that commodity" (Guillory 1993: 313). Faced with the incommensurability between the economic cost of production and desire, and unwilling to acknowledge that capitalist economy is defined by precisely a *disequilibrium* between production and consumption – i.e., by the accumulation of surplus-value – Smith and the other classical economists "were forced to shift their analysis to the terrain of production" and to bracket "the realm of consumption" and desire "as irrelevant to the determination of price" (Guillory 1993: 314). Thus political economy emerged as a field severed from aesthetics at the same moment as Smith's notorious "invisible hand" of the market is reconceptualized in his *The Wealth of Nations* (1776) without any reference to aesthetics, exclusively in the utilitarian terms of self-interest:

> Every individual is continually exerting himself to find out the most advantageous employment for whatever capital he can command. It is his own advantage, indeed, and not that of society, which he has in view. But the study of his own advantage naturally, or rather necessarily leads him to prefer that employment which is most advantageous to the society.
>
> (Smith 2000: 482)

Yet, in this way, he is "led by an invisible hand to promote an end which was no part of his intentions … By pursuing his own interest he frequently promotes that of the society more effectually than when he really intends to promote it" (Smith 2000: 485). With this withdrawal of the beautiful and desire from the economic sphere, political economy departs on its solitary route, guided by the double utilitarianism of use-value and self-interest. Here production and consumption converge once again, but this time on the basis of the principle of need (as opposed to desire). Concomitantly, aesthetic theory is birthed on the premises of the non-utilitarian character of art and the non-self-interestedness of aesthetic contemplation.

Thus, the movement of formalization is marked by an abstraction from content, in both the structuralist sense and the utilitarian sense as a material thing (use-value) and (according to Kant, pathological) interest. Kant notoriously executed this movement on three levels: reason, ethics, and aesthetics. Kant was to define aesthetic judgment as "subjectively universal," something which Caygill characterizes as "a contradictory faculty" or "aporia," insofar as "it can be deduced neither a priori nor empirically but only from a 'feeling of pleasure'" supposed to hover in between (Guillory 1993: 318; Caygill 1989: 27). As Guillory writes, Caygill "rightly aligns the aporias of judgment with the disproportion of production and consumption," that is, with the aporia of surplus-value (Guillory 1993: 318). It is in the face of this aporia that Karl Marx will eventually, in the third (structuralist) movement, shift political economy away from use-value to exchange-value. Goods, Marx writes, become "commodities" only once they obtain, with the advent of the capitalist mode of production, "a dual nature" as "objects of utility and bearers of value," thus:

> possess[ing] a double form, i.e. natural form and value form … Not an atom of matter enters into the objectivity of commodity as values; in this it is the direct opposite of the coarsely sensuous objectivity of commodities as physical objects … Commodities possess an objective character as values only in so far as they are all expressions of an identical social substance, human labour, … their objective character as values is therefore purely social.
>
> (Marx 1990: 138–9)

In this move, Marx evacuates commodities of their content (use-value) and turns them into purely abstract values, whereby each commodity *qua* exchange-value is determined in its "social," that is, purely differential, relations to all other exchange-values or commodities. It is this same move of abstraction and formalization that was executed a century earlier in Kant's three critiques on the three levels of reason, ethics, and aesthetics. His categorical imperative – "Act only according to that maxim by which you can at the same time will that it should become a universal law" (Kant 1959: 39) – and his definition of the "beautiful … as the object of an entirely disinterested satisfaction," both aim at evacuating the law of all remnants of content, in both senses established by the utilitarianism of classical political economy: material things (use-value) and (according to Kant, pathological) interests. On the level of capitalist economy, this process of formalization engenders commodity fetishism, which means that human or social relations and object relations are expressed through the same language, so that value-relations are the relations of both things and humans. Similarly art is not autonomous from the relations of things and humans, at the same time that it retains its inalienable autonomy in its ability to undermine society.

As alluded to above by reference to Caygill, Kant's understanding of the aesthetic judgment differs from his understanding of ethics and reason, insofar as the latter two are based on the objective universality of the concept. For Kant, the aesthetic judgment involves subjective pleasure, for "from concepts there is no transition to the feeling of pleasure or pain [*Unlust*; displeasure]" (Kant 2000: 56; Kant 1974: 125; §6). That the aesthetic judgment is coupled with "a claim" not to objective but "to subjective universality" means that this judgment has the character of an "*as if*": "as if beauty were a characteristic of the object," and as if one had "reason for attributing a similar satisfaction to every one" (Kant 2000: 56; §6). Once again, the material things of perception (use-values) become irrelevant, since one only "speaks of beauty *as if* it were a property of things," while subjective universality is introduced, as "the judgment of taste itself does not *postulate* the agreement of every one … it only *imputes*" it (Kant 2000: 58, 62; §7, §8). One may be tempted to hear in Kant's characterization of beauty as an "as if" quality of the object the echo of the Democritian-Lockean "secondary qualities." However, the "secondary qualities" of the object, such as color or smell, are still too bound to the materiality of an object, even as they may be perceived subjectively in a distorted way, in comparison to something as abstract or immaterial as exchange-value, in which, to repeat Marx's words, there is "not an atom of matter." Particularly from Galileo onward, the distinction between primary and secondary qualities corresponds to the distinction between objective and subjective perception of *matter* (in both cases), as opposed to Kant's distinction between any perception of matter and a judgment that is altogether independent of matter, since it is only an "as if" quality of the object. In other words, prior to Kant's formalization, the distinction was matter-bound objective or true perception versus matter-bound subjective or distorted perception. With Kant (and definitely later, with Marx) the distinction becomes matter-bound perception (objective or subjective) versus perception and conception as the result of an autonomous abstract relational network. Furthermore, since these abstract relations delineate the limits of the possible and the impossible of any subjective determination, they allow subjectivity to lay claim to universality (as in Kant's "subjective universal").

This endeavor to refer the aesthetic judgment to an autonomous abstract relational network leads Kant to turn to "totality" through his linking of the aesthetic judgment to the moral "Ideal," which, "although we are not in possession of this, we yet strive to produce … in ourselves" (Kant 2000: 85; §17). Kant thus enables a redefinition of "beauty" as "the form of the *purposiveness* [*Zweckmäßigkeit*] in an object, so far as this is perceived in it *without any representation of a purpose* [*Zweck*]" (Kant 2000: 90; Kant 1974: 155; §17). Here, beauty is defined as a kind of teleology without *telos*, based on the model of reason's demand for the totality of experience (presented in Kant's first *Critique*). While *Zweck* pertains to natural determinism and to the faculty of understanding, which is concerned with concrete experience, *Zweckmäßigkeit* – like the *Gesetzmäßigkeit* (conformity to law) of pure reason – entails purposiveness or finality only in the sense of aiming at its own *totality*, beyond any particular end or interest. When anything existent attains its own highest *Zweckmäßigkeit* (totality) it experiences the feeling of pleasure. However, no human product, artistic or not, can comply with *Zweckmäßigkeit*, since its production is motivated by its producer's *end* or purpose of producing it. This impediment will lead Kant to shift the focus in the second part of the *Critique of Judgment* from the aesthetic to the teleological judgment, where it is admitted that only a thing that "bear(s) itself alternately as cause and as effect [[muß] … sich zu sich selbst wechselseitig als Ursache und Wirkung verhalten]" – an "*organised* and *self-organising being*" that causes itself as its own "*natural purpose* [*Naturzweck*]" – can fulfill the requirement of *Zweckmäßigkeit* (Kant 2000: 275, 278; Kant 1974: 320, 322; §65). However, the "*internal natural perfection*" of "*natural purposes* … [that] are … called organized beings, is not analogous to any physical, *i.e.* natural faculty known to us … it is not even thinkable or explicable by means of any exactly fitting analogy to human art" (Kant 2000: 279–80; §65). While nature "organise[s] itself and its organised products" according to the principle of "self-preservation," art presupposes "an artificer (a rational being) external to it" (Kant 2000: 278; §65). Thus, "the organisation of nature" becomes for Kant the surface on which to project a causal model that "has in it nothing analogous to any causality we know," including in art and its subjective universality (Kant 2000: 279; §65).

Kant's favoring of natural beauty as the ideal of beauty may have served, as Caygill, and Guillory after him, point out, subsequent philosophers to repress the process of production and the "invisible hands [of] the wage-laborers of manufacture" (Guillory 1993: 312; see also Caygill 1989, particularly "Part 2: Taste and Civil Society," 38–102). Yet Kant's own "enlightened"-bourgeois approach has no difficulty in *consciously* justifying their exploitation and oppression. For instance, having established that the only "ultimate purpose" that we can adequately ascribe "to the human race," Kant states: "The culture of the *skill* is indeed the chief subjective condition of aptitude for furthering one's purposes in general" (Kant 2000: 355: §83), and then concludes, with the characteristic cynicism of self-righteous bourgeoisie:

> Skill cannot not be developed in the human race except by means of inequality among men; for the great majority provide the necessities of life, as it were, mechanically, without requiring any art in particular, for the convenience and leisure of others who work at the less necessary elements of culture, science and art.
>
> (Kant 2000: 356; §83)

By contrast, what Kant finds unbearable and is indeed forced to repress, at the very moment that he discovers it, is the conceptual "aporia" behind the "contradictory faculty" of a judgment that, to repeat Caygill's objection, "can be deduced neither a priori nor empirically" but from *a subjective, yet not empirically grounded* "'feeling of pleasure'" (Guillory 1993: 318; Caygill 1989: 27). This can be the case only if this judgment is based on an aspect of subjectivity that both precedes any experience of the subject and, since it is not *a priori*, presupposes the empirical world. In other words, the aesthetic judgment comes logically both before and after experience, it is *both a priori* and *a posteriori*, it is *both its own cause and effect*. This is to say that Kant did, as we saw above, discover that aesthetic pleasure involves this *Zweckmäßigkeit* – something that, to repeat his words, "bear(s) itself alternately as cause and as effect" – but was unwilling to accept this insight. For Kant could explain such a, to his mind, paradoxical causality only in terms or either "hylozoism" or the presupposition of "organised matter as the instrument of … [an external] soul" (Kant 2000: 279; §65) – that is, only through conclusions that would amount to the collapse of Enlightenment rationality. Now, as we have seen on several occasions in the present work, this ostensibly paradoxical causal relation is established in Marx's theory of commodity fetishism and, already more than a century before Kant, in Spinoza's *Ethics* (1677): "God is the immanent, not the transitive, cause of all things," an "immanent" cause being precisely a cause that is itself the effect of its own effects (*Ethics* IP18). However, the question remains, particularly at the peak of the Enlightenment: what is to be understood under the term "God"? Thus, this aporia will be bequeathed to the Romantics.

Their movement will consist in the reconceptualization of form as veritable structure. As we know from the third chapter here, the primary precondition of structure is the existence of a third order or symbolic element, beyond the "one" and the "two," "a third at once unreal, and yet not imaginable" (Deleuze 2004: 172). This "eminently symbolic … object = x," which, to repeat Deleuze's words, "belongs to no series" but "is nevertheless present in both," is in fact timidly pointed to already by Kant, as "the transcendental subject of thoughts = x," which is "represented," but only as a "wholly empty representation (*Vorstellung*)," "through this I, or He, or It (the thing) which thinks" (Deleuze 2004: 184–5; Kant 1998: 414; A346/B404). If Fichte, Schlegel, Novalis, and other Romantics see in Kant's advancement a failure to ground adequately thought and the phenomenon of self-consciousness, it is because of Kant's persistence on a dualistic mirroring between subject and object, the transcendental "I" and "the thing" (that thinks). Kant failed to conceive of this third, symbolic dimension, as that which is at once presupposed for conscious experience and is its effect.

The solution to this problem will come from Friedrich Wilhelm Joseph von Schelling, in his *System of Transcendental Idealism*. There Schelling claims that "in order to understand philosophy" we must presuppose that we are "at once that which is intuited … and that which intuits" (Schelling 1976: 355). This means that we must see the process of self-consciousness as an "*organization*" that encompasses in itself the passage "from simple matter to organization," through which "unconsciously productive nature returns into itself" (Schelling 1976: 377). This "organization" consists of four logical levels, of which "nature" or the object "lacks only the final," which is the exclusive prerogative of thought or consciousness (Schelling 1976: 376).

Here follow the four levels. "At the beginning the absolutely identical principle divides itself … [into] subject and object," but only a third gaze, that of "the philosopher," can intuit their difference. In the "second self-intuition … the ego intuits … the objective aspect of its activity, which occurs in sensation," and thereby becomes "*an object for itself*," whereas before "it was object and subject only for the philosopher" (Schelling 1976: 375). In the "third self-intuition," the ego intuits its own act of sensing and thus "becomes an object for itself also as sensing," whereby "the previously subjective phase in the ego [sensing] is transposed into an objective phase," and "the ego, consequently, is now … *wholly* objective," that is, nature or "simple matter": that initial "identical principle" of objectivity (presupposed and split on the first level) that is "simultaneously subject and object" (Schelling 1976: 375). To put it simply, the moment I see myself, my self becomes the object (or natural product) of my self-intuition, and then, in the next stage, I see myself seeing myself, whereupon this latter "I" becomes the new object of my self-intuition, and so on. If this process continued like this, "self-intuition could potentiate itself on and on to infinity" and "the series of products in nature would merely be increased, but consciousness would never arrive" (Schelling 1976: 376). There must, therefore, be an "intuitive activity … to the second power, i.e., a purposive activity, which is, however, unconsciously purposive" (Schelling 1976: 376). That is, this exceptional intuitive activity must be capable of intuiting all preceding phases of intuition but *incapable of intuiting its own act of intuiting*. For, if it did, it would objectify its own act of intuiting and thus recommence the series of objectifications, turning everything into nature, while consciousness never arrives.

In order to halt the sequence of intuitions or reflective acts, therefore, a "ground" must be presupposed, which "can only lie outside the ego," that is, there must be "another rational being," beyond the ego, which is unconscious of its own reflective activity (Schelling 1976: 376). In other words, a *consciousness unconscious of itself* must be presupposed in nature – "*natura prior*" (Schelling 1976: 377) – as *a thing that thinks*. This thing does not belong to any of the series of objects and subjects constituted throughout the process of reflective acts. Rather, it is present in both as that which prevents the two series of subject and object from collapsing onto one another and regressing to the "absolutely identical principle" of subject and object of nature. When we arrive at the fourth level we realize that the philosopher's gaze that Schelling felt compelled to presuppose at the outset is the real surplus to the series of both objects and subjects: not the self-consciousness of the philosopher, but that which thinks in the philosopher – the unconscious.

As is known, Paul de Man has reproached Romanticism for staging a case of "aesthetic ideology," by which he means the desire for identity between subject and object (see Paul de Man 1996). However, as follows from Schelling's invocation of the unconscious as the third requirement for accounting for both subject and object, Romanticism is not trapped in the imaginary mirroring de Man has in mind. Rather, as Jochen Schulte-Sasse puts it in his response to de Man, by "address[ing] the desire for … unity … in a way that preempts the obfuscation of that desire," Romanticism shows that this ground is a "necessary illusion," an "impossibility," or in Schlegel's words, undoubtedly "a *fiction*. But an absolutely necessary one" (Schulte-Sasse 1997: 21, 19, citing Schlegel 1958: 4; III B; see also de Man 1983). Hölderlin's premonition about developing an epistemological theory doomed to "cancel itself as something undifferentiable" and, thus, to "become an empty infinity" (Hölderlin 1988: 70–1), applies not to Romanticism but, rather, to (de Manian) irony – the eternal ironization/objectification of one's own reflective act. If such irony were indeed the ultimate ground of thought, it would preempt the possibility of any action, including the decision of undertaking the project to write on irony, whether seriously or ironically.

As necessary fiction – a transcendental function presupposed for the distinction between subject and object throughout the reflective series – unconscious consciousness (object=x) is the cause and effect of the series. To repeat, this is the secular God, as Jacques Lacan's "true formula of atheism," "God is unconscious," indicates (Lacan 1981: 59). *Qua* immanent cause, object=x is both exception to and a member of the series – not unlike capital in economic value. "By treating capital … [or] money" – which classical economists considered an absolute exception to the other commodities – "as a commodity," Marx "identifies a paradox in which a class of the meta-level [capital] descends to the object level [commodity] … to become a member of itself" (Karatani 1995: 69–70). All three, capital and (secular) language and consciousness, are self-referential – self-referentiality being in fact inseparable from structurality. However, before we focus on this point that will bring us to the next movement in the itinerary of aesthetic value, let us examine a few other aspects of Romanticism.

Regarding the acknowledged relation between Romanticism and psychoanalysis, the present exposition indicates that their commonality consists in their shared structuralist logic. Emblematic of this logic is what, through Freud, was to become known as the drive – that is, the death drive, in its inseparability from the pleasure principle or Eros. In Romanticism we find this concept in Fichte's aesthetic theory. Fichte establishes drive as the precondition and motor of artistic production as follows:

> Totally apart from all external experience and without any outside help the artist develops from the depths of his nature [Gemüth] what lies hidden from all in the human soul; … guided by his powers of divination he sets forth the characteristics common to the whole humanity, which have not shown themselves as such in any previous experience. But the one thing in man which is independent and utterly incapable of being determined from outside we call "drive" [Trieb].
>
> (Fichte 1984a: 79)

Next, Fichte defines beauty as the corollary of the feeling of pleasure, in opposition to displeasure, by invoking the analogy to magnetism:

> Let [a magnet] attract a piece of iron: its drive expresses itself and is satisfied … i.e., a feeling of pleasure[] would necessarily be aroused in it. If on the other hand we allow the weight of the iron to exceed the force of the magnet, then the drive still remains inside it … but it is not satisfied … then it must necessarily feel a resistance to … its force. In a word, it must feel displeasure. This is the sole force of all pleasure and displeasure.
>
> (Fichte 1984a: 82)

Beauty is complete "harmony," reminiscent of what Freud would call the "oceanic feeling," as "under [the artist's] influence the mass … actually comes together as one soul," so "that all individual differences in disposition and feeling disappear," and all that remains is "the common disposition [Universalsinn] of collective humanity" or materiality, magnet and iron (Fichte 1984a: 78). Recalling Deleuze, in the death drive, all individual "agents" involved in the act are "themselves annihilated," as are all temporal distinctions, so that, as Jean-Paul Sartre had put it, "Present, Past, Future" occur "all at the same time" (Deleuze 1994: 111; Sartre 1992: 202). As Deleuze continues, the "pure and empty form of time," devoid of any "temporal content," can emerge as, to use Spinoza's term, a species of eternity – the (a)temporality presupposed for the emergence of the signifier, or, inversely put, for the introduction of the subject into language (Deleuze 1994: 86, 110). This is why, again we recall, in the dimension of Thanatos or Eros, at the very moment that "the passive ego becomes narcissistic, the activity must be *thought*" (Deleuze 1994: 110), or, as Fichte intimates:

> the drive which we have just named the aesthetic … is directed toward a representation … exclusively for the sake of its determination [Bestimmung] and its determination as pure representation. As far as this drive is concerned, the representation is an end in itself. It does not derive its value from harmonizing with the object … It is not the replication of reality but a free unrestrained form of the image that is

> sought. Without any interdetermination [Wechselbestimmung] between it and an object such a representation stands isolated as the ultimate goal of the drive.
>
> (Fichte 1984a: 81)

Here we cannot fail to hear the echo of Freud's claim that, in Laplanche and Pontalis's words cited in the third chapter here, "the drive becomes auto-erotic, only after the loss of the object" (LP 2003: 132). As we have seen in that chapter, the loss of the object amounts to the transition from need to desire, the latter involving *totality*, that is, the identity of "indestructible life" (*potentia*) and "the locus of the Other, insofar as it is there that the first signifier emerges" (Lacan 1981: 197–8). In Romanticism, art becomes the blueprint for what structuralism, as the known historical movement, will later call the signifier.

So far we have formulated structuralist self-referentiality in two ways. First, Marx's account of money enabled us to describe it in terms of the not-all set in set theory, as money is both a member of the set of all commodities and its exception. This is the case not only with money but with every structure: every structure is a not-all set, which is also to say it is self-referential. For instance, natural language: we attempt to formalize it, to reduce it "to certain symbols," the "interpretation or definition of the symbolic form must be executed by natural language itself" (Karatani 1995: 62). This indicates "not only the impossibility of metalanguage, but also the impossibility of natural language as a foundation. Accordingly, we can say that natural language is itself this loop" (Karatani 1995: 62) – the loop that we have seen as the immanent relation of cause and effect. This immanent relation between cause and effect is the second way in which we have formulated the self-referentiality of structure – the two ways being expressions of one and the same logic, the logic of structure. As we shall shortly see, the fourth movement in the itinerary of value reflects direct consequences of structural self-referentiality.

Let us pause here to reflect further on the consequences of immanent causality since its philosophical formulation by Spinoza – a formulation that evidently indicates that immanent causality has, on some level, been discursively operative throughout all secular capitalist modernity since the seventeenth century. It seems to me that it is no exaggeration to argue that the other major secular invention next to subjectivity, history and historical consciousness, had to be conceived in teleological terms as precisely a defense against immanent causality – a thesis corollary to the one advanced in the preceding chapter about the correlation between monism and dialectics. It is astonishing to see the inability of the eighteenth- and (at least early) nineteenth-century discourses to conceive of any alternative to teleological historical time other than the presecular faith in a preordained divine order. For instance, Fichte states in "Of Rulers [*Regenten*]," one of the series of lectures he gave *On the Nature of the Scholar*:

"He who undertakes to guide his age and direct and order its constitution … knows the particular form that it has assumed at the present time, and the new forms through which it must be led nearer and nearer to its unattainable ideal" (Fichte 1984b: 103). Here we can already see, as David Simpson points out in his introductory remarks to Fichte's work, that "the extent to which Fichte anticipates Hegel in this respect" cannot be overstated (Simpson 1984: 72). Fichte continues to describe the ruler: "No part of its present form is, in his view, necessary and unchangeable, but is only an accidental point in a progression by which it is constantly rising towards higher perfection … He who cannot look upon human affairs with this unfettered vision is never a ruler, whatever station he may occupy, nor can he ever become one. His mode of thought itself, and his faith in the unchangeableness of the present, places him in a state of subordination and makes him an instrument of whoever created that arrangement of things in whose permanence he believes" (Fichte 1984b: 103–4). History is made out of rulers who know where the future leads, and the absence of such knowledge amounts to the static fatalism of a creationist religion. If these are the sole alternatives, then Hegel had all the good reasons to "misread" Spinoza's substance under the species of eternity as the nemesis of history.

As a consequence of structural self-referentiality, the last movement in the itinerary of modern value postulates that any human product – intellectual, manual, artistic, and their combinations – must relate to the rest of the world as its immanent cause and effect. This relation is expressed in "performativity," as understood in speech-act theory as the function of language to perform the reality it describes, whereby reality is both the cause and effect of language, and vice versa. That John L. Austin and John Searle ascribed performativity to all signification and not only to art, and that through this move the boundaries between signification and action tumbled: all of this results as much from the total economic expansion of the commodification of all production, including artistic, as from the increasing homogenization of secular historical consciousness under the aegis of immanent causality. This performativity entails a radical indeterminability regarding both the direction between cause and effect (due to their immanent relation) and the purpose of whatever is performed (due to the absence of will in the unconscious). This is the meaning of the fact that, again in Karatani's words, "a self-referential formal system … is devoid of both base and center; it is multicentered and excessive" (Karatani 1995: 62) – which is different from saying it has no center. Rather, the excessiveness of centers means that any "attempt to reduce [the self-referential formal system] to a stable form or structure inevitably results in undecidability" regarding both causes and purposes (Karatani 1995: 64). When Smith was replacing the "invisible hand" of God with that of the market, be it of artistic sensitivities or plainly utilitarian, he could still be certain that it was a benevolent hand. In the time of performative self-referentiality, the knowledge that the hand in question is our own "unconscious hand" allows for unforeseen fantasies that range from conspiratorial absolute control or the terror of radical indifference to a nightmare of humans' inhuman self-destruction. These contradictory tendencies are unified in the horrors of the various twentieth-century totalitarianisms.

In the aftermath of these forms of totalitarianism – about which both Foucault and Giorgio Agamben concur that they are manifestations of biopolitics[2] – we arrive at the era of global capital and its market. As we have seen in the first chapter, this is the era of full-fledged commodity fetishism, which means that "the constitution of the world is not … the work of a subject, but a genesis of subjectivity (*a* form of determinate historical subjectivity) as part (and counterpart) of the social world of objectivity" (Balibar 2007: 67). To refresh further our memory, this simultaneous genesis of objectivity and subjectivity is determined not by the content of these objects or "the personalities" of the subjects, which become "entirely interchangeable," but by their "relations of exchange" and the "fluctuation of values" (Balibar 2007: 58). If objects and subjects appear as bearing no inherent qualities but are rather constituted purely through "relations of exchange," then they appear only as expressions of value. Accordingly, subjects and objects appear to be constituted through formal relations with all other objects or subjects, as members of purely differential structures. This is the postmodern, global capitalist version of the ecstatic fusion with all, where everything becomes one. It is no accident that here we may hear the echoes of the Dionysian "gospel of universal harmony," the "intoxication" of the "glorious satisfaction of the primordial One," of which Nietzsche thought that we are deprived in our societies and for which art was supposed to make up (Nietzsche 1956: 23–4).

To be sure, one of the reasons for which Nietzsche was so enthusiastically received as a forerunner of modernism (and even postmodernism) is that he nailed down the mode of its suffering. This he described in his reinterpretation of the classical view of ancient Greek art. Nietzsche saw in this art an expression of blissful union with both nature and gods – but only as a schizoid reaction formation. The Greeks – "a race so hypersensitive, so emotionally intense, so equipped for suffering" – "were keenly aware of the terrors and horrors of existence"; therefore, they "had to place before them the shining fantasy of the Olympians" in order "to be able to live at all" (Nietzsche 1956: 29–30). Nietzsche's reevaluation of art as an (Apollonian) defense mechanism against life's sufferings indeed reflects something of the anxiety underpinning the movement of performative self-referentiality since modernism. Where Nietzsche fails is in grasping that what he still perceives as a (Dionysian) yearning is already happening in reality. Like totalitarianism, Nietzsche turned the fact of the trans-individual constitution of any individual (subject or object) within the world of capital into a promise of the dissolution of identity and complete self-forgetfulness, a world-to-come in which "each individual becomes not only reconciled to his fellow but actually at one with him" and "forgets himself completely," as the "shattering of [Schopenhauer's] *principium individuationis*" will finally occur. This Dionysian call hides the *fait accompli* that is the *very cause* of the modernist suffering (Nietzsche 1956: 22–4). It is because people already *were* cogs in the industrialist and bureaucratic machine that they were fascinated by the call of totalitarianism's Nietzschean twist to forget themselves in massive party rallies and in the mass destruction of World War II – for mobilizing themselves toward the attainment of *this goal* gives them the illusion that they are not yet *it*.

This misperception of the given state of affairs as a desired goal relates to the illusory inversion between cause and effect, which, according to Spinoza, is the basis of all superstition. As Spinoza writes in his breathtaking appendix of part I in the *Ethics*, this inversion produces "superstition" because people are "conscious of their volitions and desires" but "ignorant" of "the causes that have determined them to desire" (*Ethics* I appendix). This means that they mistake the *goal* of their desires for the *cause* of their desires, which is the constitutive mechanism of superstition. According to Althusser's more secular parlance, this same mechanism is the basis of ideology. Althusser acknowledges Spinoza's statements in this appendix as "the matrix of every possible theory of ideology," since it describes how "the human subject endowed with finalized desires projects himself into God as the original and final cause of the Universe," and, therefore, "of all meaning" (Althusser 1997: 7).

To return to Nietzsche and the issue of individuality, what we have here is a total repression of the fundamental constitution of individuality (whether of subjects or objects) that returns into consciousness in its inverted form, as the opposite kind of individuality, accompanied by the wish for a return to the first "lost" kind of individuality. I am presently going to spell out this process, but also note that this is a concrete application to individuality of the general mechanism of repression and its return, and that in the last chapter we shall see this mechanism applied to eternity.

To spell out the logic of repression in the context of individuality, we turn to Spinoza, one of Nietzsche's favorite philosophers and the blueprint for Schopenhauer's own understanding of individuality. According to Spinoza, individuality is, in Balibar's words, "transindividuality, or a 'transindividual process of individuation'" (Balibar 1993: 12). Equal emphasis must be placed on "trans-" and on the word "process," that is, no individual is ever a finished product but always a becoming. The unity of an individual, itself "composed of … parts," "relates [the individual] to an infinite multiplicity of other individuals" (Balibar 1993: 8, 15). Subjects are not discrete entities but are always caught up in an immanent network in which they are actively further individuated or produced. It is in this sense that Balibar argues that "'substance' and 'individuality' are reciprocal concepts," that is, "'substance' (or God, or Nature) is an infinite process of production of multiple individuals, whereas 'individuals,' being all different and all causally dependent, are the necessary existence of the substance" (Balibar 1993: 8). This is exactly what it means when Spinoza asserts that substance is the "immanent, not the transitive, cause of all things": substance does not externally cause modes or individuals to exist but, rather, substance actualizes itself as these modes of empirical existence (*Ethics* I, P18). In short, "'substance' is nothing other than the individuals" (Balibar 1993: 8).

The above is precisely what is repressed through and in the ideology of "individualism," according to which the individual is an autonomous, clearly delineated entity, in opposition to the collective. In its desperate urge to return to this "lost" (because repressed) transindividuality, the individualistically self-perceived individual will jump into any ersatz, any imitation of transindividuality, such as the mass group under the fascination of the leader or of the football team or the rock star. Who would not be fascinated by Nietzsche's "mystic philosophy" of "a recognition that whatever exists is of a piece, and that individuation is the root of all evil"? Who would not hail "a conception of art as the sanguine hope that the spell of individuation may yet be broken, as an augury of eventual reintegration"? (Nietzsche 1956: 67). That the difference between Spinoza and Nietzsche is so subtle, almost imperceptible except on the level of rhetoric – which is perhaps why this is the most philosophical level – is not irrelevant to the fact that we are in the era of performative self-referentiality with its extreme ambivalence and undecidability.

This precariousness is further intensified when performative self-referentiality becomes manifest in economics as financial capital – that is, not real, but "nominal" or "signaling" or "productive" capital, presupposed for its own production – particularly as it renders financial prognosis more uncertain than ever. The anxiety arising from the dilemma of the effect that knows that it is its own arbitrary cause finds two (more or less simultaneous) formulations in the field of aesthetics through Heidegger and Benjamin.

If Heidegger is recurrently forced to bend the German language into a grimace of the Greek μέση φωνή (middle voice), so that "*die Welt weltet* [*the world worlds*]," it is because in that "setting-into-work of truth" that we call "art," "truth is both the subject and the object of the setting," even as "subject and object are unsuitable names" for what is meant here (Heidegger 2008: 352, 357; Heidegger 1960: 41, 79–80). Heidegger's collapse of the opposition between subject and object aims at establishing the emergence of truth not as an action that involves an agent and an object, but as precisely a μέση φωνή, a process in which truth or the world is its own cause and origin, the "primal" or "founding leap" (*Ursprung*) through which truth or the world brings itself "into being out of the source of its nature" (Heidegger 2008: 357; Heidegger 1960: 80). "One of the ways in which truth" or the world "happens is the work-being of the work" of art, given that "the setting up of a world and the setting forth of earth are two essential features in the work-being of the work" of art (Heidegger 2008: 355, 353; Heidegger 1960: 54, 45).

Put differently, "men and animals, plants and things, are never present and familiar as unchangeable objects, only to represent incidentally also a fitting environment for" the work of art, "which one fine day is added to what is already there"; rather, "we think of all this in reverse order," so that it is the work of art that, "in its standing there, first gives to things their look and to men their outlook on themselves" (Heidegger 2008: 352; Heidegger 1960: 38–9, 41). Therefore, the art's "setting up" means that "*the work lets the earth be an earth*," just as it lets the world be a world in that it allows it "to liberate the Open and to establish it in its structure," which is what makes it a world and not just an undifferentiatable Open (Heidegger 2008: 353; Heidegger 1960: 44, 41–2). Thus, "the all-governing expanse of this open relational context" "acquires the shape of destiny for human being" and forms "the world of this historical people," and it is in the "decisions of our history" that the "world worlds" (Heidegger 2008: 351–2; Heidegger 1960: 37, 41). The decisions of history are the destiny of human beings. "In setting up a world," that is, history, the work of art "does not cause the material to disappear, but rather causes it to come forth for the very first time … as the work sets itself back into the massiveness and heaviness of stone" (Heidegger 2008: 353; Heidegger 1960: 42–4). "That into which the work sets itself back and which it causes to come forth in this setting back of itself we called the earth" (Heidegger 2008: 353; Heidegger 1960: 42–4). World is history, earth is nature.

Thus, "world and earth are essentially different from one another and yet are never separated" but rather constantly engaged in "a striving," "battle," or "struggle" that aims not at their "destruction" but is rather the precondition for "the opponents [to] raise each other into the self-assertion of their natures." On the one hand, the world is history and destiny, in which "the holy is opened up as holy and the god is invoked into the openness of his presence" – in exactly the same way as "the sculpture of the god … is not a portrait … [but] rather it is a work that lets the god himself be present and thus *is* the god himself." On the other hand, the earth, as "that whence the arising brings back and shelters everything that arises without violation," that is, as the irrevocable sedimentation of this "consecrate[d]" history, the "*phusis*" or "ground in which man bases his dwelling" (Heidegger 2008: 352–4, 351–2; Heidegger 1960: 46–7, 38–40). In short, nature is fossilized culture, with culture fermenting itself in a historical destiny made out of decisions.

In this *coincidentia oppositorum*, it is only a matter of a slippery inflection to see either fatalism creep in – through, for instance, statements such as "world is the ever-nonobjective to which we are subject" – or decisionism, whether of the revolutionary or the authoritarian type – such as in Heidegger's own concluding invitation to take a side regarding the "either-or and its decision," at the ever-present moment, between "whether art can be an origin and then must be a head start, or whether it is to remain a mere appendix and then can only be carried along as a routine cultural phenomenon" (Heidegger 2008: 352, 357; Heidegger 1960: 41, 81). This is more or less the general Heideggerian middle-voice version of performative self-referentiality.[3]

At the same time, focusing on particularly the technological equipment, Benjamin discovers that the "illusionary nature" of technologically reproducible art is "of the second degree," insofar as "the mechanical equipment has penetrated so deeply into reality that its pure aspect [is] freed from the foreign substance of equipment" (Benjamin 2008: 335). In a film, for instance, one can no longer say this is the extent to which the work of art represents authentic reality, and this is the extent to which this reality is adulterated by the intervention of technology. Because of this "thoroughgoing permeation of reality with mechanical equipment," technologically reproduced art "offers ... an aspect of reality which is free of all equipment," and which is structured according to "a new law" which had remained hitherto unknown or unnoticed, just as "fifty years ago," prior to psychoanalysis, "a slip of the tongue passed more or less unnoticed" (Benjamin 2008: 335–6). Technologically reproducible art, and particularly "film has enriched our field of perception with methods which can be illustrated by those of Freudian theory," that is, "the camera introduces us to unconscious optics as does psychoanalysis to unconscious impulses" (Benjamin 2008: 336–7). Echoing Heidegger's rhetoric, we can say that, in expressing the new unconscious laws (the being and truth) of humans and reality, psychoanalysis and mechanically reproducible art let impulses and reality *be* impulses and reality. The undecidability of this performative self-referentiality between art and reality is here reflected in the "either-or" with which Benjamin frames his essay.

As is well known, in this essay Benjamin attributes the "aura" of the work to "its unique existence in time and space" and then proceeds to declare its elimination due to the artwork's reduction to reproducible and exchangeable commodities, since, "by making many reproductions" art "substitutes a plurality of copies for a unique existence" (Benjamin 2008: 329).[4] In the preface of this essay, Benjamin frames this elimination of the "aura" of the work or art as having a "prognostic value" analogous to that of Marx's prophesy of "what could be expected in the future" from "the basic conditions underlying capitalist production." This prophesy, in Benjamin's and generally in the early twentieth-century left reading, is of course to "make it possible to abolish capitalism itself." Accordingly, Benjamin's own "theses about the developmental tendencies of art under present conditions of production" are heralded by himself as the unmistakable "weapon ... useful for the formulation of revolutionary demands in the politics of art" toward the realization of "the masses['] ... right to change property relations," and as "completely useless for the purposes of

Fascism" (Benjamin 2008: 327–8, 338). In the epilogue, however, the weapon seems to have changed hands in this unbridled circulation of values, as it is now "Fascism," with its "imperialistic warfare," that realizes that "mass movements, including war, constitute a form of human behavior which particularly favors mechanical equipment" and that, consequently, "war and war only can set a goal for mass movements on the largest scale while respecting the traditional property system" (Benjamin 2008: 339, 343, n. 31). Putting the preface and the epilogue together, it follows that mechanical reproducibility provides conditions that can enable the dissolution of property as much as its sustenance by means of war. Performative self-referentiality lends itself to such mirror-like reversals regarding the future.

In the same essay Benjamin introduces the logic that would become Adorno's trademark. This occurs in the epilogue, in the context of Benjamin's comments on Marinetti's futurist manifesto, whose "formulations deserve to be accepted by dialecticians," revealing the truth of "the aesthetics of today's war ... as follows":

> If the natural utilization of productive forces is impeded by the property system, the increase in technical devices, in speed, and in the sources of energy will press for an unnatural utilization, and this is found in war ... Imperialistic war is a rebellion of technology which collects, in the form of "human material," the claims to which society has denied its natural material.
>
> (Benjamin 2008: 339)

Benjamin's suggestion that in society there is a function (in this case, war) that expresses, and can even profit from, that which society denies, will eventually become the core of Adorno's negative dialectic. In Adorno's application of the negative dialectic to aesthetics, war is replaced with art. Thus, performative self-referentiality comes to mean that "art is the social antithesis of society," that is, "works of art are after-images or replicas of empirical reality, inasmuch as they proffer to the latter what in the outside world is denied them" (Adorno 1984: 11, 6). More specifically, as Adorno states, echoing Marx's conception of religion – whose logic indeed anticipates the negative dialectic[5] – "the moment of unreality and non-existence in art is not independent of the existent, as though it were posited or invented by some arbitrary will. Rather, the moment of unreality is a structure resulting from quantitative relations between elements of being, relations which are in turn a response to, and an echo of, the imperfections of real conditions, their constraints, their contradictions, and their potentialities" (Adorno 1984: 10). Or, just as in the face of a "dream of a better life," one should not forget "the fact that such dreams should recall the negativity from which they were forcibly extracted" (Adorno 1984: 17). This is why "works of art do not lie; what they say is literally true," since it is "the unresolved antagonisms of reality [that] reappear in art in the guise of immanent problems of artistic form" (Adorno 1984: 8). Hence, "all art contains in itself a negative moment from which it tries to get away" (Adorno 1984: 16). This is why art "is defined by its relation to what is different from art," its "real other," as well as why "art has a twofold essence, being both an autonomous entity and a social fact," as opposed to the idealist "absolute freedom in art," which remains blind to and "contradicts the abiding unfreedom of the social whole" (Adorno 1984: 4, 10, 8, 1). These principles of negative dialectic allow us to "conceive of the world of art in terms of its ability to hold on to the negativity of the real and to enter into a definite relation to it" (Adorno 1984: 17).

They also force us to reinterpret the Enlightenment passion for contemplative "disinterestedness" in the face of art, and to understand that "works of art necessarily evolve in a dialectic of interests and disinterestedness" (Adorno 1984: 17). By this, Adorno means that "there is a grain of validity even in the contemplative attitude toward art, inasmuch as it underscores the important posture of art's turning away from immediate praxis and refusing to play the world game" of a "society" that is "dominated as it is by brutal self-interest" (Adorno 1984: 17). The "most important taboo" of the bourgeois disinterested artistic reaction "prohibits an animal-like desire toward the object" of art (Adorno 1984: 16).

Yet, Adorno's argument remains predicated on the assumption that the market is populated by self-interested individuals – not unlike the market in Adam Smith's mind. Accordingly, Adorno infers that the goal of art is to entice individuals to act not motivated by self-interest. Adorno is here not realizing that he is referring to an already bygone era, or, differently put, that he is replicating Nietzsche's fallacy. For, as we have already seen, the myth of the self-interested individuals has long ceased to hold sway. In the era of commodity fetishism and performative self-referentiality, the anxiety of the people concerns increasingly their self-experience as anonymous pawns of the market rather than competing self-interested individuals. If eventually Adorno turns to Kafka, as an exemplary case of (progressive) modernist literature, it is because Kafka is a pioneer in sensing, and expressing, the death of this myth. At the same time that it appears that, in Adorno's words, Kafka's work "does anything but appeal to our faculty of desire," calling "forth in us responses of real anxiety … [that] seem to be the opposite of desire," in truth it only "enable[s] desire to survive in art," since "these phenomena of psychic defense and rejection have more in common with desire than with the old Kantian disinterestedness" (Adorno 1984: 18). For Adorno, Kafka stands for art in its post-bourgeois-disinterested phase because he makes an appeal to our anxiety and our psychic organization as the last haven of some sense of singularity or even humanity within our machinic collectivization. Far from being mutually exclusive, transindividuality is the precondition of singularity. Yes, when transindividuality is experienced as

Gleichschaltung – in all its more or less related variations, bureaucratic, totalitarian, biopolitical – then an extra appeal to singularity becomes necessary. Ever since, as performance art and other forms of postmodern art indulge in reconfirming, desire and self-interest are the true negative "after-image" of the capitalist mode of production.

For, brainwashed by utilitarianism and humanism alike, consumers and producers may imagine that we act according to our own interests and desires, or for that matter, the interest and benefit of the community, but, as Hegel, the master of the imaginary, shows us, this is just our defense against our fear that we are pawns in the hands of the "Spirit of History." To be sure, this is no longer the ever-young "Spirit of History" of the State-type ideology, the future Ideal to be obtained in a future that never arrives; rather this is the over-matured Spirit of a History that has long reached its end. If we perceive ourselves as pawns of anything today, it is the accumulation of surplus-value. What is worse, far from being a clear-cut external imposition on humanity, surplus-value, as the concept of performative self-referentiality indicates, is a modulation, however distorted, of our own – human, economic, and technological – unconscious.

Notes

1 This chapter pursues the itinerary in question in the mode of a leisurely stroll, as it were, establishing also connections to further concepts examined in the present work. For a considerably more concise version of the itinerary of aesthetic value in modernity, see Kordela 2016.

2 In Foucault's words: "Nazism was … the paroxysmal development of the new power mechanisms that had been established since the eighteenth century. Of course, no State could have more disciplinary power than the Nazi regime. Nor was there any other state in which the biological was so tightly, so insistently regulated. Disciplinary power and biopower: all this permeated, underpinned, Nazi society … Controlling the random element inherent in biological processes was one of the regime's immediate objectives" (Foucault 2003: 259). In the era of biopower, "the essential function of society or the State, or whatever it is that must replace the State, is to take control of life, to manage it, to compensate for its aleatory nature, to explore and reduce biological accidents and possibilities." Accordingly, "this play [of biopolitics] is … inscribed in the workings of all … modern States," "capitalist" and "socialist" alike, and, indeed, we cannot dispute that "socialism has made no critique of the theme of biopower" and that it "takes this [biopolitical play] over wholesale," certainly in the form of the "socialist States (of the Soviet Union type)" (Foucault 2003: 260–2).

Turning now to Agamben, for him biopolitics consists in the direct exercise of power on "bare life," a concept derived out of Aristotle's reference to ζωή (*zoé*), the physical life of any living being, as opposed to βίος (pronounced *vios*, but in English known as *bios*), which for Aristotle means political life. While for Aristotle human life is primarily political (βίος), Agamben maintains that in biopolitics it is precisely bare life (ζωή) that is politicized. We may witness the first most explicit politicization of "birth" – i.e., of "bare natural life as such" – in the first of the 1789 Declarations: "Men are born and remain free and equal in rights." We witness the first most brutal application of this politicization of "bare life" in the atrocities of the Nazi concentration camps, in which the Jews and others "were exterminated not in a mad and giant [sacrificial] holocaust but, exactly as Hitler had announced, 'as lice,' which is to say, as bare life" (Agamben 1998: 127–9, 114). However, there are also central differences in the relation of biopower to totalitarianism between the two thinkers. For an examination of some central differences between Agamben and Foucault, see Kordela 2013.

3 Nevertheless, as is the case also with Benjamin, despite all undecidability, one can ultimately detect metaphysical preferences in Heidegger's work that entail less ambiguous political choices than I let be inferred here (for my relevant comparison between Benjamin and Heidegger, see Kordela 2015).

4 Here I am referring to the concept of aura as defined by Benjamin only in his essay "The Work of Art in the Age of Mechanical Reproduction." Elsewhere Benjamin defines aura as our capacity "to invest [the object] with the ability to look at us in turn," that is, as the object's gaze (Benjamin 1969: 188). Moreover, unlike in this essay, in several of his other works Benjamin does not celebrate the withering of the aura. (For an insightful analysis of Benjamin's "aura," see Comay 1992; see also Kordela 2015.)

5 I am referring to the following famous passage: "*Religious* suffering is at one and the same time the *expression* of real suffering and a protest against real suffering. Religion is the sigh of the oppressed creature … It is the *opium* of the people. The abolition of religion as the *illusory* happiness of the people is the demand for their *real* happiness. To call on them to give up their illusions about their condition is to *call on them to give up a condition that requires illusions*" (Marx 1975: 244). Of course, more famous than the passage itself is the misunderstanding of Marx's simile between religion and opium. In his attempt to rectify this, Kojin Karatani writes: "Marx attempts to say that it is impossible to dissolve any religion unless the 'real suffering' upon which every religion is based is dissolved" (Karatani 1995: 187–8). For religion – like art in Adorno's negative dialectic – is not some random illusion but a negative representation of the people's "real suffering."

References

Adorno, T. (1984) *Aesthetic Theory*, Gretel Adorno and Rolf Tiedemann (eds), C. Lenhardt (trans.), London: Routledge.

Agamben, G. (1998) *Homo Sacer: Sovereign Power and Bare Life*, Daniel Heller-Roazen (trans.), Stanford, CA: Stanford University Press.

Althusser, L. (1997) "The Only Materialist Tradition, Part I: Spinoza," in *The New Spinoza*, Warren Montag and Ted Stolze (eds), Minneapolis: University of Minnesota Press, pp. 3–19.

Balibar, E. (1993) *Spinoza: From Individuality to Transindividuality*, Delft: Eburon.

Balibar, E. (2007) *The Philosophy of Marx*, Chris Turner and Gregory Elliott (trans.), New York: Verso.

Benjamin, W. (1969) "On Some Motifs in Baudelaire," in *Illuminations: Essays and Reflections*, Hannah Arendt (ed.), Harry Zohn (trans.), New York: Schocken, pp. 155–200.

Benjamin, W. (1977) *The Origin of the German Tragic Drama*, John Osborne (trans.), London: Verso.

Benjamin, W. (2008) "The Work of Art in the Age of Mechanical Reproduction," in *Aesthetics: A Comprehensive Anthology*, Steven M. Cahn and Aaron Meskin (eds), Oxford: Blackwell, pp. 327–343.

Caygill, H. (1989) *Art of Judgement*, Oxford: Basil Blackwell.

Comay, R. (1992) "Framing Redemption: Aura, Origin, Technology in Benjamin and Heidegger," in *Ethics and Danger: Essays on Heidegger and Continental Thought*, Arleen B. Dallery, Charles E. Scott, and P. Holley Roberts (eds), Albany, NY: State University of New York Press, pp. 139–167.

Deleuze, G. (1994) *Difference and Repetition*, Paul Patton (trans.), New York: Columbia University Press.

Deleuze, G. (2004) "How Do We Recognize Structuralism?," in *Desert Islands and Other Texts 1953–1974*, Melissa McMahon and Charles J. Stivale (trans.), David Lapoujade (ed.), Los Angeles, CA: Semiotext(e), pp. 170–192.

de Man, P. (1983) "The Rhetoric of Temporality," in *Blindness and Insight: Essays in the Rhetoric of Contemporary Criticism* (Second Revised Edition), Intro. Wlad Godzich, Minneapolis: University of Minnesota Press, pp. 187–228.

de Man, P. (1996) *Aesthetic Ideology*, Andrzej Warminski (ed.), Minneapolis: University of Minnesota Press.

Fichte, J.G. (1984a) "On the Spirit and the Letter in Philosophy," Elizabeth Rubenstein (trans.), in *German Aesthetic and Literary Criticism: Kant, Fichte, Schelling, Schopenhauer, Hegel*, David Simpson (ed.), Cambridge: Cambridge University Press, pp. 74–93.

Fichte, J.G. (1984b) "On the Nature of the Scholar, and His Manifestations in the Sphere of Freedom," William Smith (modified trans.), in *German Aesthetic and Literary Criticism: Kant, Fichte, Schelling, Schopenhauer, Hegel*, David Simpson (ed.), Cambridge: Cambridge University Press, pp. 96–113.

Flax, N.M. (1983) "The Presence of the Sign in Goethe's Faust," *PMLA*, 98(2): 183–203.

Foucault, M. (1970) *The Order of Things: An Archaeology of the Human Sciences*, New York: Vintage.

Foucault, M. (2003) *Society Must be Defended: Lectures at the Collège de France*, David Macey (trans.), Mauro Bertani and Alessandro Fontana (eds), New York: Picador.

Guillory, J. (1993) *Cultural Capital: The Problem of Literary Canon Formation*, Chicago, IL: The University of Chicago Press.

Heeg, G. (2000) *Das Phantasma der natürlichen Gestalt*, Frankfurt/Main: Stroemfeld Verlag.

Heidegger, M. (1960) *Der Ursprung des Kunstwerks*, Intro. Hans Georg Gadamer, Stuttgart: Reclam.

Heidegger, M. (2008) *The Origin of the Work of Art in Aesthetics: A Comprehensive Anthology*, Steven M. Cahn and Aaron Meskin (eds). Oxford: Blackwell.

Hölderlin, F. (1988) *Essays and Letters on Theory*, Thomas Pfau (ed. and trans.), Albany, NY: State University of New York Press.

Hume, D. (1975) *Enquiries Concerning Human Understanding and Concerning the Principles of Morals (Third Edition)*, L.A. Selby-Bigge and P.H. Nidditch (eds), Oxford: Clarendon Press.

Kant, I. (1959) *Foundations of the Metaphysics of Morals and "What is Enlightenment?"* Lewis White Beck (trans.), Indianapolis, IN: The Liberal Arts Press.

Kant, I. (1974) *Kritik der Urteilskraft, in Werkausgabe, Band X*, Wilhelm Weischedel (ed.), Frankfurt/Main: Suhrkamp.

Kant, I. (1998) *Critique of Pure Reason*, Paul Guyer and Allen Wood (trans., eds), Cambridge: Cambridge University Press.

Kant, I. (2000) *The Critique of Judgment*, J.H. Bernard (trans.), New York: Prometheus Books.

Karatani, K. (1995) *Architecture as Metaphor: Language, Number, Money*, Sabu Kohso (trans.), Michael Speaks (ed.), Cambridge, MA: MIT Press.

Kordela, A.K. (2013) "Biopolitics, From Tribes to Commodity Fetishism," *Differences*, 24(1) (Spring): 1–29.

Kordela, A.K. (2015) "Commodity Fetishism and the Gaze," in *Sparks Will Fly: Benjamin and Heidegger*, Andrew Benjamin and Dimitris Vardoulakis (eds), New York: SUNY Press, pp. 95–119.

Kordela, A.K. (2016) "Value," in *Keywords in German Aesthetics*, J.D. Mininger and Jason M. Peck (eds), New York: Bloomsbury.

Lacan, J. (1981) *The Seminar of Jacques Lacan: Book XI: The Four Fundamental Concepts of Psychoanalysis*, Jacques-Alain Miller (ed.), Alan Sheridan (trans.), New York: W.W. Norton.

Laplanche, J. and J.B. Pontalis (2003) "Fantasy and the Origins of Sexuality," in *Unconscious Fantasy*, Riccardo Steiner (ed.), London: Karnac.

Marx, K. (1975) *Early Writings*, Rodney Livingstone and Gregor Benton (transls), New York: Vintage Books.

Marx, K. (1990) *Capital: A Critique of Political Economy (Volume 1)*, Ben Fowkes and David Fernbach (trans.), New York: Penguin.

Nietzsche, F. (1956) *The Birth of Tragedy, and, The Genealogy of Morals*, Francis Golffing (trans.), New York: Anchor Books, Random House.

Sartre, J.-P. (1992) *Being and Nothingness: An Essay on Phenomenological Ontology*, Hazel E. Barnes (trans.), New York: Washington Square Press.

Schelling, F.W.J. (1976) *System of Transcendental Idealism*, Albert Hofstadter (trans.), in *Philosophies of Art and Beauty: Selected Readings in Aesthetics from Plato to Heidegger*, Albert Hofstadter and Richard Kuhns (eds), Chicago, IL: The University of Chicago Press, pp. 347–377.

Schiller, F. (1985) "On Naive and Sentimental Poetry," trans. Julius A. Eliot (slightly modified by H.B. Nisbet), in *German Aesthetic and Literary Criticism: Winckelmann, Lessing, Hamann, Herder, Schiller, Goethe*, H.B. Nisbet (ed.), Cambridge: Cambridge University Press, pp. 180–232.

Schlegel, F. (1958) *Kritische Friedrich-Schlegel-Ausgabe*, Ernst Behler et al. (ed.), Munich: Schöningh.

Schulte-Sasse, J. (1997) "General Introduction: Romanticism's Paradoxical Articulation of Desire," in *Theory as Practice: A Critical Anthology of Early German Romantic Writings*, Jochen Schulte-Sasse et al. (ed.), Minneapolis: University of Minnesota Press, pp. 1–43.

Simpson, D. (1984) *German Aesthetic and Literary Criticism: Kant, Fichte, Schelling, Schopenhauer, Hegel*, David Simpson (ed.), Cambridge: Cambridge University Press.

Smith, A. (2000 [1776]) *The Wealth of Nations*, Edwin Cannan (ed.), New York: The Modern Library, Random House.

Spinoza, B. (1985) *The Collected Works of Spinoza*, Edwin Curley (trans.), Princeton: Princeton University Press.

Winckelmann, J.J. (1985) "Thoughts on the Imitation of the Painting and Sculpture of the Greeks," H.B. Nisbet (trans.), in *German Aesthetic and Literary Criticism: Winckelmann, Lessing, Hamann, Herder, Schiller, Goethe*, H.B. Nisbet (ed.), Cambridge: Cambridge University Press, pp. 32–54.

6 Marx and psychoanalysis[1]

Psychoanalysis is as intrinsically interconnected with structuralism as with Marx's theory, with which it shares central conceptual, methodological, epistemological, and ontological affinities. Historically, however, thinkers did not begin to become aware of the intrinsic relation between the two theories until after the onset of Marxism's own crisis, that is, its development into the totalitarian ideologies of Bolshevism and Stalinism. The first systematic attempt to relate Marxism and psychoanalysis is attributed to the Frankfurt School. Other differences notwithstanding, its members (Theodor W. Adorno, Jürgen Habermas, Max Horkheimer, Herbert Marcuse, et al.) recuperated concerns of traditional philosophy (mainly German Idealism) – such as reason, truth, beauty – so as to address them in their relation to current cultural and socio-political power and dynamics, and in view of Freud's discoveries. However, the thinker closer to understanding the intrinsic conceptual, methodological, and epistemological relation between Marx and psychoanalysis is, as we have seen, Alfred Sohn-Rethel (who was never accepted as a member by the Frankfurt School, and his theory was not published before 1977), as well as Walter Benjamin (who was associated with the School but not a member).

In a fragment to which we shall return in the last chapter, Benjamin stated that "Freud's theory is capitalist through and through" – that is, it replicates, in ways that reveal and undermine, the logic of capital, such as that "what has been repressed … is capital itself, which pays interest on the hell of the unconscious" (Benjamin 1996: 289). The intrinsic relation between psychoanalysis and capitalist society may be reflected in Adorno's "negative dialectic" between art and society: "[w]orks of art are after-images or replicas of empirical life, inasmuch as they proffer to the latter what in the outside world is denied them" (Adorno 1984: 6). Accordingly, "[t]o the extent to which psychoanalysis decodes the social character of a work and its author," it could reveal how in "artists of the highest caliber … the keenest awareness of reality was joined to an equally acute sense of alienation from reality" (ibid., 12–3). However, Adorno did not discern how Freud's theory points to such an analysis and instead saw it as "reducing art to an absolutely subjective system of signs" and as analyzing it "in terms of a purely subjective language of the unconscious" (ibid., 12, 14). This assumption of the unconscious as a subjective category perpetuates the early Freudian and Marxian dualisms between interiority and exteriority (which we shall examine below) within the very attempts to produce a psychoanalytic Marxism. Under this assumption, any such attempts remain trapped within a perceived need to "reconcile" the two theories. Wilhelm Reich, for instance, rightly attributed neurotic symptoms to the socio-economic conditions of capitalism but failed to see the homology between these conditions and psychological processes (see Reich 1972). The social psychologist Erich Fromm, who had studied with Wilhelm Reich and was initially a member of the Frankfurt School, saw an intrinsic interdependency between Marxism and psychoanalysis. Both, he noted, are concerned with the subconscious driving forces of the human and of society, adapting Rosa Luxembourg's definition of the "subconscious" as designating "blindly acting historical forces" (Fromm 1966: 5). For Fromm, the core of Spinoza's ethics, Marxist revolutionary action, and Freudian psychoanalysis converge in the insight that humans cannot be free if other forces beyond their own reason and will control their fate. Understanding these forces is, therefore, the necessary step toward liberation from the confines of capitalist society and its distortion of human nature. Nevertheless, Fromm also sees a need for reconciliation between the two theories, insofar as Freud falls prey to a "mechanistic materialism" that reduces the human subject to psychological processes, opposed by the world and society, whereas Marx achieves a humanistic philosophy of history (Fromm 1966).

It was Jacques Lacan's structuralism-inflected reading of Freudian psychoanalysis, beginning in the 1930s, that revealed the objectivity of the unconscious, eventually enabling Marxist theorists working in the 1960s – notably Louis Althusser and Étienne Balibar – to discern the intrinsic interconnection of Marx and psychoanalysis, and to revise Marxist theory accordingly. In the following I would like to foreground certain salient points of affinity between psychoanalysis and Marx's theory, including some that are central in conceiving of being as both value and as power of self-actualization.

Conceptual, methodological, epistemontological affinities

Beginning with some conspicuous affinities, Freud's conceptual repertory draws largely on economic and mechanical models, as he began with an "economic model" of the mind to develop terms such as the cathexis (investment, occupation) of the libido, the latter being conceived as a form of energy or that has its own economy and undergoes gains and losses. Similarly, the Freudian subject takes recourse to mechanisms such as overcompensation or withdrawal and is itself governed by the conflicting laws of the pleasure principle and the death drive. The pleasure principle is conceived as a homeostatic mechanism or an economy of equilibrium that maintains the value of the libido on the same level, without any surplus or loss – not unlike Marx's conception of precapitalist economies. Juxtaposed to it is the death drive, an entropic tendency or an economy of disequilibrium that produces an excess that can become lost or be reappropriated as surplus – as in capitalist economy. Lacan's structuralist reading added to Freud's homology between economic and sexual value (libido), the linguistic value (see Kordela 2007). Methodologically, a central Marxian and Freudian principle is that the logic of the norm is revealed in the exception or "pathological symptom" (e.g., economic crisis, slip of the tongue, respectively) (Žižek 1989: 21, 128; see also Lacan 1975).

A fundamental epistemological affinity between Marx and Freud consists, in Balibar's words, in the "theoretical, non-empirical character of the constitution" of the "object" of their theories, which is what makes each theory a new science (Althusser and Balibar 2009: 277). The object of a science is thus not pre-given but – like "the object in desire" (Lacan 1977: 28) – is rather constituted in and through the emergent science. This same idea underlies Althusser's psychoanalytically inspired concepts of the "problematic" and the "symptomatic reading." A "problematic" is the "terrain" or "horizon" of a given scientific "theoretical structure" that determines what questions can be posed and what answers can be given within that scientific theory (Althusser and Balibar 2009: 25). A structuring condition of any problematic, therefore, is that there are "problems [that] are necessarily *invisible* in the field of the existing theory, because they are not objects of this theory, because they are *forbidden* by it" (ibid., 26–7). These invisible or unthinkable problems constitute the theory's silences and contradictions – or its symptoms, in the psychoanalytic sense: codes in need of interpretation. To interpret these symptoms is to perform a "symptomatic reading," and any symptom invites its reading because the "symptom" does not simply hide or repress but "acts as a language that enables repression to be expressed" (Lacan 1997: 60). This is why for Althusser, the text's "silence is *its own words*" (Althusser and Balibar 2009: 23) – not unlike "negation" in Freud, which enables the repressed to "make its way into consciousness [but only] on condition that it is denied" (Freud 1974d: 235). Like negation, the symptom of the problematic "at bottom" says: "[t]hat is something that I would rather repress" (Freud 1974d: 236).

An eminent example of symptomatic reading is Marx's interpretation of the "inextricable confusions and contradictions" (Marx 1990: 679) of classical political economy through the concept of "labour-power." In Althusser's words, this concept "*is the correct answer to a question that has just one failing: it was never posed*" (Althusser and Balibar 2009: 22) – and the same is true, as we shall see, of Freud's concept of sexuality. Of course, the correctness of the answer becomes visible only after the "transformation of the *entire* terrain" or the problematic (ibid., 25). The new problematics demarcated by Marx and Freud consist in the introduction of a new "*type of object*," which, properly speaking, is a structural object, insofar as, in Balibar's words, (a) it is constituted by the varying "forms" of a given "combination" of "elements" that are themselves changing as a result of these changing forms; and (b) the different "forms" may appear to take place in different stages of either historical or individual development of the elements, when in truth the "continuity" of the combination owes neither to the elements nor to stages of development but to "functions" (Althusser and Balibar 2009: 277, 272).

For instance, in Marx the object "labour process" consists of the combination of three elements: the "personal activity" of "labour"; the "object of labour"; and the "means of labour" (ibid., 270–1). The difference between handicraft (and manufacturing) and industrial production consists in a transformation of the form in which the three elements of labor combine. Handicrafts rely on a "'*technique*'" as "*the indissoluble ensemble* of a means of labour or tool, *and a worker*, moulded to its use by apprenticeship and habit," just as the tool must itself "be adapted to the human organism" (ibid., 267). With the introduction of the industrial "machine-tool" this "relationship is inverted," so that the human "organism must adapt itself to the instrument," as it is now "*the unity of the means … and the object of labour*" under which the labor activity (and the laborer) is now entirely subordinated (ibid., 268). However, as a result of "the transformation of the relationship between the elements of the combination, the nature of those elements themselves are transformed"; for "fixed machines [are now] ready to receive any workers," that is, the laborer as the bearer of a technique is now replaced with the "collective worker" (ibid., 268–9).

Similarly, in Freud, the presumed stages of sexuality within the development of the individual are in truth different forms of libidinal organizations that acquire the "sexual character" only "because analysis discovers for them *the same* function," namely the "search for pleasure" (ibid., 273). Accordingly, for Freud "there is hardly any part of the body that" is not "invested with a sexual 'value'" and does not serve one "single sexual instinct," the latter having thereby been radically redefined as something ("search for pleasure") that far exceeds genital or procreative sexuality (ibid., 273–4).

Here we see a central Spinozian aspect in Marx's and Freud's approach. For their conception of the scientific object (e.g., labor process) as a system of immutable functions (e.g., labor *qua* personal activity, object of labor, and means of labor) whose combination alters the elements occupying these functions corresponds to Spinoza's immutable substance and its manifestation in historically or individually varying modes. This comment points to the intrinsic connection between epistemology and ontology that marks the theories of all three.

Beyond sexuality itself, this is evident in Freud's reconceptualization of several other elements in adjacent combinations, notably of the "biological" and the "psychological" elements. For, if instincts are defined not by their "somatic source" but "by their aim" (pleasure) (Freud 1974a: 122–3), and if knowing them involves an "analysis of forms," then "the biological is ... absent as such." It follows that, in Balibar's words, "the psychological, too, is absent," for "in its traditional conception it ... was defined by its opposition and relation to the biological," so that if "the latter disappears as such, the psychological is transformed into something" else, namely "what Freud called the 'psychical'" (Althusser and Balibar 2009: 276). This reconceptualization corresponds to the redefinition of the "natural" and the "social" in Marx. On the one hand, "[l]abour is, first of all, a process between man and nature, a process by which man ... confronts the materials of nature as [himself] a force of nature" (Marx 1990: 283); that is, "man has the role of a natural power with respect to nature" (Althusser and Balibar 2009: 276); and, on the other hand, through the commodification of nature, "nature [too] has the role of a social element" (exchange), so that "nature as such is [also] absent" (ibid., 276). Just as Freud "ends by defining instincts as a *frontier* between the biological and the psychological" (ibid., 275), Marx's theory entails that being and life (bios) are a frontier between the natural and the social.

Commodity fetishism and materialist epistemology: from bourgeois ideology to the constitutive imaginary, and from interiority-exteriority to extimacy

To turn to the core of the relation between Marx and psychoanalysis, the above (and an abundance of further) points of affinity are ultimately explainable through Marx's own theory of commodity fetishism. As we have seen in the second chapter, the most evident common element between this theory and psychoanalysis is the unconscious. To recapitulate briefly, human activity under capitalism consists mainly in exchanging the products of our labor as quantities of abstract homogenous labor, that is, as pure exchange-values; and insofar as we "do this without being aware of it" (since we consciously assume that we are exchanging objects of utility), Marx's theory of commodity fetishism introduces the unconscious into political economy (Marx 1990: 166–7). This theory entails the re-demarcation of political economy itself. For if our functioning within, and our subordination to, the capitalist system depends on our not knowing what we actually do, then the sustenance of capitalism depends on imaginary representations of reality. As an obvious consequence, this means that capitalism depends on ideology, understood as a distorted representation of reality that endeavors both to make our lives appear more meaningful than mere mediators in the exchange of value, and to legitimize unequal power relations. However, Marx had discerned the centrality of ideology in this sense already in his early writings, while his later theory opens up a new direction in understanding the mediation of the imaginary in the relation between subjects and economy. Here we need to differentiate between two conceptions of the imaginary (and ideology) that correspond to two different phases in the development of Marx's thought – a distinction which we have already seen in Balibar's commentary on the distinction between ideology and fetishism in the first chapter. As we shall presently see, the characteristics of these two phases are reflected also in the development of Freud's thought.

Marx's initial phase consists of two sub-stages: the first, with Hegel and Feuerbach as points of reference, lasts until the mid-1840s; and the second, in which Marx and Engels developed historical materialism, lasts until 1857, when Marx eventually turns to the analysis of more economic concepts, such as value and labor. Throughout this first phase, Marx gradually conceives of both religion and the ideology of the State as "an inverted consciousness of the world" that, nevertheless, is required for people to compensate for the fact that they live in "an inverted world" (Marx 1970). In other words, the inversion of ideology is not a random imaginary construction but one owing to an actual inversion within reality itself. If, for instance, Hegel conceives of the political State as the manifestation of the Spirit within reality, this is due to the real "abstraction" of the State, that is, to the fact that the State functions as an entity transcendent to the civil society. For, as we saw in the first chapter, under "the mode of domination inherent in the State" ideology involves a dualism between immanence and transcendence, between the earthly world and the "idol" or the "ethereal realm of ideas (Freedom, Justice, Humanity, Law)" or the State. This is why ideology is here accompanied by its corollary view regarding "the conditions and objectives of the revolutionary struggle" as the "overthrowing a bourgeois domination which has entered into contradiction with the development of civil society" (Balibar 2007: 76–8). Marx expands the Manichean dualism of his early conception of ideology to the clear division between intellectual and manual labor, the former pertaining to the dominant bourgeois ideologues, and the latter to the dominated masses. This division entails that even as the ideological distortions derive from real distortions, ideology or the (bourgeois) mind always offers distorted representations of (the true, proletarian) material reality – whence Marx's assumption that the proletarians "are fundamentally *external* to the world of ideology, whose abstractions and ideal representations of the social relation 'do not exist' for them" (Balibar 2007: 54). Accordingly, ideology cannot be overcome through theoretical criticism; rather, only if the real social contradictions are practically eliminated will ideology then also disappear – the assumption being that in a non-exploitative society there would be no ideology.

Marx's early conception of ideology and the imaginary corresponds methodologically to Freud's work in the period from 1893 to 1897, in which, as we saw in the third chapter, he developed the "seduction theory." To recapitulate briefly, as long as the "guiding principle" of the seduction theory was "the search for chronology, going backwards into time towards the first real, verifiable elements," Freud remained "prisoner of … theoretical alternatives" such as "internal-external, imaginary-real" (Laplanche and Pontalis 2003: 119) – like Marx's opposition between ideology and material reality. Here Freud still conceives of the phenomena of the unconscious in terms of such oppositions, which in truth are posited only by consciousness. Eventually, as we have seen, through his discovery of autoeroticism or human sexuality (sexuality predicated on desire, as opposed to need), Freud formulates the unconscious as "a pre-subjective structure, beyond both the strict happening and the internal imagery" (Laplanche and Pontalis 2003: 118), in which there is "no negation" (Freud 1974b: 179) or "No" (Freud 1974d: 235).

In Freud it is auto-eroticism – and in Marx, capitalism – that dislodges the living being away from need into desire and thereby makes it human, that is, a being of the imaginary and, hence, of linear time. This is the time which, to repeat Spinoza's words cited in the first chapter here, "is a product of the imagination" (*Ethics* IIP44S), and which, to repeat Kojève's words from the fourth chapter here, Hegel raises to "the *Concept* itself" (Kojève 1980: 101). For Freud, the initial (pre-human) situation is that of the infant, which involves "non-sexual functions," but functions that fulfill needs, such as "the taking of food" (Laplanche and Pontalis 2003: 132). Similarly, for Marx, the initial situation is that of precapitalist economy, in which the sole purpose of exchange is "selling in order to buy" so as to fulfill needs, whereby money is "nothing more" than the mediator in the "exchange of products": C – M – C (Marx 1990: 200). Here, "the repetition or renewal of the act of selling in order to buy [C – M – C] finds its measure and its goal (as does the process itself) in a final purpose which lies outside it, namely consumption, the satisfaction of definite needs" (ibid., 252). This means that time is circular, consisting of the repetition of the same within a finite duration, its limit being posed by need: should the need be extinguished (as in death), then there would be no reason for exchange either. "But in buying in order to sell [M – C – M], on the contrary, the end and the beginning are the same, money or exchange-value and this very fact makes the movement an endless one" (ibid., 252). The repetition becomes infinite, for the goal of the exchange is no longer to satisfy any specific need but the interminable accumulation of capital. This is the drive of capital: an (ideally) infinite repetition of the act of exchange that opens up duration to infinity. Like the subject of desire, capital is governed not by the (homeostatic) pleasure principle but by repetition compulsion – understood not in its proper sense as death drive (which, as we have seen in the third chapter, does not pertain to linear time) but in imaginary terms, as an infinite prolongation of duration.

The corollary of the notorious secular introduction of historical time is, for both Marx and psychoanalysis, the introduction of time as infinite repetition. Of course, the link of time with infinity also enables fantasies such as progress and other evolutionist and teleological conceptions of history. Such teleological conceptions of history can vary from the idealization of human agency to its total subjugation under a Spirit of History, whether fathomable or unfathomable, as the motor of history. Postmodern Hegelianism, as we have seen, attempts, however successfully, to avoid this double bind.

However, I should also add here that the link of time with infinity introduced by surplus-value also enables secular fantasies of immortality. For, as follows from the theory of commodity fetishism, if value – which, we recall, is according to Marx the dominant subject in capitalism – exists in infinite duration, then should not the subjects living in the system of the accumulation of surplus-value (imagine that they) also live in infinite duration? This is a crucial question but, as I have addressed it in several of my other works, I will not expand on it here.[2] In the last chapter, however, we shall return to the question of the subject's relation to the various temporalities that pertain to capitalism to examine both their role in biopower, as well as the alternatives indicated through Spinoza's conception of the humans' relation to time and eternity and of secular salvation.

As we have seen in the third chapter, the introduction of the subject to the signifier entails also its introduction to duration or linear time, the corollary of which is the loss of the undifferentiated totality of immortal life and signifier (see Lacan 1981: 198). This totality is one of the meanings of Lacan's *real*. Similarly, in Marx's ontology of capital, a sole substance – value – is the undifferentiated totality of actual material or physical objects and bodies (use-values, including labor objectified as a commodity) and of abstract exchange-values (including homogeneous abstract labor or labor-time). This undifferentiated totality of value appears, due to commodity fetishism, as the sole presupposition for both use-values and exchange-values (whereby labor-power – "labour which is still objectifying itself" (Marx 1993: 272) – falls entirely out of the picture). In Marx's words, "the money [exchange-value] and the commodity [use-value] function only as different modes of existence of value itself, the money as its general mode of existence, the commodity as its particular or, so to speak, disguised mode … [C]apital is money, capital is commodities. In truth, however, value is here the dominant" and "automatic" "subject … of this process" (Marx 1990: 255). Value can exist empirically either as money or as a commodity, but the two are undifferentiated in value in itself as the dominant subject, and as an (ostensible) economic equivalent of Lacan's aforementioned real. Just as value can be empirically apprehended either as use-value or as exchange-value, the "method of apprehending an object is split in two."

On the one hand, Laplanche and Pontalis continue, we have the "non-sexual functions" that satisfy needs; and, on the other hand, we have the capitalist or "sexual drive." The drive propels the (theoretically) infinite repetition of the exchange of one exchange-value or "idea" (signifier) for another, while the "external object [use-value] is abandoned," so that the drive's "aim and … source assume an autonomous existence with regard to feeding." Accordingly, the drive's "prototype is not the act of sucking, but the enjoyment of going through the motions of sucking" (Laplanche and Pontalis 2003: 132–3). Similarly, the drive of capitalist exchange (M – C – M′) renders "value" "a self-moving substance," which, instead of "representing the relations of commodities, it now enters into a private relationship with itself" (Marx 1990: 256). Just as the "ideal … of auto-erotism is 'lips that kiss themselves'" (Laplanche and Pontalis 2003: 132–3), "the circulation M – C – M′ presents itself … in its final result and without any intermediary stage, in a concise style … as M – M′," "'money which begets money'" (Marx 1990: 256–7).

The above analysis of value, developed by Marx in his later phase (starting with *Grundrisse*, 1857/1858) and corresponding to Freud's later period, culminates, as we have seen in the first chapter, in a radical reconceptualization of ideology through the fetish. In contrast to the "idol," the fetish is an earthly "material thing" that assumes a supernatural "irresistible power over individuals (the commodity and, above all, money)" (Balibar 2007: 76). Fetishism folds transcendence (domination) fully within the plane of immanence (civil society). Thus, whereas the earlier model of ideology is a theory of the State, "fetishism is fundamentally a *theory of the market*," that is, a theory of "the mode of subjection or constitution of the 'world' of subjects and objects inherent in the organization of society as market and its domination by market forces" (ibid., 78). With the shift from State-type ideology to market-type fetishism, we pass from the question of domination to the problematic of "subjection" in the sense of a concomitant "constitution" of both subjects and objects (ibid., 77). At this point, ideology expands its meaning beyond an imaginary distortion in the service of domination (or of revolution) to *the imaginary as constitutive* in the structuring of the world. There is, as we have seen in the second chapter, a level on which the imaginary distortion is in fact objective – a distortion occurring in the objects. Then, on top of this, there are further illusions that are maintained only in the subjects' minds, but even they are not subjective – in the sense of depending on one's will. Rather, they are collective, insofar as the whole reality is organized in such a way that tends to induce these illusions in the human mind. This saturation of subjectivity with the imaginary reflects the shift in the workings of power, which Lacan indicates through the shift from the discourse of the Master to that of the University (to which we shall return below), and which became the focus of Michel Foucault's analysis of biopower.

However, we must not forget that commodity fetishism and biopolitics do not announce a post-ideological era, since ideology is from the outset *constitutive* of subjectivity (see Althusser 1971). Rather, commodity fetishism reconceptualizes ideology so as to grasp its logic when transcendence (*qua* idol and locus of power) is folded within the plane of immanence (market). This logic includes: (a) that ideological interpellation or "calling" emanates from an Other that is imagined by the subject; (b) that effective interpellation presupposes a kernel of non-sense within ideology and the subject's distance from its own ideology; and (c) that the idol is increasingly replaced by affect.[3]

As we have seen in the second chapter, the imaginary becomes in capitalism constitutive of subjectivity and objectivity because in commodity fetishism (which, we recall, is "inseparable from the production of commodities"; Marx, 1990: 165), the imaginary (as well as abstract thought and the unconscious) is not merely a subjective but an objective formation. We also saw there that beyond the division of labor within production, commodity fetishism involves a division between manual and intellectual labor *within the realm of exchange*, which corresponds to the psychoanalytic split between the unconscious and consciousness. In exchange, the sole activity of manual (i.e., unconscious) labor is to exchange exchange-values. Therefore, Lacan's "the unconscious is structured like language" (Lacan 1981: 149) also means that the unconscious is structured as the network of exchange-values. By discerning that abstraction occurs within social objectivity, Marx pointed to the socio-objective genesis and formation of the subject's abstract thought and its unconscious preconditions. To recall Balibar's words, as opposed to idealist transcendentalism, which posits "a consciousness [that] 'constitutes a world' … by means of its own categories … of representation," commodity fetishism means that "the constitution of the world is not … the work of a subject, but a genesis of subjectivity (*a* form of determinate historical subjectivity) as part (and counterpart) of the social world of objectivity … [or] 'nature'" (Balibar 2007: 65–7). This materialist epistemology is entailed in both Marx's and Freud's interlacing of the internal (abstract thought) and the external (objective material reality) – an interlacing which Lacan expresses through the neologism of "extimacy" ("intimate exteriority") (Lacan 1992: 139). This intimate exteriority introduced by commodity fetishism in capitalism relates to the experience of the "uncanny" (das Unheimliche) – not recognizing one's own most intimate core – and the fascination with the human-machine (automata, robots, golems), particularly since industrial capitalism (see Freud 1974c).

From surplus-value to surplus-enjoyment

A culminating point of psychoanalysis as the realization of a materialist theory of metaphysics as postulated by Marx's theory of commodity fetishism is Lacan's concept of "surplus-enjoyment" (*plus-de-jouir*). This concept intertwined Marx and psychoanalysis in ways that corrected each according to the findings of the other. The connotations of *jouir* ("to come" or "reach orgasm"; see Fink, in Lacan 1998: 3, n. 8) already expand the referential field of Marx's economic counterpart. Generally speaking, *jouissance* (enjoyment) and *plus-de-jouir* (surplus-enjoyment) are the same, insofar as enjoyment is always a surplus or excess to what in utilitarian terms is required for productivity (see Lacan 1998, particularly the first chapter). Nevertheless, the term *plus-de-jouir* has the advantage of making as much an allusion to surplus-value (*plus-value*) as to the loss of all enjoyment, since it also means "no more enjoyment." This ambiguity of the term points, as we shall see, to enjoyment's relation to labor-power and the latter's historical function (or non-function) as an economic category.

Soon after the 1968 Paris events, Lacan explicitly indicates the need to fathom the true meaning of Marx's "surplus-value": "It's not because one nationalizes the means of production at the level of socialism in one country that one has thereby done away with surplus value, if one doesn't know what it is" (Lacan 2007: 108). For Lacan, Marx's discovery goes beyond the reductionist conception of surplus-value as a purely economic category specific to capitalism. First – directly following from Marx's theory of commodity fetishism – surplus-value must be conceived as much as an economic category as a category pertaining to the human subjectivity constituted under economic conditions that involve such an accumulation of surplus-value. Second – directly following from the Spinozian/structuralist principle that defines any scientific object as a combination of elements that mutate as a result of the historical changes of the form of their combination – capitalist surplus-value is only one, historically specific modulation of surplus. That is, any system of values (economic and/or semantic) is an entropic system, involving an excess, for always when the "signifier" or "knowledge ... is at work, what it produces is entropy" (Lacan 2007: 50), that is, excess. However, this excess may be entirely wasted as pure loss or partly recuperated as a surplus that accumulates within the system, as is the case of surplus-value. Marx's "surplus value ... has the same ambiguous place as ... surplus work" (Lacan 2007: 20) – "ambiguous," as it can be work whose exchange-value is in excess to its wage (as in capitalism) or work that does not compute at all within the sphere of values, surplus as pure waste (precapitalism). Labor-power points to a surplus beyond surplus-value: a transhistorical surplus that historically can be either waste (as in antiquity or feudalism) or surplus-value (as in capitalism). That is, capital or surplus-value is only one of the historically possible modulations of this excess. Excess as such is transhistorical, yet capable of enabling the formation of societies as diverse as archaic societies, the slave economy of pagan antiquity, theocratic feudalism, capitalism, and beyond (see Kordela 2007, 2013).

In fact, strictly speaking, enjoyment or "[j]ouissance is what serves no purpose (*ne sert à rien*)"; it is a "loss" or "wasting" as an "effect of entropy" (Lacan 1998: 3; Lacan 2007: 50). To be a "loss" means to not be "counted" within what "can possibly be articulated as signifier" (Lacan 2007: 50) – whether a signifier pertaining to knowledge or to the counting of exchange-values. In short, enjoyment is discursive – epistemic and economic – waste. Only what is not useful, that is, what does not contribute to the discursive (epistemic and economic) sustenance can count as enjoyment. By this token, throughout all modes of production based on slavery or serfdom, labor has always pertained to the level of enjoyment, as a sheer waste that was not counted. In Lacan's words, "people who had slaves didn't realise that one could establish equations for the price of their food and what they did in their *latifundia* … There is not the hint of an equation as to their output" (Lacan 1991b: 75). The capitalist revolution consists precisely in the shift in the status of labor from waste to being counted as the very precondition for the accumulation of surplus-value which is the defining characteristic of capital. One refers to this historically relatively new phenomenon as the commodification of labor.

Now, this reference to "labor" is vague, for in capitalism labor involves three aspects – labor as a specific activity, labor-power, and labor-time. This is a crucial point in grasping the workings of biopower, to which we shall return in the last chapter.

For now let us stay with the 1969 seminar, in which Lacan performed a further re-demarcation of the problematic of psychoanalytic Marxism through the introduction of a new object: the discourse. Discourses designate varying relations between enjoyment and the rotating concatenations of four mathemes that stand for the effects of the signifier: knowledge, truth, subject, and master (power). The formal restructurings of these "mathemes" result in different (social and subjective) effects and modes of efficacy, depending on "the effect allowed by" each discursive combination and "the obstacles and shortcomings endemic to that discourse" (Fink 1995: 129–30). In Spinozian terms, the four mathemes and topological functions constitute the immutable substance of discourse as such, while their specific combinations, and the corollary crystallization of the content of the mathemes, are the modes in which discourse can manifest itself empirically. Given that there are four "mathemes" and four functions, a total of "twenty-four different discourses are possible," but Lacan focuses on the discourses of the Master, the University, the Hysteric, and the Analyst (Fink 1995: 198). Even as he also presented a discourse designated as that of the Capitalist (Lacan 1972), he clearly links the University discourse to capitalism, and the discourse of the Master to any pre-capitalist system in which the discursive topological configuration brought about economic equilibrium (i.e., no accumulation of surplus-value), and labor and enjoyment were wasted (i.e., not counted or not commodified).

The transition from the Master to the University involves a shift in which, beyond the fact that the waste (labor-power and enjoyment) begins to be reappropriated as surplus-value, "surplus enjoyment [plus-de-jouir]" begins to be conjoined "with the master's truth" (Lacan 1991a: 207; Lacan 2007: 177–8, translation modified). This means that the modern, capitalist, master appears as "nothing other than knowledge," not mastery or power, but *pure* knowledge, which, as such, is said to be "objective knowledge ... science ... bureaucracy" (Lacan 2007: 31). This radical transformation in the relation between power and knowledge marks the era of biopower with the so-called "(objective) laws of the market," in which power bases itself on the illusion that knowledge reveals objective, scientific or purely procedural truths, rather than sustaining its authority.

Lacan's discourses offered a new impetus in the development of psychoanalytic Marxism and in theorizing biopower. As we shall see in the last chapter, there is a correlation of labor-power, *jouissance*, and substance or potentiality that indicates the need for a monist Marxist-psychoanalytic reconceptualization of biopower that goes beyond the conceptions of "bios" in extant theories.

Notes

1 A much shorter, modified version of this chapter will be included as an entry on "psychoanalysis" in the *Bloomsbury Companion to Marx*, edited by Jeff Diamanti, Andrew Pendakis and Imre Szeman, Bloomsbury (forthcoming).

2 See Kordela 2013a, 2013b, 2013c, 2016.

3 These statements are based on Althusser 1971, Žižek 1989, and Pfaller 1998, and I elaborate on them in more detail in Kordela 2016. Note also that they comply entirely with Spinoza's anthropo-logy as presented in his *Ethics*, according to which: (a) individuals are constituted transindividually on the basis of what affects they imagine other individuals experience (see also Balibar 1993); (b) our passive affects are inadequate ideas; and (c) although Spinoza advocates for the cultivation of more rational subjects, he deviates radically from the dominant assumptions of the Enlightenment, seeing in reason an impotent remedy against affects and imagination. For Spinoza, affects are controlled and manipulated not through reason but by means of other affects, just as "imaginings do not disappear at the presence of what is true in so far as it is true, but because other imaginings that are stronger supervene to exclude the present existence of the things we imagine" (*Ethics* IVP1S). In fact, reason itself (and consciousness), far from being the basis or measure of our affects and imaginings, is their effect formation, since "we do not endeavor, will, seek after or desire because we judge a thing to be good" but rather "we judge a thing to be good because we endeavor, will, seek after and desire it" (*Ethics* IIIP9S).

References

Adorno, T. (1984) *Aesthetic Theory*, Gretel Adorno and Rolf Tiedemann (eds), C. Lenhardt (trans.), London: Routledge.

Althusser, L. (1971) "Ideology and Ideological State Apparatuses (Notes Toward an Investigation)," in *Lenin and Philosophy and Other Essays*, Ben Brewster (trans.), New York: Monthly Review Press, pp. 127–242.

Althusser, L. and E. Balibar (2009) *Reading Capital*, Ben Brewster (trans.), New York: Verso.

Balibar, E. (1993) *Spinoza: From Individuality to Transindividuality*, Delft: Eburon.

Balibar, E. (2007) *The Philosophy of Marx*, Chris Turner and Gregory Elliott (trans.), New York: Verso.

Benjamin, W. (1996) "Capitalism as Religion," in *Selected Writings Vol. 1, 1913–1926*, Rodney Livingstone (trans.), Cambridge, MA: Belknap Harvard Press.

Fink, B. (1995) *The Lacanian Subject: Between Language and Jouissance*, Princeton, NJ: Princeton University Press.

Freud, S. (1974a) "Instincts and their Vicissitudes," in *The Standard Edition of the Complete Works of Sigmund Freud* (vol. 14), James Strachey (ed. and trans.), London: The Hogarth Press and the Institute of Psychoanalysis, pp. 109–140.

Freud, S. (1974b) "The Unconscious," in *The Standard Edition of the Complete Works of Sigmund Freud* (vol. 14), James Strachey (ed. and trans.), London: The Hogarth Press and the Institute of Psychoanalysis, pp. 161–215.

Freud, S. (1974c) "The Uncanny," in *The Standard Edition of the Complete Works of Sigmund Freud* (vol. 17), James Strachey (ed. and trans.), London: The Hogarth Press and the Institute of Psychoanalysis, pp. 219–256.

Freud, S. (1974d) "Negation," in *The Standard Edition of the Complete Works of Sigmund Freud* (vol. 19), James Strachey (ed. and trans.), London: The Hogarth Press and the Institute of Psychoanalysis, pp. 235–239.

Fromm, E. (1966) "Marxism, Psychoanalysis, and Reality," first published in *Tagebuch: Monatshefte für Kultur, Politik, Wirtschaft*, vol. 21 (no. 9): 5–6, Florian Nagde (trans.), CreativeCommons: www.marxists.org (2011).

Kojève, A. (1980) *Introduction to the Reading of Hegel: Lectures on the Phenomenology of Spirit*, Allan Bloom (ed.), Ithaca, NY: Cornell University Press.

Kordela, A.K. (2007) *$urplus: Spinoza, Lacan*, New York: SUNY Press.

Kordela, A.K. (2013a) *Being, Time, Bios: Capitalism and Ontology*, Albany, NY: SUNY Press.

Kordela, A.K. (2013b) "Biopolitics, From Tribes to Commodity Fetishism," *Differences*, 24(1) (Spring): 1–29.

Kordela, A.K. (2013c) "(Marxian-Psychoanalytic) Biopolitics & Bioracism," in *Penumbr(a)*, Sigi Jöttkandt and Joan Copjec (eds), Melbourne: Re.Press.

Kordela, A.K. (2016) "Monsters of Biopower: Terror(ism) and Horror in the Era of Affect," *Philosophy Today*, 60(1): 193–205.

Kordela, A.K. (forthcoming) "Psychoanalysis," in *Companion to Marx*, Jeff Diamanti, Andrew Pendakis and Imre Szeman (eds), New York: Bloomsbury.

Lacan, J. (1972) "On Psychoanalytic Discourse," in *Lacan in Italia, 1953–1978*, Milan: La Salamandra (1978, pp. 32–55), English translation by Jack W. Stone available online at http://stonejtrans.eu.pn/Milan_Discourse2.pdf (accessed 31 May 2017).

Lacan, J. (1975) *Livre XXII: R.S.I. 1974–1975*, Ornicar? 4, Paris.

Lacan, J. (1977) *Écrits: A Selection*, Bruce Fink (trans.), New York: W.W. Norton & Co.

Lacan, J. (1981) *The Seminar of Jacques Lacan: Book XI: The Four Fundamental Concepts of Psychoanalysis*, Jacques-Alain Miller (ed.), Alan Sheridan (trans.), New York: W.W. Norton.

Lacan, J. (1991a) *Le Séminaire. Livre XVII: L'envers de la psychanalyse*, Paris: Seuil.

Lacan, J. (1991b) *The Seminar of Jacques Lacan: Book II: The Ego in Freud's Theory and in the Technique of Psychoanalysis, 1945–1955*, Sylvana Tomaselli (trans.), Jacques-Alain Miller (ed.), New York: W.W. Norton & Co.

Lacan, J. (1992) *The Seminar of Jacques Lacan: Book VII: The Ethics of Psychoanalysis, 1959–1960*, Dennis Porter (trans.), Jacques-Alain Miller (ed.), New York: W.W. Norton & Co.

Lacan, J. (1997) *The Seminar of Jacques Lacan: Book III: The Psychoses*, Russell Grigg (trans.), Jacques-Alain Miller (ed.), New York: W.W. Norton & Co.

Lacan, J. (1998) *The Seminar of Jacques Lacan: Book XX. Encore, 1972–1973: On Feminine Sexuality; The Limits of Love and Knowledge*, Bruce Fink (trans.), Jacques-Alain Miller (ed.), New York: W.W. Norton.

Lacan, J. (2007) *The Seminar of Jacques Lacan: Book XVII: The Other Side of Psychoanalysis*, Russell Grigg (trans.), Jacques-Alain Miller (ed.), New York: W.W. Norton & Co.

Laplanche, J. and J.B. Pontalis (2003) "Fantasy and the Origins of Sexuality," in *Unconscious Fantasy*, Riccardo Steiner (ed.), London: Karnac.

Marx, K. (1970) *Critique of Hegel's "Philosophy of Right"*, Annette Jolin and Joseph O'Malley (trans.), Cambridge: Cambridge University Press.

Marx, K. (1990) *Capital: A Critique of Political Economy (Volume 1)*, Ben Fowkes and David Fernbach (trans.), New York: Penguin.

Marx, K. (1993) *Grundrisse: Foundations of the Critique of Political Economy (Rough Draft)*, M. Nicolaus (trans.), London: Penguin Books.

Pfaller, R. (1998) "Negation and its Reliabilities: An Empty Subject for Ideology?," in *Cogito and the Unconscious*, Slavoj Žižek (ed.), Durham, NC: Duke University Press, pp. 215–218.

Reich, W. (1972) "Dialectical Materialism and Psychoanalysis," in L. Baxandall (ed.), *Sex-Pol*, New York: Vintage Books, pp. 3–74.

Spinoza, B. (1985) *The Collected Works of Spinoza*, Edwin Curley (trans.), Princeton, NJ: Princeton University Press.

Žižek, S. (1989) *The Sublime Object of Ideology*, London: Verso.

7 The other side of value

Substance, labor and enjoyment, or biopolitics according to Spinoza, Marx and Lacan

I begin this last chapter by recapitulating a line of thought that traverses the present work. As we know from Spinoza, being or substance is that which is the cause of itself, that is, it is the power of being to actualize itself. The conception of being as the power of self-actualization is the only possible secular conception of being, that is, one that does not presuppose a creator of being. This substance *qua* power-of-self-actualization pertains not to duration but to a species of eternity, and humans partake in substance and its eternity most directly through their labor-power, insofar as the latter is the potentiality of labor to actualize itself. In capitalism, this power of labor's self-actualization is for the first time commodified, as a result of which surplus-value is, again, for the first time in history, accumulated.

Marx also shows us that this phenomenon is necessarily accompanied by commodity fetishism, that is, the fact that while we consciously assume that we exchange concrete objects of utility, unconsciously we are vehicles for the circulation of abstract exchange-values. While we consciously actualize our labor-power in concrete forms of labor, unconsciously we deposit congealed labor in the commodities we produce, as abstract labor (labor-time), whereby our labor becomes alienated and autonomous (from the laborers). All this is part of the phenomenon we call commodification. The result of this mechanism is that commodities (both things and laboring bodies and minds) no longer matter as concrete objects of utility (products of concrete modes of actualization of labor-power) or as singular producers (of concrete modes of actualization of labor-power); rather they matter only insofar as they are the manifestations of value, as "both the money and the commodity function only as different modes of existence of value itself, the money as its general mode of existence, the commodity as its particular or, so to speak, disguised mode" (Marx 1990: 255). In other words, the result of commodity fetishism is that the being or substance of which both concrete things and people *and* abstract exchange-values are "different modes of existence" appears to be exclusively value – and not the power of self-actualization.

However, we also have seen (in both the first and second chapters) that this appearance is not a subjective illusion but an objective reality. It is an objective fact that the commodification of labor-power is presupposed for the accumulation of surplus-value, and commodity fetishism reflects this central fact: capitalism renders the essence of being *qua* power-of-self-actualization subservient to the domination of value. However, in this last chapter I would like to turn to the question: What is the function of the commodification of being *qua* power-of-self-actualization *beyond* serving the accumulation of economic surplus-value? Differently put, what is its function, beyond economy in the narrow sense, as a factor in the constitution of subjectivity and political power? To respond to this question we need to grasp the power of self-actualization (and labor-power) as something that is useless to the accumulation of value. As we shall see below in more detail, this conception of the power of self-actualization as useless relates to enjoyment, insofar as enjoyment lies outside that which a society considers to be useful to productivity.

Before continuing, let us note that raising the question about the function of the commodification of being *qua* power-of-self-actualization beyond serving the accumulation of economic surplus-value does not mean that we extricate ourselves from the hold of commodity fetishism (which would be tantamount to extricating ourselves from the imaginary, i.e., something impossible). Rather it means switching our perspective to the underside of commodity fetishism by inverting its dynamic. What if the accumulation of value were not the ultimate law governing the universe of capitalism? What if value is the law governing our experience only insofar as it is itself sustained by another transcendental law, as its logical presupposition – not unlike the empirical law of the pleasure principle and its presupposed transcendental law of the death drive? As Deleuze puts it:

> What we call a principle or law is, in the first place, that which governs a particular field; it is in this sense that we speak of an *empirical* principle or law. Thus we say that the pleasure principle governs life universally and without exception. But there is another and quite distinct question, namely, in virtue of what is a field governed by a principle; there must be a principle of another kind, a second-order principle, which accounts for the necessary compliance of the field with the empirical principle. It is this second-order principle that we call transcendental … [The death drive is] not the exception to the [pleasure] principle but … its "*foundation.*"
>
> (Deleuze 1994b: 112–3)

Therefore, to understand fully the law of the pleasure principle requires understanding its foundation, its underside. By the same token, turning to the underside or foundation of commodity fetishism is essential in understanding it and, hence, in understanding being both as value and as the power of self-actualization.

This was actually Lacan's intent in his XVII Seminar, *The Other Side of Psychoanalysis*, when he focused on the need to fathom the true meaning of Marx's surplus-value, admonishing: "It's not because one nationalizes the means of production at the level of socialism in one country that one has thereby done away with surplus value, if one doesn't know what it is" (Lacan 2007: 108). Having grasped that the intertwining of subjectivity and objectivity underlies as much Freud's psychoanalytic theory as Marx's theory of commodity fetishism, Lacan understood that surplus-value goes far beyond its reductionist conception as a purely economic category. Surplus-value is also a category of the human subjectivity and socio-political formations that constitute, and are constituted under, economic conditions that involve the accumulation of surplus-value. In a consummating gesture of psychoanalysis as the realization of a materialist epistemontology as postulated by Marx's theory of commodity fetishism, Lacan designated this category "surplus-enjoyment" (*plus-de-jouir*). The connotations of *jouir* ("to come" or "reach orgasm"; see Fink in Lacan 1998: 3, n. 8) already expand the referential field of Marx's economic counterpart. As we shall see below, *jouissance* (enjoyment) and *plus-de-jouir* (surplus-enjoyment) are effectively the same, insofar as enjoyment is always a surplus or excess to what in utilitarian terms is required for productivity. Nevertheless, the term *plus-de-jouir* has the advantage of, on the one hand, making an allusion to surplus-value (*plus-value*) as the corollary of a presumed excess of enjoyment, and, on the other hand, indicating the loss of all enjoyment under capitalist conditions, since the French term also means "no more enjoyment." This ambiguity of the term points, as we shall see, to enjoyment's relation to labor-power – both being manifestations of the power of self-actualization – and their historically mutable function as an excess beyond what counts as useful or as an excess that is recuperated within the realm of the useful.

To respond to the question animating this chapter, I shall first explore (surplus-)enjoyment by bringing together certain common elements in Lacan's exposition of this concept in Seminar XI – *The Four Fundamental Concepts of Psychoanalysis* (1964), Seminar XVII – *The Other Side of Psychoanalysis* (1969–1970), and Seminar XX – *Encore* (1972–1973). While one often tends to speak of a shift in Lacan's conceptualization of enjoyment throughout his Seminars, particularly between Seminars XI and the later seminars, I here endeavor to trace a line of continuity.[1] In what follows I shall approach enjoyment and its temporality so as to focus on its relation to labor and labor's temporal dimensions. As we shall see, labor in capitalism involves different aspects with distinct temporalities. Through labor's aspect as concrete physical and mental activity within time, human beings relate to duration and mortality, while through its aspect as labor-power – which pertains to what Spinoza defines as singular essence – human beings relate to eternity. This distinction will allow us to understand the biopolitical administration of the temporalities of labor and enjoyment both in the constitution of subjectivity and in the sustenance of objectivity, that is, the sustenance of the *status quo* of capitalism and its biopower. In turn, this will lead us to the central biopolitical reproduction of what Lacan calls "imitation" or "semblance of surplus *jouissance*" (Lacan 2007: 81), as the religious practice of capitalism – in contrast to Spinoza's third kind of knowledge, which is the path to secular salvation, and to "joy" or the "love of God."

Jouissance of the real

In this section we shall see that *jouissance* is the psychoanalytic term for Spinoza's substance or the power of self-actualization. To be more specific, as Jacques-Alain Miller has pointed out, in Seminar XI Lacan obtains "the passage from *jouissance* of the imaginary to [*jouissance*] of the real" (Miller 1995: 11) – and it is the latter that stands for substance. The difference between these two kinds of *jouissance* can be better clarified through the distinction between two levels of the real in Lacan's theory. As Bruce Fink states, there are:

> two different levels of the real: (1) a real before the letter, that is, a presymbolic real, which, in the final analysis is but our own hypothesis (R1), and (2) a real after the letter which is characterized by impasses and impossibilities due to relations among the elements of the symbolic order itself (R2), that is, which is generated by the symbolic.
>
> (Miller 1995: 27)

It is important to add that the Real 2 is generated by the symbolic but not actualized within the symbolic, which is why it remains *real*. This Real 2 can also be said to be imaginary – like that which fills in the *objet a* (the unattainable object of desire) – *insofar as* it has *real* effects. What Miller calls *jouissance* of the real pertains to the level of Real 1, whereas the *jouissance* of the imaginary pertains to the Real 2.

The "*jouissance*" of the real, Miller continues, is that "which is present" in the "asexual real," that is, it is the "libido," insofar as we refer to the libido "of the real level." Further, since for Lacan there is a "link between libido and … the death drive," the real *jouissance* is "drive," which is why "*jouissance* [is always] beyond the pleasure principle" – the death drive being defined as precisely the beyond of the pleasure principle. Summing up, real *jouissance* is the libido of the "asexual real" or of the "real level," and it is "drive" (Miller 1995: 10–4). Lacan specifies the drive further in Seminar XI by adding that "the activity of the drive is concentrated in this *making oneself* (*se faire*)" (Lacan 1981: 195). The real *jouissance* or drive, at once death drive and "pure life instinct" (Lacan 1981: 198), is something that is not created, produced, constructed, or made, for it is itself the pure activity of making itself (*se faire*). In other words, *jouissance* or drive is the cause of itself, not unlike Spinoza's substance. Because *jouissance* is a sheer power or potential, its "characteristic is not to exist" actually (Lacan 1981: 197). It is a potential unlimited by both the intensity of its power and time; in Lacan's words, "*jouissance*" is "pure life instinct … immortal … irrepressible … indestructible life" (Lacan 1981: 197).

Here Lacan makes a twist of a biological term and speaks of the "lamella," conceived as a mythic "amoeba" that is "immortal … because it survives any division, any scissiparous intervention," to make clear that *jouissance* is alien to any division or differentiation; it is an undifferentiated totality (Lacan 1981: 197). It is for this reason that the real *jouissance* or libido coincides with "the locus of the Other, insofar as it is there that the first signifier emerges" (Lacan 1981: 198). This is to say, prior to the emergence of this signifier, pure indestructible life and the Other – the locus from which the signifier, as "that which represents a subject," *will* emerge (Lacan 1981: 198) – are one. This is why Lacan can make within two subsequent pages the same point twice, once using the word "libido," the other the word "Other." First iteration: "the libido, *qua* pure life instinct … immortal life, or irrepressible life … is precisely what is subtracted from the living being by virtue of the fact that it is subject to the cycle of sexed reproduction" (Lacan 1981: 198). Second iteration: "The relation to the Other is precisely that which, for us, brings out what is represented by the lamella … the relation between the living subject and that which he loses by having to pass, for his reproduction, through the sexual cycle" (Lacan 1981: 199).

In short, real *jouissance* is the undifferentiated totality of indestructible life or libido and of the signifying structure, in the midst of which the first actual signifier will emerge, or, rather, distinguish itself from indestructible life. The emergence of the signifier introduces sexuality and mortality, that is, time as finite diachrony or duration. The *jouissance* of the real is substance as the *undifferentiated* power of self-actualization, whereas the first actual signifier designates "that which the intellect perceives of substance as constituting its essence," that is, the "attribute" (*Ethics* ID4). The intellect cannot perceive substance in its undifferentiatedness but rather it perceives it under the attribute of either extension or thought – either as Body or as Mind. As Beth Lord remarks, "a substance is pure, indeterminate being," that is, nothing can be said about it except that it is the "'cause of itself', the eternal activity of causing existence," in short, "*being as such* is the power of making itself actual" (Lord 2010: 21). By contrast, the "attributes are the different ways in which a substance *can be* perceived" by the intellect, for the "intellect can truly perceive a substance, but not as pure, indeterminate being"; rather, the "intellect always perceives of a substance *as* one of its attributes" and, therefore, an "attribute *is the substance itself*, as perceived in a certain way" (Lord 2010: 21). Although substance consists of infinite attributes, the human intellect can perceive only two, Mind and Body, or signifier and physical being.

The moment of the emergence of the signifier, sexuality, and duration bars or splits the subject, thereby introducing for the first time an "antinomy between subject and *jouissance*"; from then on the "barred subject calls for a complement of being" (Miller 1995: 10–4). That is, by identifying with the signifier, the subject lacks being, and this is why it is barred. In other words, once the *jouissance* of the real – the undifferentiated totality of life or the potential of self-actualization and the signifying structure – has been destroyed through the emergence of the signifier as distinct from life, *jouissance* becomes being as that which the subject lacks. For "the disappearance of being [is what is] induced by the very function of the signifier" (Lacan 1981: 211). This is to say that the being or *jouissance* that the subject lacks after the emergence of the signifier and duration is not to be conflated with the body or extension. Being, like substance, is undifferentiated power, neither Body nor Mind, and it is this that the subject lacks from within duration (and hence from the perspective of the imaginary). That "time … is a product of the imagination" (*Ethics* IIP44S) is the corollary of the imaginary character of lack or imperfection; for "things have been brought into being by God with supreme perfection, since they have necessarily followed from a most perfect nature" (*Ethics* IP33S2).

Recapitulating, the entrance of the subject to language is also the subject's entrance to sexed reproduction and mortality, and both entail the loss of this primary pre-symbolic undifferentiated absolute immanence (Real 1). The referent of Lacan's *jouissance* of the real is this purely hypothetical, yet (logically) necessarily presupposed absolute immanence of life and signifier, as the precondition for the emergence of the split subject. On this level (Real 1), if we speak of "being" we mean life *qua* libido, that is, as the indestructible power of being to actualize itself – rather than being as a lack (Real 2). The status of (the lack of) being and of the sexual difference is that of the Real 2 – that is, they are effects of the emergence of the signifier, of its failure to represent adequately that necessarily presupposed hypothesis of undifferentiated totality (or, in the Spinozian parlance, the attribute's failure to express substance as such, in its pure, indeterminate state). Both sexual difference and the imaginary owe to the intellect's impossibility to grasp the Real 1 as such – that is, as undifferentiated power of self-actualization.

Needless to say, this *jouissance* of the real is no empirically possible enjoyment but something that needs to be presupposed logically for any empirically possible enjoyment – not unlike Spinoza's substance that is necessarily presupposed for the existence of modes.

Temporality of the *jouissance* of the real

As the unvarying power of being to actualize itself, real *jouissance* is an indestructible potential that lies outside chronological time or duration. *Jouissance* or, in Spinoza's terms, substance is of an "eternal nature" and exists "under a species of eternity [*sub species aeternitatis*]" (*Ethics* IIP44C2D). It is important to note that eternity has nothing to do with any conception of chronological time or duration, including infinite duration. In Spinoza's words, eternity "cannot be explained by duration or time, even if the duration is conceived to be without beginning or end" (*Ethics* ID8E). It is only the actualization of an action and its actualized product that pertain to duration, whereas sheer potentiality or, as Gilles Deleuze puts it, the "full, unvarying *power* of acting," cannot involve duration and pertains instead to eternity (Deleuze 1988: 62–3).

Lacan stresses the atemporal or eternal status of real *jouissance* (R1) by juxtaposing it to the *jouissance* of the imaginary (R2), which presupposes the separation between being and signifier, or, what amounts to the same, the introduction of sexuality, duration, and mortality. In his words, real *jouissance* or "being is the *jouissance* of the body as such, that is, as asexual (*asexué*)" (Lacan 1998: 6). The "asexual" is outside time, for only the introduction of sexuality can introduce time – to reiterate in its more complete form Lacan's afore-cited words: "what the *sexed* being loses in sexuality … is … the libido, *qua* pure life instinct, that is to say, immortal life, or irrepressible life … [this] indestructible life … is precisely what is subtracted from the living being by virtue of the fact that it is subject to the cycle of sexed reproduction" (Lacan 1981: 197–8). The signifier introduces duration, which, in the Spinozian idiom, means that we are now on the level of finite modal existence, which, beyond mortality, for the human being involves sexual difference, the distinction between Body and Mind, and the introduction of lack and the imaginary.

Let us note here the crucial distinction of the imaginary of R2, as opposed to any other imaginary idea that will emerge as its effect. On the level of R2, imaginary only indicates our impossibility of grasping the undifferentiated being as such. Given this impossibility, the two attributes, Mind and Body, like the two sexes, female and male, are the sole real ways in which we can grasp and experience being. This is why we call this imaginary – *Real* 2.

Jouissance *and labor: singular essences, in distinction to substance*

The unvarying power of self-actualization *sub species aeternitatis*, this "*jouissance*," Lacan tells us in Seminar XX, "is what serves no purpose (*ne sert à rien*)" (Lacan 1998: 3). In this context Lacan mentions the notion of usufruct, to make the point that *jouissance* is by definition something that cannot serve any utilitarian or pragmatist purpose, however this may be historically defined. "Usufruct" (from the Latin *usus* and *fructus*, which mean "use" and "enjoyment," respectively), is "a legal notion," introduced around 1630 to indicate the right to use and enjoy the profits of something belonging to another. Specifically, Lacan continues, to "have the usufruct of an inheritance" means that "you can enjoy the inheritance (*en jouir*) as long as you do not use up too much of it," that you "can enjoy (*jouir de*) your means, but must not waste them" (Lacan 1998: 3).[2] Through usufruct, the law's task becomes to constrain enjoyment within the boundaries of the useful, to make sure that it is not wasted. The "essence of law" in utilitarianism is "to divide up, distribute, or reattribute everything that counts as jouissance," so that the latter "is forbidden to him who speaks, as such," since "to speak" presupposes that the subject is subjected to the law, and "the Law is grounded in this very prohibition" of "jouissance" (Lacan 1998: 3; Lacan 1977: 319). "This is why," Lacan says already in Seminar XVII, "I introduced [*jouissance*] by the term '*Mehrlust*,' surplus *jouissance*," in the sense of a wasted excess, for it "is precisely through being perceived in the dimension of loss," "through this effect of entropy, through this wasting, that *jouissance* acquires a status and shows itself" (Lacan 1991a: 56; Lacan 2007: 50). Always when the "signifier" or "knowledge … is at work, what it produces is entropy," that is, *jouissance qua* loss (Lacan 2007: 50). This means that even in capitalism, where everything seems to be put in the service of the accumulation of surplus-value, there still must be something that is lost, that does not serve this accumulation. This is a tricky point, both because it can easily appear that capital lets nothing be wasted *and* because we may miss the actual function of either that which is wasted or that which is counted – "counted" meaning what "can possibly be articulated as signifier" (Lacan 2007: 50), whether signifier in the field of knowledge or in economy (i.e., exchange-value).

Now, given that *jouissance* is defined as an uncounted loss or waste, it might appear strange that, as Alenka Zupančič remarks, in Seminar XVII "Lacan … poses (and presupposes) a certain equivalence between work and enjoyment," so that "the status of work (or labor) … is identical to the status of enjoyment" (Zupančič 2006: 162). In fact, Zupančič attributes this equivalence or identity to the fact that both labor and enjoyment "essentially appear[] as entropy, as loss, or as an unaccounted-for surplus (by-product) of signifying operations" (Zupančič 2006: 162). Labor, however, was an unaccounted-for surplus only prior to the capitalist commodification of labor, as in the slaved labor of antiquity or in feudal serfdom, that is, during the era dominated by what Lacan calls the discourse of the "classical master [*maître antique*]" (Lacan 2007: 31). By contrast, in capitalism, far from being wasted, labor is reappropriated as surplus-value – in fact, it is its very precondition. The same is true of enjoyment, since in capitalism not only are the forms of entertainment commodified but leisure is itself a requirement for the producers in order both to replenish their energy, so as to be productive, and to consume. In short, labor and enjoyment can be either lost or reappropriated as productive surplus, depending on the historical economic and social conditions. Since both labor and enjoyment share the same historical fate as to whether they are wasted or reappropriated, there must exist a further, essential, link between them – a shared essence that remains historically immutable.

However, in order to address this question we must first return to Lacan's account of the discourses in seminar XVII, mentioned in the preceding chapter, so as to see the historical itinerary of labor from the precapitalist to the capitalist economy. Only the discourses of the Master and the University are relevant here, since Lacan links them directly to precapitalism and capitalism, respectively.[3] Each of these two discourses expresses a specific relation between the signifier and *jouissance*, as well as a specific relation between knowledge and politico-economic power. In the discourse of the Master, "the entire function of the episteme … as transmissible knowledge" – that is, not as practical knowledge (*savoir-faire*) but as theoretical or abstract knowledge, such as philosophy (*connaissance*) – "is always borrowed from the techniques of craftsmen, that is to say of serfs. It is a matter of extracting the essence of the knowledge in order for it to become the master's knowledge" (Lacan 2007: 21–2). Lacan references here Plato's dialogues, but think also of Aristotle: to develop his concept of *entelechy* – the idea that everything bears within itself its own telos, its proper purpose – Aristotle turns to the shoemaker who has to adjust all his labor activity to the purpose of the shoes, which are to be worn for walking. So, shoes bear within themselves their telos – to be used for walking – and this can then be generalized as the abstract thesis that everything has in itself its own telos, its *entelechy*. Out of the concrete knowledge of the shoemaker, Aristotle extracts an abstract concept, *entelechy*, which was destined to impact centuries of philosophical, religious, ethical, and legal thought. In this way the ancient philosopher instills the unquestionable assumption of a ubiquitous *entelechy*, which in the case of the human translates as the soul that guarantees that humans know what is good for them and strive after it.

This assumption remained unquestioned up until Freud's introduction of the death drive, but the relevant point here is that in the discourse of the Master, the practical knowledge of the slave worker (e.g., the shoemaker) was distilled and appropriated by the master as abstract knowledge, while the laborer's actual labor went wasted, that is, it was not counted by the signifier, in both senses of the word, knowledge and exchange-value. It is in this sense that Lacan says that in the discourse of the Master, the master appropriated not the slaves' labor as such but, rather, "it is a matter of robbing the slave of his function at the level of knowledge" (Lacan 2007: 22). Zupančič succinctly foregrounds this point: "a knowledge that 'does not know itself' and that works passes into articulated knowledge that can be written down and thought independently of the work which it is bound up with at the outset" (Zupančič 2006: 161). Of course, the capitalist revolution lies precisely in the fact that this labor as such that was never before counted began to be counted and be accumulated as surplus-value. As Zupančič also recognizes, "in order for capitalist exploitation to function, the entropy or loss, the amount of work not accounted for, or simply not counted, has to start to be counted (and 'valued')" (Zupančič 2006: 170).

Marx had of course made the same point; what Lacan adds, as we saw in the preceding chapter, is the insight that the transition from the discourse of the Master to that of the University entails a radical shift in the relation between power and knowledge. To repeat, with the advent of capitalism, "the impotence of conjoining surplus enjoyment with the master's truth [l'impuissance à faire le joint du plus-de-jouir à la vérité du maître] … is all of a sudden emptied" (Lacan 1991a: 207; Lacan 2007: 177–8, translation modified); that is, surplus enjoyment – the waste (i.e., labor) – can now be conjoined not only with surplus-value but also with *the truth* of the master. Truth is a category pertaining not to economy but to knowledge. This is to say that Lacan recognized that the new, modern or capitalist, master is knowledge itself, specified as "not knowledge of everything … but all-knowing [non pas *savoir-de-tout* … mais *tout-savoir*]," that is, "nothing other than knowledge," not mastery or power, but *pure* knowledge, which, as such, is said to be "objective knowledge" or "science" or what "in ordinary language is called the bureaucracy" (Lacan 2007: 31). We have entered the era in which power bases itself on the illusion that knowledge reveals objective, scientific or purely procedural truths, rather than sustaining authority. In short, the discourse of the University or the "modern master" represents the era of capital as that of biopower: the power that succeeds in hiding itself behind what passes as the "globalizing logic of the market and procedures" (Brousse 2006: 259). This imaginary perception of power as scientific or objective knowledge rather than mastery is part and parcel of the phenomenon of commodity fetishism that we have examined in earlier chapters here.

Just as labor as such was wasted and unaccounted, so was the slaves' or serfs' enjoyment. That is, as Lacan already had put it in his second seminar, "people who had slaves didn't realise that one could establish equations for the price of their food and what they did in their *latifundia*" (Lacan 1991b: 75) – whether what they did was an activity of the kind of producing shoes or, say, enjoying staring at the stars or getting drunk; as long as, of course, the shoes were timely ready. If the shoes were not ready, one could always dispose of the slaves in question and buy new ones. Which is why, Lacan continues, "[t]here are no examples of energy calculations in the use of slaves. There is not the hint of an equation as to their output." Then he adds, "[i]t took machines for us to realize they had to be fed. And more – they had to be looked after" – and, as we know, it took capitalism to have the machines he has in mind, namely, machines based on the calculation of energy, such as the "steam engine." So, it took this kind of machine, which also means the kind of science and technology that was developed under capitalism, to realize that workers "tend to wear out," even though "[s]laves do as well." For in the case of slaves, "one doesn't think about it, one thinks that it is natural for them to get old and croak" (Lacan 1991b: 74–5). By contrast, in capitalism and its "free" (i.e., commodified) labor, where the employers pay laborers/employees in a calculated manner (in terms of labor-time), and eventually, through biopolitics, they bear responsibility for the expenses regarding the laborers' health, etc., the employers are concerned with the mode of the laborers' enjoyment insofar as it can affect their productivity and the employers' own expenses for sustaining the laborers. By now it is clear that when Zupančič states that labor and enjoyment constitute the discursive waste, she means this as a statement that applies only to precapitalism, whereas in capitalism both labor and enjoyment are counted as, in fact, indispensable factors for the accumulation of surplus-value.

Now we can return to the question regarding labor's and enjoyment's essential, historically immutable, link, because of which the two share the same destiny – as wasted or counted excess – in different historical socio-economic organizations. Their profound, essential, affinity owes to the fact that both *jouissance* and labor are *potentiality*. Though here we must be precise and point out that this is true not of vaguely "labor" but specifically of labor-power. Labor-power is the potentiality of labor to actualize itself or – to reiterate Lacan's equivalent verb in the context of libido or enjoyment – "*se faire*." Recalling Marx's words, "labour-power exists only as a *capacity* of the living individual" (Marx 1990: 274, emphasis added); it "is his [the laborer's] vitality itself," that is, it "is not materialized in a product, does not exist apart from him, thus exists not really, but in *potentiality*, as his *capacity*" (Marx 1993: 267, emphasis added).

However, it is now time to differentiate between the potentiality of substance and that of labor-power and enjoyment. For only substance is the cause of itself, whereas labor-power and enjoyment, being potentialities of finite modes (living beings), are not self-caused. Put differently, yes, labor-power is the power of labor to actualize itself, but this labor depends entirely on the existence of a being with Body and Mind, whose existence depends on other finite modes, and so on. To examine more closely the difference between labor-power and enjoyment, as well as their relation to eternity despite this difference, we must turn to Spinoza's distinction among three kinds of knowledge.

The "first kind of knowledge" derives "from singular things which have been presented to us through the senses" or "from signs … without order for the intellect," and through which we form our "opinion or imagination." The "second kind of knowledge" or reason consists of our "common notions and adequate ideas of the properties of things." While the first kind of knowledge pertains to imagination and "is the only cause of falsity," "knowledge of the second and third kind is necessarily true," with the second pertaining to reason and the third forming what Spinoza calls "intuitive knowledge" (*Ethics* IIP41 and P40S2). While imagination perceives everything within time, reason and intuition know things *sub species aeternitatis.* Spinoza stresses the difference between "duration" and the "species of eternity" by stating: "Whatever the Mind understands under a species of eternity, it understands not from the fact that it conceives the Body's present actual existence, but from the fact that it conceives the Body's essence under a species of eternity" (*Ethics* VP29).

To understand how it is possible that the human mind can conceive the body's essence under a species of eternity we need to recall the identity of God and Nature (Spinoza's famous "Deus, seu Natura," "God, or Nature"); given that God is Nature, "the very necessity of God's eternal nature" entails that it "is of the nature of Reason to perceive of things under a certain species of eternity," and hence "to regard things as necessary, not as contingent." This also means that "the foundations of Reason are notions … which explain those things that are common to all, and which … do not explain the essence of any singular thing" but of the universal, which therefore "must be conceived without any relation to time, but under a certain species of eternity" (*Ethics* IIP44C2 and P44D). Reason and its common notions explain things under a certain species of eternity only insofar as they explain things as universal and necessary. Like a geometrical law or a pure structural formula, reason or the second kind of knowledge grasps what is common in all things (e.g., in all triangles) but, to repeat, not what is "the essence of any singular thing" (e.g., a singular triangle). "*Nevertheless,*" Spinoza adds while explaining the third kind of knowledge, "*in God there is necessarily an idea that expresses the essence of this or that Body, under a species of eternity*" (*Ethics* VP22). For, "God is the cause not only of the existence of this or that Body" within duration "but also of its essence" *sub species aeternitatis,* insofar as this singular essence is "conceived through the very essence of God … by a certain eternal necessity" (*Ethics* VP22P). In other words, through the third kind of knowledge our mind conceives of our body as an eternal and singular essence, insofar as we are necessary effects of God.

Thus, although both reason and intuition are the source of truth and consider things under a species of eternity, their objects do not coincide entirely. Reason accounts for everything that follows from the necessity of God – whether directly or indirectly – whereas intuition accounts only for what follows from God indirectly, which is to say only for things and ideas with actual existence. These latter things and ideas have "God … [as] a cause not insofar as he is infinite, but insofar as he is considered to be affected by another idea of a singular thing which actually exists, and of this [idea] God is also the cause, insofar as he is affected by another third [idea], and so on, to infinity" (*Ethics* IIP9). In other words, within reason "singular things do not exist, except insofar as they are comprehended in God's attributes," that is, "their objective being, *or* ideas, do not exist except insofar as God's infinite idea exists" – i.e., for reason, it suffices that things and ideas follow from the necessary nature of God in order for them to "exist." By contrast, intuition pertains to "singular things [that] are said to exist, not only insofar as they are comprehended in God's attributes, but insofar as they are said to have duration" (*Ethics* IIP8C).

Thus, in Spinoza's own example, we can know from reason (specifically, geometry) that "the rectangles formed from the segments of all the straight lines intersecting" within a circle "are equal to one another," and that, therefore, a circle contains "infinitely many rectangles that are equal to one another." Nevertheless, "none of them can be said to exist except insofar as the circle exists," that is, insofar as they follow by necessity from the nature of the circle (the equivalent of God's attributes in the afore-cited passages). In short, *for reason*, all these infinite rectangles "exist." By contrast, if we draw two "of these infinitely many" rectangles – as Spinoza does in the *Ethics* – the "ideas" of these two rectangles "also exist now, not only insofar as they are only comprehended in the idea of the circle, but also insofar as they involve the existence of those rectangles" and "[b]y this they are distinguished from the other ideas of the other rectangles" (*Ethics* IIP8S). While the other rectangles exist only for reason, these two, actually existing, rectangles exist also for intuition. In other words, while reason considers things as eternal insofar as they are simply necessary (as are the infinite equal rectangles within a circle), intuition considers things with regard to their *singular* essence, that is, not simply with regard to what follows by necessity from the nature of God but also with regard to that which determines their existence or non-existence. For "to the essence of any thing belongs that which, being given, the thing is [NS: also] necessarily posited and which, being taken away, the thing is necessarily [NS: also] taken away" (*Ethics* IID2). Unlike reason, which disregards the question of existence and focuses entirely on universal necessity, intuition links the existing mode with its singular necessity, that is, its essence *sub species aeternitatis.*

Yet, although the essence of singular determined things (finite modes) is and is conceived under a species of eternity, it must not be conflated with substance itself. In Spinoza's words, "*[t]he being of substance does not pertain to the essence of man*," for "the being of substance necessarily involves existence," so, "if the being of substance pertained to the essence of man, then substance being given, man would necessarily be given … and consequently man would exist necessarily, which is absurd" (*Ethics* IIP10 and P10D).

We can now understand the difference between the potentiality of substance and that of labor-power or enjoyment, that is, singular essences. What differentiates substance and its essence from any singular essence is that the substance's essence necessarily entails existence, that is, it is the sole cause of itself or is self-actualized. By contrast, a singular essence does not necessarily involve existence. It follows that, insofar as a mode's singular essence is the eternal expression of substance through that singular mode, *singular essence must be the potentiality or power of actualizing whatever that mode can actualize – it is the power of actualizing that mode's singular potential.* Therefore, the singular essence of a human being consists in the power of its Body and Mind to actualize whatever they can. They actualize whatever they can either in the form of labor-power or in that of enjoyment, depending on what counts historically as recuperable excess or waste. To distinguish it from the absolute potentiality of the substance, I shall refer to the potentiality of labor-power and enjoyment as *singular potentiality.* Despite their difference, however, both the necessity of singular potentiality or essence and the necessity of the substance's potentiality or essence are eternal, that is, both partake in exactly the same eternity.[4]

Now, the essence of labor-power and of *jouissance* (of the real) as singular potentiality remains the same under any historico-economic circumstances. It is only in capitalism that this labor-power becomes "the use-value which the worker" sells to the capitalist in the market, insofar as he or she (the worker) is "free" (Marx 1993: 267). Slaves and serfs did not sell their labor-power, for they were not free; their vitality – their life or bios – itself did not belong to them but to their masters. In capitalism, by contrast, as we have seen, labor-power is commodified, that is, it is counted by the signifier toward the accumulation of surplus-value.

However, the realization that the link between enjoyment and labor applies to labor only in its aspect as labor-power indicates that we have to examine labor's distinct aspects, as well as their respective temporalities.

Aspects of labor and their temporalities

The term "labor" subsumes three distinct forms of labor: (a) labor-power, the singular potential of labor to actualize itself; (b) concrete labor, the specific set of physical and mental activities practiced in the process of the labor-power's self-actualization or expenditure (for example, the labor of the baker versus the labor of the teacher); and (c) abstract labor or labor-time, homogenous and quantified labor, which serves as the unit for measuring the exchange-value of a commodity based on the labor-time that is socially necessary for the production of a given commodity at a socially given average productivity of labor. "Socially necessary labour-time," as Marx puts it, "is the labour-time required to produce any use-value under the conditions of production normal for a given society and with the average degree of skill and intensity of labour prevalent in that society." It is the "expenditure" of this "abstract," "identical," "equal" or "homogeneous" labor – that is, "human labour-power expended without regard to the form of its expenditure" – "that forms the substance of value" in capitalism (Marx 1990: 128–9).

Only the abstract, homogeneous, quantifiable and measurable aspect of labor, objectified in the commodity, constitutes the substance of value. In Marx's words:

> A use-value, or useful article, therefore, has value only because abstract human labour is objectified (*vergegenständlicht*) or materialized in it. How, then, is the magnitude of this value to be measured? By means of the quantity of the "value-forming substance," the labour, contained in the article. This quantity is measured by its duration, and the labour-time is itself measured on the particular scale of hours, days etc.
>
> (Marx 1990: 129)

This is why as "values, the coat and the linen have the same substance, they are the objective expressions of homogeneous labour" (Marx 1990: 134). On the one hand:

> [t]ailoring and weaving are the formative elements in the use-values coat and linen, precisely because these two kinds of labour are of different qualities; but [on the other hand] only in so far as abstraction is made from their particular qualities, only in so far as both possess the same quality of being human labour, do tailoring and weaving form the substance of the values of the two articles mentioned.
>
> (Marx 1990: 136)

Again: "commodities possess an objective character as values only in so far as they are all expressions of an identical social substance, human labour" (Marx 1990: 138). Only as abstraction does human labor constitute this social substance that is value. Its other aspect, the fact that labor-power always actualizes itself through particular activities – i.e., the fact that labor always comes as *concrete* labor required for a particular kind of use-value – falls out. In addition to the labor that is abstracted and objectified in the commodity so as to contribute to the accumulation of surplus-value, there is another surplus: one that is not conducive to the accumulation of surplus-value, that is not measured, and that is not counted in the formula of capital – in short, an aspect of labor that is lost, wasted. This last point is actually Heiko Feldner and Fabio Vighi's wager. The authors differentiate between concrete and abstract labor, and maintain that only abstract labor is counted, whereas concrete labor falls out of the discourse of capitalism as waste. From this they infer that capitalism's waste is ultimately "*the subject itself*," in the form of the "sub-proletariat, [the] masses of segregated people who are simply in excess," the unemployed masses who fall out of the discourse as loss.[5] These masses are "increasingly rendered superfluous (jobless)" through the technologization of the mode of production (Feldner and Vighi 2014: 43–4). Now, beyond Zupančič's and Feldner and Vighi's insightful accounts of labor in Marx, I want to foreground that at stake here is also the commodification of labor-power (and of enjoyment) – which above all means the commodification of singular essence or of the power of every mode to actualize its potential, whose temporality is eternity.

As we have seen, concrete labor was also wasted already in the discourse of the Master. What is new to capitalism is the following. While singular labor-power and concrete labor (specific activity) are phenomena that have existed throughout history, it is only through the capitalist commodification of labor-power that abstract labor (value or the capitalist social substance) emerges. That is, while the loss of concrete labor marks both precapitalist and capitalist discourses, the phenomenon specific to capitalism consists in the emergence of abstract labor as the corollary of the commodification of labor-power (singular essence).

Now let us spell out the distinct temporalities pertaining to each of the three forms of labor in capitalism. Labor-power, as the singular potentiality of labor to actualize itself, pertains to eternity. By contrast, concrete labor – the specific activities through which labor-power is expended – takes place within diachrony or duration, the temporality of physical mortal bodies and minds. Abstract labor, which, to repeat Marx, is "the substance of value," pertains to synchrony, the temporality of differential values.[6] Thus, we can infer that the exclusively capitalist commodification of labor-power means also the historically unforeseen commodification of eternity. Further, abstract labor – a form of labor emerging for the first time in history with capitalism – is of course counted, as exchange-value (this is its essential function), and so is its temporality, synchrony. The sole aspect of labor that continues also in capitalism to be wasted – i.e., does not *per se* contribute to the accumulation of surplus-value – is the expenditure of labor-power, that is, the concrete labor performed by particular physical and mental activities within finite duration.

What is unique in capitalism – particularly in its advanced technological and mediatized era – is (a) the ever-increasing *"counting"* or *commodification of eternity*, accompanied by (b) a new, *properly secular, fate* for the temporality that is not counted, that is, the temporality of concrete labor, *finite duration.*

Labor and the historical modes of its "loss" and "counting"

The loss of finite duration amounts to mortality falling out of the discourse. By contrast, that the other two temporalities of labor – synchrony and, more crucially, *eternity* – are for the first time in history counted means that they become part of the discourse. To understand the significance of becoming "lost" or "falling out" of the discourse and of "counting" within the discourse let us schematically compare the situation of the secular capitalist era to that of the discourse of the Master, as the blueprint for presecular/precapitalist organizations.

If, as we have seen, according to Lacan, "the formula of atheism" – that is, of the properly secular – is that "*God is unconscious*" (Lacan 1981: 59), then the characteristic of the presecular is that God (or the gods or spirits of any sort) is conscious, that is, an acknowledged function with epistemontologically legitimate effects on bodies and minds. As such an acknowledged function, the divine or spiritual is conceived as supernatural, and it is in this sense that it transcends natural bodies and minds. This supernatural transcendence could take the form of the transcendent spirits being incorporated in these bodies and minds, as in archaic societies in which spirits inhabited everything on earth. Or it could take the more dualist form of monotheism, as in Judeo-Christianity, where supernatural transcendence was relegated to the heavens, with the human soul becoming the link enabling the transition from earth to the heavens. This is to say that the discourse of the Master, in one form or another, always assumed a supernatural transcendent realm parallel to its natural world. Hence, this parallel universe could also become a depository for whatever falls out of the natural world, whereby the lost element would be acknowledged as a quality of the supernatural entities in question (spirits, gods, God, and their qualities such as eternity, immortality, etc.). So, returning to labor's forms and their temporalities, in the discourse of the Master there existed only labor-power and specific kinds of labor, as well as their respective temporalities, eternity and duration, both of which were lost. Eternity was projected into the realm of transcendence, whether that of the archaic spirits, the pagan gods or the monotheistic heavens. This displacement of eternity into the parallel universe of transcendence determined the fate of duration: mortal life did not matter, except as a transitory bridge toward eternal afterlife – this is what it means in the discourse of the Master that duration fell out of the discourse.

Still, this does not mean that the discourse of the Master or the presecular precapitalist paradigm constitutes a monolithic block with only one mode in which duration could fall out of the discourse. In fact, in order to pursue the historical itinerary of enjoyment next to that of labor, we need to acknowledge at least one central distinction: that between the era of polytheism, with its spirits and gods, and the era of the God of monotheism. In the former case – the case of archaic societies and the pagan societies of antiquity – the difference between humans and gods consists in the following. The "gods are simply mythical spirits, without any substratum of reality"; a "spirit that is not subordinated to the reality of a mortal body is a god, is purely *divine* (sacred)"; and, "[i]nsofar as he is himself a spirit, man is divine (sacred), but he is not supremely so, since he is real" (Bataille 1989: 37). The logic of archaic and pagan societies involves "the positing of the things as subjects," that is, the "virtues of a *thing*" consist in that it is "'capable of acting, thinking, and speaking' (just as men do)" (Bataille 1989: 32–3). This pan-animism entails pantheism, that is, the "positing … of a 'supreme being'" can occur only as a positing "in the world" (Bataille 1989: 33) – something which indicates that in spite of the assumption of a supernatural transcendence, this world is not yet as dualist as monotheism was to become. To be sure, "there is doubtless, in the invention of a supreme being, a determination to define a value that is greater than any other" so that "there is no ultimate equality between" that being and any other being, for, "by definition, the supreme being has the highest rank." Yet "all [beings] are of the same kind, in which immanence and personality are mingled; all can be *divine* and endowed with an operative power; all can speak the language of man. Thus, in spite of everything, they basically line up on a plane of equality" (Bataille 1989: 34). This is why archaic societies subscribe to what we could call a 'soft dualism' insofar as they still remain closer to a world of "immanence without a clear limit (an indistinct flow of being into being …)," like "water in water" (Bataille 1989: 33, 17).

Of course, only an "animal *is in the world like water in water*," knowing nothing of the transcendence of the subject to the object – like we, humans, "distinguish an object from ourselves" – acknowledging "no transcendence between the eater and the eaten" (Bataille 1989: 17–9). Yet, attaining this immanence or intimacy is a fundamental human yearning, manifesting itself in the most primal expression of human life, "[r]eligion, whose essence is the search for lost intimacy" (Bataille 1989: 57). This is a crucial point to which we shall return below.

For now let us note that the fact that the dualism of archaic and pagan societies is "soft," so that beings basically line up on a plane of equality, means that the division between profane and sacred is inscribed within one and the same world. That is, being in archaic societies necessitates an internal split between "the reality of a profane world, of a world of things and bodies" and "a holy and mythical world" of spirits (Bataille 1989: 37). Accordingly, "insofar as it is spirit, the human reality is holy, but it is profane insofar as it is real" (Bataille 1989: 38). This, in turn, entails that when it comes to redemption, beings have to pay their debts to themselves. It is the being in its paltry aspect as a body or "profane tool" that pays its debt to its noble aspect as a "sacred" spirit (Bataille 1989: 35). Since the body-thing must be destroyed, the debt can be paid only in the form of a bloody sacrifice. Sacrifice is the door of redemption that leads to the return to divinity: "the thing – only the thing – is what sacrifice means to destroy in the victim," as "it draws the victim out of the world of utility and restores it to that of unintelligible caprice" (Bataille 1989: 43).

Here it becomes clear that the excrement or waste that falls out of the world of utility – the "lost" enjoyment – can be anything that transgresses the laws of utility and productivity, the laws that govern what counts within (the natural aspect of) a discourse. Anything beyond these laws, from excessive pleasure to the most atrocious violence, constitutes "unintelligible caprice" – enjoyment. In the archaic and pagan variations of the discourse of the Master, the "world of utility," the real world of bodies *qua* things and tools, excretes all enjoyment into the world of the spirits – by which, crucially, is meant the world of the *same* bodies, insofar as they become the object of the "unintelligible caprice" of sacrifice, orgiastic rituals, and so on.

If the distinction between profane tool and sacred spirit threatened to introduce a split in the continuity of being, the sacrificial festival offers the antidote as a "return to *intimacy*," to the "immanence between man and the world, between the subject and the object," to the "*intimacy* of the divine world" of "violent and uncalculated generosity" (Bataille 1989: 44). In "a world that creates and preserves (that creates for the benefit of a lasting reality) ... with a view to the future," "[s]acrifice is the antithesis of production ... it is consumption that is concerned with the moment" (Bataille 1989: 49), without any relation to duration. Enjoyment is here excluded from the world of utility, but it is still practiced *in* this world, in the sacrificial festivals, those institutionalized intervals that interrupt the normal everyday life or the duration of the world of utility. In other words, archaic social life includes within itself both the discourse or productive life and its exception or loss, the festival of exuberant enjoyment, that moment of "breaking loose ... into violence" that the "normal" "order of things holds in check" for "the sake of duration" (Bataille 1989: 52).

Ironically, it is the Judeo-Christian "hard dualism" between body and spirit that will eventually lead to a social organization that claims to abhor bloody sacrifices. Whereas in archaic societies, the circulation of debts and their redemptions took place within the body – between its two aspects, the biological and the spiritual – in monotheism this is no longer possible because the latter introduces absolute transcendence. By absolute transcendence I mean not only that the spirit is supernatural (which was already the case in archaic/pagan societies) but also that the supernatural is now severed from nature, as its otherworldly or heavenly antipode. This metaphysical organization becomes also the model of sovereignty, the sovereign being conceived as the representative of God on earth. In this paradigm, as Richard Dienst puts it in his succinct recapitulation of Deleuze and Félix Guattari's account of the "despotic/barbarian system" – i.e., what "Foucault will call 'sovereign society'" – "all debts are exercised as dispensations of the infinite credit of the divine ruler" (Dienst 2011: 124). In the history of redemption, this is a shift that enables new, blood-free, forms of payment of one's debt, forms that trained the biological body to withdraw in the background and let the mind ascend, however asymptotically, to spiritual transcendence – forms such as prayer, confession, meditation, and solitude, both as asceticism and as incarceration. The possibility of replacing blood as the currency for payment with other means was already intimated through the concept of transubstantiation – drinking wine *qua* blood.

Of course, it took many centuries of development, including within the secular era up until the mutation of power into the specifically capitalist form of biopower, until the sacrifice of human life eventually became a taboo. Nevertheless, it is the logic of Christianity that sowed the seed of biopower's possibility. "This is why," as Marx writes, "Christianity is … the special religion of capital. In both it is only men who count. One man in the abstract is worth just as much or as little as the next man. In the one case, all depends on whether or not he has faith, in the other, on whether or not he has credit" (Marx 1963: 448). Already in the Middle Ages, credit and money began to function as the exemplary blood-free means of redemption, as is evidenced, in Marx's words, in "the imposition by the Popes of church tax" (Marx 1993: 839). As Alberto Toscano notes, these church taxes "can be linked to the emergence of money as the universal equivalent and the corrosion of," again in Marx's words, any "absolute values, since, for money, value as such is relative" (Toscano 2010: 17, n. 48; Marx 1993: 839). Still, as we know, biopower's Christian seed would be unable to yield anything without being fertilized by the commodification of labor which entails the need to take care of the productivity of bodies and minds.

However, to return to the itinerary of enjoyment, what we have in the monotheistic variation of the discourse of the Master is a development in which enjoyment – whether in the form of excessive bliss or of excessive violence – is gradually delegitimized in the earthly world. Initially, the privilege of enjoyment shifts from almost the whole community, as was the case of the sacrificial festival, to the clerical and political elite, who could still enjoy, both in the hedonistic and the violent senses, with impunity. Such privileges kept waning, but they remained legitimate as long as the heavens, as the parallel supernatural world, could sustain itself as an epistemontologically legitimate category.

Turning now to the modern capitalist era, we need to take heed of its internal historical shift that we noted in the first chapter, namely: the shift from State-type ideology to the primacy of commodity fetishism and biopower in a society dominated by the market. According to this distinction, as Slavoj Žižek has suggested, one can read Lacan's discourses of the Master and the University as providing the matrix of "the historicity of modern European development," reflecting the shift from State to the market. Thus, the "master's discourse stands not [only] for the premodern master, but [also] for the absolute monarchy," while the discourse of the University stands for the subsequent era of "the expert rule of bureaucracy that culminates in the biopolitics of … what … Adorno [called] 'the administered world'" (Žižek 2006: 109). This is to say that absolute monarchy is a residual form of that power that characterizes the discourse of the Master, within capitalism. As the King continues to represent God on earth, the transcendence of the Ideal (Nation, State) over and above civil society becomes the new substitute of the Heavens. Transcendence shifts from the religious realm *per se* to the political realm; nevertheless, there still remains a kind of parallel, transcendent world in which the waste of eternity can be deposited. The King is dead, long live the King! – just as we are mortal but the Ideal is immortal. The subjects' lives remain the means toward the realization of the Ideal and, therefore, sacrifices are still legitimate, as Hegel's philosophy emphatically asserted:

> Compared to the universal, the particular is for the most part too slight in importance: individuals are surrendered and sacrificed. The Idea pays the ransom of existence and transience – not out of its own pocket, but with the passions of individuals.
>
> (Hegel 1988: 35)

In his account of modern power, Foucault also acknowledges this, to put it in Wilhelm Pinder's and Ernst Bloch's terms, *Ungleichzeitigkeit des Gleichzeitigen* (the non-simultaneity of the simultaneous), noting that up until the late eighteenth century power's principle ultimately remained that of sovereignty, as "the right to take life and let live." During this earlier phase of capitalism, the "very essence" of this "right of life and death is actually the right to kill," for "it is at the moment when the sovereign can kill that he exercises his right over life" (Foucault 2003: 240–1). During that period death had to be "made … so spectacular and ritualized" because "it was a manifestation of a transition from … one power – that of the sovereign of this world – to another – that of the sovereign of the next world … from a civil or public right over life and death, to a right to either eternal life or eternal damnation" (Foucault 2003: 247).

The shift to the era of commodity fetishism and capitalist biopower occurs when "power is decreasingly the power of the right to take life, and increasingly the right to intervene to make live" or "to improve life." At that point "death becomes, insofar as it is the end of life, the term, the limit, or the end of power too … Death is beyond the reach of power, and power has a grip on it only in general … statistical terms." Now that "power has no control over death … it can control [rates of] mortality." At this point "death … become[s] the most private thing of all," and "[p]ower no longer recognizes death" (Foucault 2003: 248). Through commodity fetishism we understand that also the subjects under this form of power and discourse do not recognize mortality as physical death; it is only the death that is counted – in statistical data – that is registered in consciousness. If sovereignty mastered death by being its physical cause, biopower masters it by treating it as an agglomeration of data devoid of any physicality.

The drastic shift between all variations of the discourse of the Master, precapitalist and capitalist, and the discourse of the University proper, that is, the domination of commodity fetishism and biopower, consists in the fact that in the latter there is no parallel supernatural space for the loss to emigrate, whether in this world or in the beyond. A drastic epistemontological and political reconfiguration has occurred by that historical point, in which the presecular (soft or hard) dualist parallelism, as well as its secular residue in the form of ideology, all yield to the properly secular parallelism between body and mind within the plane of immanence. Or, what amounts to the same, transcendence is folded within immanence, as a result of which the spirit or Ideal is devoid of its supernatural aura and can claim only the modest status of the signifier and exchange-value.

However, all this occurs at the same time as *everything in the world obtains a fetishistic aura.* As we have seen in the second chapter, fetishism involves the unconscious and repression: the entire economic system is predicated on our not being aware of what we are doing. The loss of the space that could afford the supernatural yields to repression – and even to foreclosure – as Lacan's aforementioned formula of atheism indicates ("*God is Unconscious*"). In other words, the waste is now either repressed or foreclosed. If, as we have seen, duration and, hence, mortality are wasted, this means that they fall out of the conscious conception of human life. This is the subjective correlative of the fact that the biopolitical discourse (of the University), as Foucault remarks, "literally ignores death" (Foucault 2003: 248). In the past, death provided the occasion for "one of those spectacular ceremonies in which individuals, the family, the group, and practically the whole of society took part." With the advent of capitalist biopower, death's "great public ritualization … gradually began to disappear, or at least to fade away, in the late eighteenth century and … it is still doing so today," so "much so that death has become, in contrast, something to be hidden away," to the point that "ultimately, it is now not so much sex as death that is the object of a taboo" (Foucault 2003: 247).

Imitation enjoyment as a religious practice

At the same time that death as such becomes a taboo, *eternity* is counted within the discourse, which is to say, it operates in human consciousness as a category of everyday life, as *an empirically attainable dimension.* Of course, just as we continue to die even as our mortality falls out of our consciousness, eternity remains truly unattainable and what we empirically experience is actually an imitation of eternity.[7] As Lacan remarks, the commodification of *jouissance* means that "surplus *jouissance* is no longer surplus *jouissance*" – waste – but an "imitation surplus *jouissance* [semblant de plus-de-jouir]"; it is "the homogeneous equivalent of whatever surplus *jouissance* is produced by our industry" of our "'[c]onsumer society'" (Lacan 1991a: 92–3; Lacan 2007: 80–1). The same is true of eternity, which now becomes an *imitation eternity* that is produced and marketed by the industry of our consumer society, above all the media industry. Lacan clearly sensed the massive appeal of such an enterprise: one "can do a semblance of surplus *jouissance*" or of eternity that "can catch on" – "it draws quite a crowd" (Lacan 2007: 81).

Aldous Huxley discerned the connection between the distractions provided in a mediatized society and religion, for even as the "other world of religion is different from the other world of entertainment … they resemble one another in being most decidedly 'not of this world'" with its "realities of the social and political situation" – that is, not of the world of duration (Huxley 1985). We recall that Bataille pointed out that the "essence" of religion "is the search for lost intimacy" or immanence (Bataille 1989: 57) – an ecstatic state of the dissolution of the self and of the sense of lived time. Already sociologists such as Émile Durkheim and Marcel Mauss had made clear that religion is motivated by this yearning for a "lost intimacy" and that therein lies the function of archaic and pagan religious festivals, those ecstatic lacunae that interrupted the linear time of purposeful and socially productive activity, and of which the later monotheist religious rituals were the residues. It is this same experience that is sought by the distractions of our hyper-mediatized society.

As Neil Postman and others have argued, Huxley's dystopic vision seems to represent more adequately the mechanisms of control in contemporary Western capitalist democracies than George Orwell's coercively totalitarian dystopia. In chapter IV, "Propaganda in a Democratic Society," of his *Brave New World Revisited*, Huxley succinctly formulates the shift from the phase of capitalism dominated by the State-type ideology to the full-fledged biopolitical phase of the global market by writing:

> In regard to propaganda the early advocates of universal literacy and a free press envisaged only two possibilities: the propaganda might be true, or it might be false. They did not foresee what in fact has happened, above all in our Western capitalist democracies – the development of a vast mass communications industry, concerned in the main neither with the true nor the false, but with the unreal, the more or less totally irrelevant.

The concern with the alternatives between truth and falsity voiced within the era of the State-type ideology has yielded to the devotion to the unreal.[8] The advocates of the free press during the early modern era, still in Huxley's words, "failed to take into account man's almost infinite appetite for distractions," which like a new version of religious rituals, continue to transpose people to the ecstatic world of self-forgetfulness. Transposed outside duration and the self, one experiences the commodified imitation-*jouissance* of the distraction industry in the dimension of fake eternity. This is the closest our society can come to the ecstasy of a kind of boundless flow of non-differentiation between subject and object or being and language, in a nirvana-like timeless eternity.

This form of biopower that functions by means of distraction or imitation *jouissance*-eternity is not *like* religion but of an *essentially religious* character. First, we may note that the issue is not simply that today the festival has been replaced by all the means of providing imitation *jouissance*, that is, distraction, as the empirical state closest to experiencing something like eternity. In our society the sources of such distraction are ubiquitous and incessant, ranging from mass communication and entertainment media, addictive substances and drugs (including, tellingly, Ecstasy), to consumerism, entertainment, workouts and sports, up to and including workaholism. All of these modes of distraction are part and parcel of the accumulation of surplus-value. It is in this sense that, as Benjamin astutely discerned:

> [c]apitalism is the celebration of a cult *sans rêve et sans merci* [without dream or mercy [i.e., without a break]]. There are no "weekdays." There is no day that is not a feast day, in the terrible sense that all its sacred pomp is unfolded before us; each day commands the utter fealty of each worshiper.
>
> (Benjamin 1996: 288; interior set of brackets inserted by me)

This means that, as Benjamin continues to state, capitalism is "not a formation conditioned by religion," as in Max Weber, or at least, it is not simply this. Rather, capitalism is "an essentially religious phenomenon" which, nevertheless, differs from *all* other religions in four respects. The first, as we just saw, lies in its "permanence of the cult." The second lies in the fact that "capitalism is a purely cultic religion," that is, it "has no specific body of dogma, no theology" (Benjamin 1996: 288). This point relates to several matters we have addressed in the present work, from the fact that the present society presents itself as post-ideological and the concomitant fact that biopower presents itself as no mastery but as objective knowledge, to the power's self-presentation as pluralist and tolerant. The sole exception in all this remains, of course, the dogma of "utilitarianism," which here "acquires" directly "religious overtones," in opposition to any other religion.

Third, "capitalism is probably the first instance of a cult that creates guilt, not atonement"; in fact, it "makes guilt pervasive," as "a vast sense of guilt that is unable to find relief seizes on the cult, not to atone for this guilt but to make it universal" (Benjamin 1996: 288). To understand more easily Benjamin's statement here it helps to know that the German word for "guilt" is "*Schuld*," which is the same word for "debt." By employing this inevitable double-entendre in his language, Benjamin points out, first, that any socio-symbolic order consists above all of all forms of exchange between debts and redemptions, in all their forms: economic, juridical, and ethico-metaphysical. Second, he ventures that, faced with this transhistorical fact, past socio-symbolic orders sustained themselves more or less successfully through the promise of atonement, whereas capitalism does the same through an ideally universal dissemination of *Schuld*.

Lastly, fourthly, in "the religion of capitalism … its God must be hidden from it," which is why "what has been repressed … is capital itself, which pays interest on the hell of the unconscious" (Benjamin 1996: 288). This is Benjamin's premonition of two by now well-known Lacanian theses, "*God is unconscious*" and "the unconscious is structured like language" (Lacan 1981: 59, 20), or – through my intervention via Marx's commodity fetishism – the unconscious is structured like the network of values. In short, Benjamin's thesis is that the secular capitalist biopower is one among other forms of religion, only more pervasive, more totalitarian.

The insight that the essence of religion lies in the search for the lost immanence of *jouissance* raises the question of whether, depending on historical conditions, the model for the sought *jouissance* can be either that of the real or of the imaginary. For it is evident that the former would lend itself to a social organization of the monist or soft dualist type, while the latter would lend itself to hard dualism. Indeed both monotheism and the era of the State-type ideology were governed by (hard dualist) oppositions such as truth-falsity and immanence-transcendence. By contrast, archaic societies – in which physical life itself was imbued with spirits – and the full-fledged biopolitical capitalism, with its unceasing everyday experience of *jouissance qua* distraction – both seem to bear more affinity with the immanence of the *jouissance* of the real. This affinity between archaic societies and capitalism might be not irrelevant to the fact that, as Marcel Mauss has argued in his analysis of the potlatch, excessive waste was part of the archaic manifestation of the discourse, that is, it was counted (as a currency for accumulating prestige and power), rather than being wasted, not unlike capitalism's surplus-value.[9] This, in turn, might indicate that social organizations predicated on the potlatch should be considered as discrete manifestations of the discourse of the University rather than that of the Master. However, rather than exploring these rough hypotheses, I want to conclude with a brief comparison between contemporary biopolitics with its imitation *jouissance*, and Spinoza's conceptions of democracy and secular salvation.

Spinoza's democracy and secular salvation

We recall that, in Spinoza, intuition or the third kind of knowledge links the existing mode with its singular necessity, that is, its essence *sub species aeternitatis*. As we have seen in the first chapter, for Spinoza intuition is the path to secular salvation. To refresh our memory, I will reiterate here the passage from that first chapter that includes Yovel's commentary on Spinoza's conception of secular salvation:

> For Yovel, Spinoza's third kind of knowledge provides access to secular redemption, conceived as the "realization of eternity within time" through a kind of ecstatic experience like those attained by mystics – but obtained instead through knowledge (Yovel 1989: 170). This is the knowledge of the community between one's singular essence and

> substance. Like substance, my essence is eternal, whereas my body and mind are finite (mortal). Given that "particular essences are eternal while minds are perishable," salvation "consists in uniting … the perishable mind and the eternal essence" through intuition, that is, through Spinoza's "rational translation of the ideal of *unio mystica*" (Yovel 1989: 170, 168). This is also to say that secular salvation can be obtained only while alive: "Thus Spinoza keeps to his strict immanent philosophy even when offering a theory of salvation" (Yovel 1989: 170).

By contrast, as we saw also in the first chapter, in the context of the third kind of knowledge and its relation to salvation Deleuze fails to keep to Spinoza's strict immanent philosophy. Nevertheless, it is Deleuze himself who approximates most Spinoza's secular salvation, and does so in a way that also frees it from Yovel's residues of mysticism. Here I will remind us of a passage in the third chapter of the present work, which has also the advantage of foregrounding the aforementioned connection between enjoyment and the drive:

> Having been introduced by Freud in his *Beyond the Pleasure Principle* as the compulsion to repeat (*Wiederholungszwang*), the death drive or the "pure and empty form of time" can emerge only through an actual repetition that not only collapses all empirical oppositions, such as reality-imaginary or object-subject, but eliminates "all content," including any "temporal content" (Deleuze 1994a: 86, 110). This radical eradication of concrete contents is the very task of repetition since, as everyone knows from "love's repetition," in repeating, "we realize that our sufferings do not depend on their object" (Deleuze 2000: 72). This is why, although the "phenomena" we repeat "are always unhappy and particular," "the phenomenon of repetition forms a general joy" (Deleuze 2000: 72) – comparable to the Spinozian "Joy" of "*the third kind of knowledge*," extracted from the "intellectual Love of God," that is, "the idea of God as its [Joy's] cause … not insofar as we imagine him as [a] present" concrete entity, but "as eternal" (*Ethics* VP32D and P32C).

In that chapter, I concluded that paragraph by noting: Repetition is Deleuze's method for transcending any concrete content, as the foremost precondition of structure, and, thus, for enabling "the repetition of the future, as [the] eternal return" of the "new, complete novelty" (Deleuze 1994a: 90). Then I proceeded to examine further the requirements of a structure in general – which (structure), as we know by now, is the object of reason, not of intuition. To make the transition from reason to intuition (i.e., from structure to singular essence) we need to add that through repetition we realize not only that our sufferings do not depend on the particular objects of our love but also that they depend not on a universal structure – say, a structure meant to formalize human love in the abstract, something like the structure or law of a (love) triangle. The latter is indeed what reason does. However, in intuition, we grasp the structure of our singular essence, that is, the singular structure or pattern that we repeat regardless of our love objects, and because of which we have the singular behavior that leads us to our sufferings. This is the path to the knowledge of the causes of our action, as opposed to imagining that these causes lie in the object of our love. Knowing the causes of our actions constitutes both our freedom and our salvation. That is, on the level of intuition Deleuze's "new, complete novelty" can refer to anything, from the acceptance of the structure or pattern that causes our sufferings to the possibility of its modification, up to and including its destruction and the emergence of a new one. This is our secular redemption.

This also means that our singular essence is not reducible to any of the particular structures or patterns we extract from our repetition. Rather, it is the law of our singular itinerary through the universe of structures or – bringing together the terminology of both the third and the present chapters here – the law of our itinerary of actualizations of virtual structures.

It is important here to point out the difference between this conception of salvation and what Zupančič felicitously calls today's "world-scale burlesque psychoanalysis," according to which, "[b]efore you come around complaining about anything, try to resolve your personal problems, since it is they, and only they, that stand in the way of your happiness!" (Zupančič 2006: 176). As Zupančič remarks, "this is a very powerful and ingenious ideological maneuver," which actually pertains specifically to the capitalist-biopolitical or commodity-fetishism kind of ideology and consists of two moves:

> in the first move, [it] makes the traditionally personal issue of happiness a public, social, and political concern … and then, in a second move, pushes it back to our personal lives precisely as inseparable from these concerns. That is to say, in a caricature, that the global economic problems will be resolved when we all resolve our personal problems and frustrations.
>
> (Zupančič 2006: 176)

On a first level, this maneuver is based on a fundamental ignorance, or rather misattribution (intentional or not) of causes, that is, the assumption that the causes of our global economic problems are our personal problems and frustrations. However, if examined more closely it becomes clear that the desire underlying this double maneuver is not in the least to resolve our global economic problems; rather it is to accept them unconditionally as the just punishment for our personal problems and frustrations. Here some form of redemption is indeed obtained – but through the universalization of guilt/debt (*Schuld*) in the hell of our global economy. This is the Christian and capitalist conception of redemption, as paying for one's debts. The issue of debt is foreign to Spinoza's third kind of knowledge and salvation.

It is equally important to distinguish Spinoza's conception of secular salvation from the imitation enjoyment of distraction, in whatever form the latter may be induced. It must have become evident in this last section that, far from obtaining an ecstatic state and of "losing" oneself, connecting to eternity from within time is rather a matter of (as Spinoza put it, another form of) *knowledge*. This knowledge, intuition, explains the first kind of knowledge and duration in terms of the second kind of knowledge and structure. In the third kind of knowledge the apparent contingency of the imaginary reveals itself, through the extraction of structures by reason, as necessity.

That is, as Yovel among others has observed, "there is no additional information gained through the third kind of knowledge. All the information we need and can possess of the object of our inquiry has already been supplied by ratio [reason]" and by our imaginary (Yovel 1989: 156). The third kind of knowledge amounts rather to "a change of perspective" in which, "without addition or subtraction," we gain "a deeper insight of the same thing through a new processing, or synthesis, of the same informative ingredients." Through the imaginary we pursued a particular thing through (apparently) contingent encounters. Then, through reason, we get to know the same thing as still determined by "external causes" but now these causes are conceived as "universal laws." Or, put differently, reason enables us to see "the way this thing instantiates a set of abstract common properties." On the level of intuition, "however, all previous information coalesces to produce a singular item, the particular essence of this thing as it follows immanently" from God "according to a logical principle of particularization" (Yovel 1989: 156). A principle of particularization (or rather, in my terminology) singularization, *is* a *principle*, that is, something that renders the (ostensibly) contingent temporal itinerary of a modal existence into a necessity deriving from eternal substance.

We could also explain intuition in Lacanian terms through the relation need-demand/love-desire. Both desire and love are to be distinguished from need which, in Joan Copjec's succinct juxtaposition of the three terms, "requires for its satisfaction a *particular* object, nourishment, for example, *or* warmth. It is not a matter of indifference which; one cannot be substituted for another" (Copjec 2015: 148). Love is situated "on the next level, that of demand." Here, "whether one gives a child whose cry expresses a demand for love a blanket or food, or even a scolding, matters little. The particularity of the object is here annulled; almost any will satisfy – as long as it comes from the one to whom the demand is addressed" (Copjec 2015: 148). If need particularizes – requiring a particular object – demand or love singularizes: the objects become indifferent and what matters is the singular subject of love. Here, "the indifferent objects are all received as signs of the Other's love" (Copjec 2015: 148) – the singular Other to whom the demand for love is addressed. That the objects become indifferent to the Other/subject means that "the objects come to represent something more than themselves, that the Other *now* appears to give something more than just these objects." This "something more is the indeterminate part of its being (in Lacanian terms the object *a*)" – and in Spinozian terms the singular essence – "which the Other (or subject) *is* but does not *have*, and therefore cannot give" (Copjec 2015: 148). Now, in the relationship with another subject – or, for that matter, with oneself or with the absolute Other – as long as this is experienced on the imaginary level:

> Love's deception … is that the object *a* can be given, that the other can surrender the indeterminate part of its being to the subject who thus becomes the Other's sole satisfaction, its reason to be. This relation is reciprocal, with the subject also surrendering that which it lacks to the Other.
>
> (Copjec 2015: 148)

On the level of the third kind of knowledge, this deception is dissolved and thereby the subject does not surrender its singular essence. This is the level of "desire," understood not as an imaginary relation but such as in Lacan's ethical imperative – "do not cede your desire!" – and its corollary question: "have you acted in accordance with your desire?" (Lacan 1992: 311). On this level, "the Other retains what it does not have [its object *a*] and does not surrender it to the subject." Desire thus conceived strips love from its deception and combines its singularity with the particularity of need on a sublimated level, as it were, that is, as the non-exchangeability of the object *a*. In Copjec's words, the "subject's desire is aimed … at a *particular absolute* [or singular], *absolute* [or singular] in the sense that, like demand, it aims beyond particular objects to that 'something more' that exceeds them, *particular* in that the refusal to surrender it means that it remains unique to the Other – it is nontransferable" (Copjec 2015: 148–9). On this level, the subject recognizes another subject as unique and not replaceable, at the same time that it recognizes that the other subject has its singular way of constructing meaning and of organizing its own enjoyment.

These remarks allow us to stress once more the distinctiveness of the third kind of knowledge so as to specify the biopolitical function of the commodification of labor-power and enjoyment or singular essence. Beyond reason, which, as we have seen, is not concerned with the actual existence of things, "[w]e conceive things as actual in two ways." In the one way, Spinoza continues, "we conceive them to exist in relation to a certain time and place," that is, through imagination or the first kind of knowledge. In the other way, "we conceive them to be contained in God and to follow from the necessity of the divine nature" not only in universal terms but also in terms of their singular essence and existence – and this is intuition or the third kind of knowledge (*Ethics* VP29S). This is why, in Balibar's words, far from referring "to a *general idea* of humanity, an abstract concept under which all individuals are subsumed and their differences neutralised," singular essence "refers precisely to the power that *singularizes* each individual" (Balibar 1998: 107). Now, the distinctive characteristic of commodification is the elimination of the singularity of whatever it is that is being commodified, as commodification renders things precisely exchangeable. In other words, the commodification of eternity and essence amounts to the elimination of singularity.

It is not irrelevant that the biopolitical development moves from the various more or less modern conceptions of love, from marriage in its Catholic, Protestant, and bourgeois versions to the passionate love of Romanticism, to its reduction to neuro-chemical processes and a sexuality conceived in medical terms and administered through a large array of institutions and statistical data.

This reference brings us back to the intrinsic link between biopower and statistics. As I argue elsewhere, there is a striking similarity between modern biopower and Spinoza's conception of democracy as the best and "most natural" of all political systems (*TTP* XVI11). For Spinoza, a real democracy would be a system in which power would be in the hands of everybody (the entire multitude), something which would fulfill Spinoza's ideal of absolute dominion, for "if there be any absolute dominion, it is, in fact, that which is held by an entire multitude" (*TP* VIII3). Absolute dominion is one in which one would not even conceive the idea of overthrowing the political authority since all would feel that power is in their hands and that they are free, that is, they operate according to the laws of reason, and not the decrees of some master to whom they are subjected. For, according to Spinoza, "a man is free, in so far as he is led by reason" (*TTP* 276, n. 27). Accordingly, "in a state or kingdom where the weal of the whole people, and not that of the ruler, is the supreme law," the sovereigns themselves, on the one hand, are "acting according to the dictates of reason," while, on the other hand, "every member of it may … live with full consent under the entire guidance of reason." This, in turn, means that "obedience to the sovereign power does not make a man a slave" but a free man (*TTP* 205–6). In short, in democracy people are governed by "objective" knowledge and are all free, which also means there is no master. All this, however, is undermined by the following:

> Whatever be the cause which leads a man to obey the commands of the sovereign, whether it be fear or hope, or love of his country, or any other emotion – the fact remains that the man takes counsel with himself, and nevertheless acts as his sovereign orders … [A]s a matter of fact, all actions spring from a man's deliberation with himself,

> whether the determining motive be love or fear of punishment; therefore … dominion … extends over every instance in which it can prevail on men to decide to obey it.
>
> (*TTP* 215)

Consequently, "every action which a subject performs in accordance with the commands of the sovereign, whether such action springs from love or fear … or, indeed, any motive whatever" – even if this indeed is, or is perceived as being, reason and freedom – "is performed in virtue of his submission to the sovereign, and not in virtue of his own authority" (*TTP* 215). For what ultimately matters "is the fact of obedience, not the motive for obedience" (*TTP* 215). Well, if this is the case, then we realize that it makes no difference whether people are *actually* free and governed by eternal laws of objective reason, *or imagine* that this is the case.[10] It follows that Spinoza's dream of an ideal democracy might simply coincide with the imaginary perception of contemporary biopower.

This possibility is further supported by the fact that, as Pierre-François Moreau indicates, Spinoza's conception of political power anticipates the modern state apparatuses and is, in Balibar's words, "not so much juridical as numerical or, if you will, *statistical* (preserving for the term its initial double meaning …) … both as a 'science of the state' and as a 'science of the population'" (Balibar 1994: 22–3; see also Moreau 1985).[11]

However, one might object, how can one reduce Spinoza's trans-individual (i.e., at once personal and collective) salvation to the current biopolitics? What does Spinoza's persistence on the knowledge of singular essence have to do with a society that commodifies this singular essence and sustains itself through the constant ritual of distraction? I am on the side of the objection: it has nothing to do with it. Except, I will add, it also has everything to do with it – which is also why the above had to be written – because it provides us with the conceptual tools to see the difference.

*

I'll end all this in a rather impressionistic tone. The brilliance of the other three (Marx, Freud, Lacan) aside, what is mind-blowing about Spinoza – and all the more so, since he preceded them in time – is that he both anticipated with remarkable precision his nasty future, and (possibly) provided the coordinates to navigate out of it.

Notes

1 See, for instance, Paul Verhaeghe (2006), and Russell Grigg (2006), who, additionally, offers an excellent account of the myths of Oedipus and of the primal father as responses to hysteria and obsessional neurosis, respectively.

2 Note also that, as Bruce Fink comments in his translation of Lacan's seminar XX, the syntactical pattern "jouir de" also "means to enjoy, take advantage of, benefit from, get off on, and so on" (Lacan 1998: 3, n. 8).

3 Strictly speaking Lacan's discourses are not conceived as historically successive discourses, but as distinct organizations of the same elements depending on their position within one and the same topology, and these organizations or discourses may be operative at one and the same historical time. As Bruce Fink puts it, "Lacan's 'four discourses' seek to account for the structural differences among discourses" and focus on the differences regarding the "efficacy," "function," or "effect" they can have "on others" (i.e., on the subjects they address), depending on "the effect allowed by" each discourse and "the obstacles and shortcomings endemic to that discourse" (Fink 1995: 129–30). Nevertheless, a discourse may represent the matrix that is dominant in the organization of a historically specific social formation, such as the discourse of the University which Lacan explicitly links to capitalist modernity.

4 In terms of the distinction introduced in the first chapter here between two kinds of eternity, both substance and singular essence pertain to the eternity of intuition (third kind of knowledge), as opposed to the common notions that grasp abstract, universal, structural relations and pertain to what Deleuze identifies as the eternity of reason (second kind of knowledge) and what I call synchrony.

5 That the loss amounts to the foreclosure of the subject understood as disenfranchised groups of people is also one of Tomšič's conclusions. In his words, that the "subject is foreclosed" means that it "*is* misrepresented … not as a decentralized negativity" that it really is, so that "the relations of production are represented without any trace of negative production, such as of indebted subjects, surplus populations and so on" (Tomšič 2015: 224).

6 Synchrony emerged as an effect of the commodification of labor-power, which is why only in capitalism could language be conceived as consisting of differential, arbitrary signs.

7 While in the following I focus on this experience of imitation eternity, in other works, as I briefly mentioned in the sixth chapter, I have examined further aspects of the biopolitical administration of the subject's relation to duration and eternity (including the latter's conflation with infinite duration), and hence to mortality and (the secular illusions of) immortality. Some of these works explore also the role of these subject-time configurations in the construction of biopolitical racism (see Kordela 2013a, 2013b 2013c, 2016). However, my attempts to describe the biopolitical administration of the subject's relation to duration and eternity through the experience of imitation eternity go back to the publication of my "Religion of Enjoyment" (see Kordela 2015).

8 Not that there is no longer censorship; on the contrary, there is huge "economic censorship," as "the media of mass communication are controlled by members of the Power Elite" (Huxley 1985). Yet, "[c]ensorship by rising costs and the concentration of communication power in the hands of a few big concerns is less objectionable than State ownership and government propaganda" (Huxley 1985).

9 See Mauss 2000.

10 In my understanding, this is the point that Frédéric Lordon's recent book elaborates (see Lordon 2014).

11 This numerical-statistical character of Spinoza's conception of power was already noted by Alexandre Matheron (1969). For my closer examination of the relation between contemporary biopower and Spinoza's philosophy, see Kordela 2017.

References

Balibar, E. (1994) *Masses, Classes, Ideas: Studies on Politics and Philosophy Before and After Marx*, James Swenson (trans.), New York: Routledge.

Balibar, E. (1998) *Spinoza and Politics*, Peter Snowdon (trans.), Warren Montag (ed.), New York: Verso.

Bataille, G. (1989) *Theory of Religion*, Robert Hurley (trans.), New York: Zone Books.

Benjamin, W. (1996) "Capitalism as Religion," in *Selected Writings Vol.1, 1913–1926*, Rodney Livingstone (trans.), Cambridge, MA: Belknap Harvard Press.

Brousse, M.H. (2006) "Common Markets and Segregation," in *Jacques Lacan and the Other Side of Psycho-analysis: Reflections on Seminar XVII*, Justin Clemens and Russell Grigg (eds), Durham, NC: Duke University Press.

Copjec, J. (2015) *Read my Desire: Lacan Against the Historicists*, London: Verso.

Deleuze, G. (1988) *Spinoza: Practical philosophy*, Robert Hurley (trans.), San Francisco, CA: City Lights Books.

Deleuze, G. (1994a) *Difference and Repetition*, Paul Patton (trans.), New York: Columbia University Press.

Deleuze, G. (1994b) *Masochism: Coldness and Cruelty & Venus in Furs*, Jean McNeil and Aude Willm (trans.), New York: Zone Books.

Deleuze, G. (2000) *Proust and Signs: The Complete Text*, Richard Howard (trans.), Minneapolis: University of Minnesota Press.

Dienst, R. (2011) *The Bonds of Debt: Borrowing Against the Common Good*, London: Verso.

Feldner, H.M. and F. Vighi (2014) "The Matrix Cannot Be Reloaded," in *States of Crisis and Post-Capitalist Scenarios*, Heiko Michael Feldner, Fabio Vighi, and Slavoj Žižek (eds), Burlington, VA: Ashgate Publishing Company, pp. 11–58.

Fink, B. (1995) *The Lacanian Subject: Between Language and Jouissance*, Princeton, NJ: Princeton University Press.

Foucault, M. (2003) *Society Must be Defended: Lectures at the Collège de France*, David Macey (trans.), Mauro Bertani and Alessandro Fontana (eds), New York: Picador.

Grigg, R. (2006) "Beyond the Oedipus Complex," in *Reflections on Seminar XVII: Jacques Lacan and the Other Side of Psychoanalysis*, Justin Clemens and Russell Grigg (eds), Durham, NC: Duke University Press.

Hegel, G.W.F. (1988) *Introduction to the Philosophy of History*, Leo Rauch (trans.), Indianapolis, IN: Hackett.

Huxley, A. (1985) *Brave New World Revisited*, www.huxley.net/bnw-revisited/.

Kordela, A.K. (2013a) *Being, Time, Bios: Capitalism and Ontology*, Albany, NY: SUNY Press.

Kordela, A.K. (2013b) "Biopolitics, From Tribes to Commodity Fetishism," *Differences*, 24(1) (Spring): 1–29.

Kordela, A.K. (2013c) "(Marxian-Psychoanalytic) Biopolitics & Bioracism," in *Penumbr(a)*, Sigi Jöttkandt and Joan Copjec (eds), Melbourne: Re.Press.

Kordela, A.K. (2015) "Religion of Enjoyment," in *The Lacanian Review Online*, the issue of 16. 10. 2015:). http://thelacanianreviews.com/lacanian_review_online161015.html.

Kordela, A.K. (2016) "Monsters of Biopower: Terror(ism) and Horror in the Era of Affect," *Philosophy Today*, 60(1): 193–205.

Kordela, A.K. (2017) "Spinoza's Biopolitics," in *Spinoza's Authority, Volume I: Resistance and Power in the Ethics*, A.K. Kordela and D. Vardoulakis (eds), New York: Bloomsbury.

Lacan, J. (1977) *Écrits: A Selection*, Bruce Fink (trans.), New York: W.W. Norton & Co.

Lacan, J. (1981) *The Seminar of Jacques Lacan: Book XI: The Four Fundamental Concepts of Psychoanalysis*, Jacques-Alain Miller (ed.), Alan Sheridan (trans.), New York: W.W. Norton.

Lacan, J. (1991a) *Le Séminaire. Livre XVII: L'envers de la psychanalyse*, Paris: Seuil.

Lacan, J. (1991b) *The Seminar of Jacques Lacan: Book II: The Ego in Freud's Theory and in the Technique of Psychoanalysis, 1945–1955*, Sylvana Tomaselli (trans.), Jacques-Alain Miller (ed.), New York: W.W. Norton & Co.

Lacan, J. (1992) *The Seminar of Jacques Lacan: Book VII: The Ethics of Psychoanalysis, 1959–1960*, Dennis Porter (trans.), Jacques-Alain Miller (ed.), New York: W.W. Norton & Co.

Lacan, J. (1998) *The Seminar of Jacques Lacan: Book XX. Encore, 1972–1973: On Feminine Sexuality; The Limits of Love and Knowledge*, Bruce Fink (trans.), Jacques-Alain Miller (ed.), New York: W.W. Norton.

Lacan, J. (2007) *The Seminar of Jacques Lacan: Book XVII: The Other Side of Psychoanalysis*, Russell Grigg (trans.), Jacques-Alain Miller (ed.), New York: W.W. Norton & Co.

Lord, B. (2010) *Spinoza's Ethics*, Bloomington: Indiana University Press.

Lordon, F. (2014) *Willing Slaves of Capital: Spinoza and Marx on Desire*, Gabriel Ash (trans.), London: Verso.

Marx, K. (1963) *Theories of Surplus Value: Volume IV of Capital*, Emile Burns (trans.). S. Ryazanskaya (ed.), Moscow: Progress Publishers.

Marx, K. (1990) *Capital: A Critique of Political Economy (Volume 1)*, Ben Fowkes and David Fernbach (trans.), New York: Penguin.

Marx, K. (1993) *Grundrisse: Foundations of the Critique of Political Economy (Rough Draft)*, M. Nicolaus (trans.), London: Penguin Books.

Matheron, A. (1969) *Individu et Communauté chez Spinoza*, Paris: Les éditions de minuit.

Mauss, M. (2000) *The Gift: The Form and Reason for Exchange in Archaic Societies*, W.D. Halls (trans.), New York: W.W. Norton.

Miller, J.A. (1995) "Transference, Repetition, and the Sexual Real: Reading the Four Fundamental Concepts of Psychoanalysis" and "Silet," lectures given as part of "The Lacanian Orientation" (1994–1995) unpublished. Text and notes have been edited by Anne Lysy, authorized by J.A. Miller, not reviewed by the author.

Moreau, P.-F. (1985) "La notion d'Imperium dans le Traité politique," in *Proceedings of the First Italian International Congress on Spinoza*, Emilia Giancotti (ed), Naples: Bibliopolis.

Spinoza, B. (1985) *The Collected Works of Spinoza*, Edwin Curley (trans.), Princeton: Princeton University Press.

Tomšič, S. (2015) *The Capitalist Unconscious: Marx and Lacan*, London: Verso.

Toscano, A. (2010) "Beyond Abstraction: Marx and the Critique of the Critique of Religion," *Historical Materialism*, 18(1): 3–29.

Verhaeghe, P. (2006) "Enjoyment and Impossibility: Lacan's Revision of the Oedipus Complex," in *Reflections on Seminar XVII: Jacques Lacan and the Other Side of Psychoanalysis*, Justin Clemens and Russell Grigg (eds), Durham, NC: Duke University Press.

Yovel, Y. (1989) *Spinoza and Other Heretics: The Marrano of Reason*, Princeton, NJ: Princeton University Press.

Žižek, S. (2006) "Objet a in Social Links," in *Jacques Lacan and the Other Side of Psychoanalysis: Reflections on Seminar XVII*, Justin Clemens and Russell Grigg (eds), Durham, NC: Duke University Press.

Zupančič, A. (2006) "When Surplus Enjoyment Meets Surplus Value," in *Jacques Lacan and the Other Side of Psychoanalysis: Reflections on Seminar XVII*, Justin Clemens and Russell Grigg (eds), Durham, NC: Duke University Press.

Index

Adorno, Theodor 96–103, 113, 122, 145–6, 151, 185 *see also* dialectics; negative dialectic
aesthetics 27, 126–31, 142–5; aesthetic theory 9, 126–135ff; beauty 129–137, 151; formalism 16, 31, 102; judgement 129
affect 31–4, 44–50, 123, 160–3, 176–7
Agamben, Giorgio 140; bare life 147–8 *see also* biopower
alienation 45, 68, 99, 106, 119, 151
allegory 15–16, 98–9, 122, 127
Althusser, Louis 21–4, 44–8, 75, 91–9, 141, 152–60 *see also* ideology; symptomatic reading
antinomies 114, 122–5, 171
Aristotle 61–2, 120, 147, 174
attribute 16–17, 32–41ff, 64–73ff, 100, 144–152, 170–8; extension 16–25ff, 40–9ff, 53–5, 100–7, 171; thought 13–21, 25–34ff, 40–7, 52–4, 100, 170
authority 49, 63, 163, 175, 195–6
auto-erotism 73, 81–9, 159 *see also* narcissism

Badiou, Alain 14, 29–31, 46, 48–9
Balibar, Étienne 17–26, 43–8, 92, 141–2, 152–6, 159–63, 195–6 *see also* transindividuality
Bataille, Georges 11, 182–4, 188
Baumgarten, Alexander Gottlieb 9, 126
Benjamin, Walter 15–16, 27–32, 46, 54, 126–7, 142–151, 189–90
Benz-Overhage, Karin 59
biopolitics 43–9, 52, 71, 140–7, 160–9ff, 185–196ff; bioracism 49 *see also* biopower
biopower 41–50ff, 147–8, 158–67ff, 175, 185–194ff
Bloch, Ernst 186
bourgeois 44–53ff, 67, 121–30ff, 146, 155–6, 195
Brousse, Marie-Hélène 175
Brown, Nicholas 120
Butler, Judith 86

capitalism 20–7, 42–3, 53–62ff, 119–21, 144, 152–61ff, 173–82ff
Carrol, Lewis 107, 110
cathexis 152
causality 19, 62–73ff, 88, 113–22, 133–9
Caygill, Howard 29, 129, 131–4
Cillario, Lorenzo 71
Comay, Rebecca 148
coincidentia oppositorum 117, 122, 143 *see also* dialectics
commodity 19–23, 42–4, 54–63ff, 121–30ff, 179–88ff; commodification 25, 41–2, 62–5, 129–38ff, 159–68ff, 181–90ff; commodity fetishism 13–22ff, 35–44ff, 68–71, 131–40ff, 155–64ff, 185–94ff; commodification of labor 42, 62–5, 162–7, 173–81ff, 194–7
common notion 32–4, 176–7, 197 *see also* knowledge, second kind of; reason (Spinoza)
consciousness 14–23ff, 35–41ff, 67–76ff, 83–92ff, 117–123, 134–43ff, 160–3, 186–7; false consciousness 98, 103
Copjec, Joan 193–4
correlationism 35
Curley, Edwin 1

De Man, Paul 9, 13–6, 136 *see also* deconstruction
death drive 75, 87, 136–7, 152–7, 167–74, 191 *see also* drive; entropy, pleasure principle
deconstruction 13–4, 16, 44
Deleuze, Gilles 17–8, 21–30ff, 40–9, 69, 73–9, 81–90ff, 99–108ff, 120–3, 134–7, 167, 172, 184, 191–7; Deleuze and Guattari 85; *see also* object = x; repetition compulsion; series; structuralism; virtual
Derrida, Jacques 13 *see also* deconstruction
Descartes, René 78; cogito 78 *see also* dualism
desire 36, 73, 86–95ff, 127–136ff, 153–162ff, 193–4 *see also* lack
diachrony 23, 33–4, 40–2, 54, 77, 170, 181; duration 34, 92, 157–8, 166–75ff, 193–7; linear time 42, 53, 74, 84–9, 157–8, 188
dialectics 27, 95–104ff, 116, 138; antithesis 95–9, 145, 184; binary opposition 96; synthesis 63, 75–84ff, 95–104ff, 123, 193; thesis 13–22ff, 46–55ff, 71–6, 95–104ff, 120–9ff, 174, 190
Dienst, Richard 184
differential 14–23ff, 38–9, 53–62ff, 77, 106–11, 128–37ff, 181, 197
discourse 43–50, 126–35ff, 159–62ff, 180–9ff, 197
drive 75, 81–90, 136–8, 152–9, 167–74, 191 *see also* desire
dualism 15, 34–43, 53–62ff, 87–99, 118, 142–51ff, 183–90
Durkheim, Émile 188

Eagleton, Terry 120
ego 39, 75, 80–7, 98–9, 110, 120–2, 135–7
enjoyment 42–4, 82–7, 159–168, 175–84ff, 197 *see also* *jouissance*
Enlightenment 14, 126, 134, 146, 163
entelechy 174
entropy 161–2, 173–5
episteme 18–27, 38, 127, 174
epistemology 13–6, 27, 53–62ff, 91, 154–60
epistemontology 13–20, 27, 35–7, 41–7, 53–62ff
essence 15, 33, 47, 74, 82–9, 98–107ff, 146, 167–76ff, 183–92ff; singular essence 24, 33, 93, 168, 177–81, 190–7
eternity 31–40ff, 88, 92, 120, 137–46ff, 166–175ff, 190–7
Euclid: Euclidean geometry 110
excess 24, 108–16, 153–62ff, 173–80
exchange-value 41–50ff, 66–70, 121–30ff, 157–161, 173–182ff *see also* value

fantasy 24, 49, 73–82ff, 118, 123, 140 *see also* narcissism
Feldner, Heiko 180
feudalism 13, 48, 128, 161
Feuerbach, Ludwig 156
Fichte, Johann Gottlieb 9, 128, 134, 136–9 *see also* German Idealism
Finelli, Roberto 69
Fink, Bruce 50, 161–2, 168–9, 197
Foucault, Michel 14–18, 42–50, 106, 127–8, 140–8, 159, 184–7 *see also* biopower; episteme
Frankfurt School 9, 151–2 *see also* Adorno, Theodor; Fromm, Erich; Habermas, Jürgen; Horkheimer, Max; Marcuse, Herbert
Freud, Sigmund; 41, 49, 70–79, 89–92, 116–122, 138–144, 151–160, 168–174, 191; Eros 84–87, 136–7; Thanatos 84, 87, 137 *see also* death drive; drive; Oedipus complex; pleasure principle; psychoanalysis; repetition compulsion, repression; seduction theory, uncanny
Fromm, Erich 152

German Idealism 14, 151
God 14, 31–40ff, 64–73ff, 88–92, 112–8, 134–43ff, 169–178ff, 190–5 *see also* self-actualization
Goethe, Johann Wolfgang von 9; *Faust* 127 *see also* Romanticism
Goux, Jean-Joseph 22
Guattari, Félix 111, 184; Deleuze and Guattari 85 *see also* Deleuze, Gilles
Guillory, John 9, 129–31, 133–4

Habermas, Jürgen 151
Hansen, Jim 15–6, 32
Hardt, Michael 70, 120
Heeg, Günther 128
Hegel, G.W.F. 26–7, 48–53, 64–9, 77, 87–8, 95–104, 115–23, 139, 147,

156–8, 186; Spirit 67–8, 97, 103–4, 114, 117 *see also* dialectics; German Idealism; negation
Heidegger, Martin 13, 27–9, 126, 142–4, 148
Hölderlin, Friedrich 9, 77, 85, 136
Homer 116
Horkheimer, Max 151
Hughes, Joe 30, 48–9
Hume, David 9, 129
Huxley, Aldous 187–8, 197

idealism 14–20, 36–45, 53–9ff, 134
identity 21, 34, 82–4, 96–105ff, 136–140, 173–7
ideology 14, 36, 43–50, 69, 91, 118, 136–45ff, 155–60, 185–192
imaginary 20–9ff, 46–9, 74–8, 105–14ff, 136–45ff, 156–65ff, 190–6
imagination 31–4, 49, 70–9ff, 100–6, 157–166ff, 194 *see also* knowledge, first kind of
immanence 18, 43–6, 69, 115, 156–60, 171–80ff; immanent causality 65, 138–9 *see also* causality
immateriality 53, 63, 70–1
infinity 39, 82–3, 121, 135–6, 157–8, 177
intuition (Spinoza) 24–33ff, 77–80, 92–3, 128–35, 177–8, 190–7 *see also* knowledge, third kind of

Jameson, Fredric 95–104ff, 109–118ff *see also* dialectics
jouissance 41–3, 161–70ff, 187–90 *see also* enjoyment; excess; loss; waste

Kafka, Franz 106, 111–4, 122, 146; Prometheus 9, 111–6, 122
Kant, Immanuel 13–4, 35, 49, 58, 69–78, 114–22, 128–134; a priori categories 14, 53; categorical imperative 131; purposiveness (Zweckmäßigkeit) 132–4; thing-in-itself 15, 18, 127 *see also* antinomies; German Idealism
Karatani, Kojin 121, 136, 138–9, 148
Kaufman, Eleanor 92
Kazarian, Edward P. 92
knowledge 16–25ff, 40–49ff, 74–5, 92–99ff, 120–7, 139, 161–70ff, 189–92ff; first kind of 24, 176–7, 193; second kind of 24, 92–3, 176–7, 193, 197; third kind of 24, 31–2, 42, 75, 92–3, 169, 177, 190–7
Kojève, Alexandre 74, 87–8, 93–7, 104, 120, 157 *see also* Hegel G.W.F.; negation
Kordela, A. Kiarina 49–50, 69–71, 120–3, 153–61ff, 197

labor: abstract- 42, 65–70, 158–67, 179–81; concrete- 70, 179–81; congealed- 65,166; homogenous- 155, 179; manual- 54–8, 6770, 156; -power 41–2, 64–7, 158–67ff, 180–9ff, 197; -time 42, 65, 70, 158–67, 176–9
Lacan, Jacques 27, 38–43, 67–73, 81–7, 91–100ff, 115–123, 136–8, 153–62ff, 166–75ff, 190–7 *see also* imaginary (Lacan); negation; not-all (set); *objet a*; psychoanalysis; repetition compulsion; repression; symbolic
lack 28, 70, 82–9, 108–16, 171–2 *see also* negation
Laplanche, Jean: Laplanche and Pontalis 8–9, 73–7, 80–1, 89–92, 138, 157–9
Larrain, Felipe Bascuñán: Sachs and Larrain 63
Leibniz, Gottfried Wilhelm 100, 111 *see also* monad
Lenin, Vladimir 96
Lessing, Gotthold Ephraim 9, 100, 126
Lévi-Strauss, Claude 5, 79, 116, 122 *see also* structuralism
libido 81–7, 152–3, 169–76
Lord, Beth 47–8, 65, 170
Lordon, Frédéric 197
loss 28–34, 81, 138, 152–61ff, 168–77ff, 181–7ff *see also* auto-erotism; void
Lukács, Georg 27, 96, 101–3, 107–10
Luxembourg, Rosa 152

Macherey, Pierre 6, 9, 18, 24, 88–9, 123 *see also* Hegel G.W.F.; negation; Spinoza, Baruch/Benedict de
Marcuse, Herbert 151
Marx, Karl 13–22ff, 35–44ff, 53–62ff, 79, 91, 121–30ff, 144–153ff, 166–175ff, 190–196 *see also* capitalism; commodity; labor; money; political economy
materialism 13, 35, 38–40, 58–59, 67–68, 152–156
materialist epistemology 53, 57, 69, 155, 160 *see also* epistemology
Matheron, Alexandre 197

Mauss, Marcel 188, 190, 197
Meillassoux, Quentin 2, 7, 13, 25–40 *see also* correlationism; speculative materialism
mercantilism 128
metaphysics 20, 35, 39, 44, 160
Miller, Jacques-Alain 169, 171
mode (Spinoza) 32–6, 46–9, 75–84ff, 111, 142–51ff, 176–81ff
monad 111, 114
money 14–23ff, 43–52ff, 118–27ff, 136–8, 157–9, 185 *see also* commodity
monism 1–9, 15–18, 27, 100, 138 *see also* Spinoza
Montag, Warren 17, 21, 24
Moreau, Pierre-François 196
multitude 71, 120, 195

narcissism 80–7 *see also* auto-erotism
negation 88, 97, 104, 123, 153–7
negative dialectic 145–8, 151
Neroni, Hilary 50
Nietzsche, Friedrich 24, 78, 126, 140–2, 146
not-all (set) 66, 122, 138

object = x 76, 82–4, 134 *see also* Deleuze, Gilles
objet a 81, 169
Oedipus complex 77–9, 86,
ontology 16, 27, 46, 53–4, 64–9, 122, 154–8
Orwell, George 188
O/other (Lacan) 38, 81–90, 138, 151, 160–9ff, 194

parallelism 17–18, 39, 186–7
Parmenides 62–4, 97
Peden, Knox 48
Pendakis, Andrew 163
Pfaller, Robert 120
phenomenon 26–35, 58, 70–5, 84–92ff, 129, 134, 144, 162–171ff, 181–90ff
Pinder, Wilhelm 186
Plato 13, 29–30, 120, 174
pleasure principle 75, 87, 136, 152–7, 167–9, 191 *see also* psychoanalysis
political economy 53, 60, 70, 129–31, 153–5
polytheism 182
Pontalis, Jean-Bertrand: Laplanche and Pontalis 8–9, 73–7, 80–1, 89–92, 138, 157–9
Postman, Neil 188
postmodernism 110, 140
post-structuralism 23
potentiality 28–34, 49, 64–70, 163–72ff, 181
power 13–24ff, 42–9, 64–70, 84, 135–46ff, 151–60ff, 170–9ff, 195–7 being qua power-of-self-actualization 27, 41–8, 167; power of self-actualization 25–7, 41–8, 65–7, 152, 166–72
proletariat 180
psychoanalysis 26–35ff, 73–82ff, 91, 123, 136–44, 151–60ff, 192
pure reason 53, 57–8, 133

real (Lacan) 16–20, 39–43, 61–9, 74–83ff, 91–9ff, 120–3, 146–55ff, 168–78ff, 183–90
reason (Spinoza) 24, 32–5, 49–57ff, 92–3, 122, 163–172ff, 191–7 *see also* knowledge, second kind of
redemption 33, 183–92ff *see also* salvation
Reitter, Karl 59
Reich, Wilhelm 152
repetition compulsion 157; compulsion to repeat (*Wiederholungszwang*) 75, 92, 191; "empty form of time" (Deleuze) 75–84ff, 137, 191 *see also* drive
representation 13–21, 27–35, 43, 74, 89–90, 126–35ff, 148–57ff
repression 42, 129, 141, 153, 187
Romanticism 71, 126, 136–8, 195

Sachs, Jeffrey David: Sachs and Larrain 63
salvation 33, 42–5, 158, 169, 190–6; secular salvation 5,11
Sartre, Jean-Paul 73, 82–3, 87–9, 137; for-itself 83; in-itself 83
Saussure, Ferdinand de 14, 23, 96, 102, 206 *see also* structuralism; signified; signifier
Schelling, F.W.J. 9, 37, 39, 134–5 *see also* German Idealism
Schiller, Friedrich 9 *see also* Romanticism
Schlegel, G.H. 9, 134, 136
Schulte-Sasse, Jochen 9, 136
science 20, 30–39ff, 56–9, 71–3, 92, 119, 133, 153, 163, 175–6, 196
secular capitalist modernity 13–22ff, 48, 57, 68, 138; secular thought 16, 20–439, 45, 64

seduction theory 73–9, 86, 157
self-actualization 25–7, 41–8, 64–7, 152, 166–175ff
self-consciousness 53, 103, 118, 134–6
self-referentiality 15, 126, 136–45ff; performative 92, 126, 139–147
series 15–23, 45–9, 73–82ff, 92–103ff, 113–22ff, 134–8
sexuality 77–86ff, 153–7, 170–2, 195
sign 14–23ff, 31–40ff, 77–9, 85–90, 127–8, 137–142ff, 176, 194
signified 14, 80, 106–10, 127
signifier 14–21, 79–85, 137–8, 158–167ff, 187
Simmel, Georg 39
Simpson, David 139
Smith, Adam 9, 129–30, 139, 146; invisible hand 130, 133, 139
Sohn-Rethel, Alfred 4, 7–9, 53–62ff *see also* materialist epistemology
Sophocles 78
speculative materialism 13, 35–39
Spinoza, Baruch/Benedict de 18–27ff, 37–46ff, 53–62ff, 74, 88–97ff, 119–123, 138–142, 163–72ff, 190–6; God or Nature 64, 142, 177; *see also* attribute; common notion; God; imagination; intuition (Spinoza); knowledge; mode (Spinoza); monism; parallelism; potentiality; self-actualization; *sub specie aeternitatis*; substance
state 43–4, 69, 129, 147, 156–9, 185–8, 190–7 *see also* authority, biopower
Stolze, Ted 91, 92
structuralism 17–26ff, 40–9ff, 69–78ff, 90–9ff, 110–19ff, 138, 151–2; structure 14–23ff, 31–40ff, 62–71ff, 80–89ff, 100–9ff, 126–35ff, 153–62ff, 190–3
sub specie aeternitatis 67 *see also* eternity
subconscious 152
subject 14–23ff, 34–43ff, 53–62ff, 74–83ff, 90–99ff, 123–32ff, 140–9ff, 160–9ff 180–9ff; subjectivity 13–22ff, 35, 56, 68, 132–40, 159–68ff; transcendental- 14, 35–40, 134
substance 13–22ff, 32–41ff, 54–63ff, 88–97ff, 120–9ff, 141–50ff, 163–72ff, 180–9ff, 197 *see also* self-actualization; Spinoza
superego 85–6
superstition 141 *see also* imagination
surplus 43, 130–6, 153, 161–9, 173–80, 197 *see also* excess; waste; loss
surplus-enjoyment 160–1, 168 *see also* enjoyment; excess; *jouissance*; loss, surplus-value; void; waste
surplus-value 65–6, 130–1, 147–156ff, 166–175ff, 190 *see also* value
symbolic 21–6, 70–9ff, 91–100ff, 120–9ff, 169–71, 189
symptom 153
symptomatic reading 153
synchrony 23, 34, 42–9, 54, 92–3, 181, 197

teleology 99, 120, 132
temporality 30–4, 40–9, 54–6, 70–9ff, 120, 137, 168–177ff
Tomšič, Samo 5–6, 197
Toscano, Alberto 69–71, 185
totality 21, 37–9, 58, 77–9, 81–9, 98, 119, 122, 132–8, 158, 170–1
transcendence 16–8, 43–4, 69, 79, 156–60, 182–90; transcendentalism 19, 68, 160
transindividuality 141–2, 146
transitive causality 64–5, 111, 134, 142

uncanny 161
unconscious 38–48ff, 54–63ff, 75–84ff, 135–144ff, 151–160ff, 182–190
use-value 41–2, 53–9, 61–70, 121–129, 130–2, 158, 179–80 *see also* value
usufruct 172–3
utilitarianism 45, 129–31, 147, 173, 189; utility 41–55, 66–7, 129–31, 155, 166, 183–4

value 13–22ff, 35–44ff, 53–62ff, 83–92ff, 121–130ff, 152–161ff, 173–182ff
Verhaeghe, Paul 196
Vighi, Fabio 180
Virno, Paolo 65, 71, 120
virtual 40, 70, 75–84, 86–92, 192
void 56, 117–118

waste 161–3, 173–180, 183, 185, 187, 190
Weber, Max 44, 189
Winckelmann, Johann Joachim 126–7

Yovel, Yirmiyahu 32–4, 190–3

Žižek, Slavoj 96–98, 104, 117, 153, 185
Zupančič, Alenka 173–6, 192–3

